Michigan Herb
❧ Cookbook ❧

Anna & Matt
Thanks for all
your hospitality.
Happy Cooking
Suzanne

Michigan Herb
Cookbook

Suzanne Breckenridge & Marjorie Snyder

Ann Arbor
The University of Michigan Press

Published in the United States of America by
The University of Michigan Press
Manufactured in the United States of America
♾ Printed on acid-free paper

2004   2003   2002   2001   4   3   2   1

A CIP catalog record for this book is available from the British Library.

Designed and produced by Flying Fish Graphics, Blue Mounds, Wisconsin
Old engravings from *Food and Drink: A Pictorial Archive from Nineteenth-Century Sources,* Jim Harter. Reproduced by
permission, Dover Publications, Inc., New York

Library of Congress Cataloging-in-Publication Data

Breckenridge, Suzanne.
   Michigan herb cookbook / Suzanne Breckenridge & Marjorie Snyder.
      p. cm.
   ISBN 0-472-08694-4 (pbk. : alk. paper)
   1. Cookery (Herbs) 2. Herbs. 3. Herb gardening—Michigan. I. Snyder, Marjorie. II.
Title.

TX819.H4 B695   2001
641.6'57—dc21   2001023069

Preface

In more than 30 years of cooking and gardening, we have come to realize the importance of a special book on growing and cooking with herbs here in Michigan. Michigan offers unique gardening opportunities. Its geographical location spans the Hardiness Zones from 3 to 6. In some coastal areas the climate is comparable to that of Southern states, making it possible to grow fruits like sweet cherries, nectarines, apricots, and peaches, and even almonds and pecans. Knowing this, and rejoicing in the knowledge that we actually do have good earth, we wanted to write a book about what to expect from this growing season, a book that would provide recipes for all tastes and all levels of cooking ability—recipes to challenge and recipes to start you on your way to confident cooking; a book written with the hope that home cooking and home gardening are the future; a book that would help teach how to use herbs effectively in everyday cooking. Most of all, we hope that with this book all your questions get answered and your senses heightened.

Although neither Suzanne or I was born in Michigan, nor do we live there now, we still have strong feelings for the Wolverine State. We both spent much of our youth in various cities throughout the state. Suzanne's early elementary school years were spent in Grand Rapids, where instead of recalling food and smells, she remembers the next door neighbor's cocker spaniel that bit her! But food did play an important part in her childhood. Family reunions happened regularly on both sides of her family. Potlucks were the tradition—and pie making was the specialty. Fresh peach and fresh cherry pies were favorites of the family. Those pies are probably why Suzanne is so skilled at pastry making today.

I spent every summer till I was 14 in the Muskegon-Ludington area. I remember going with my mother's family, who still live in the area, to peach orchards and picking bushels and bushels of this fragile, delicious fruit. Then the assembly line would begin—quarts of canned peaches, peach preserves, and chutneys were made—always on the hottest days of the summer. Later, toting picnic baskets, the family would pile into cars in search of blueberry patches. Some attempts were more successful than others, but one thing is for sure—we always came home with blue-stained shorts and at least one bucket of blueberries for pie!

Our husbands also share ties with Michigan—my husband, Chuck, also summered in the Ludington area, where many of his relatives live. It's funny we never ran into each other then—or did we? We didn't meet till college, but I bet we passed each other in the dining room of Win Schuler's! Now my husband spends a great deal of time fishing the beautiful trout streams of Michigan—both in the Upper and Lower Peninsulas. He claims some of the finest trout fishing east of the Mississippi is in Michigan.

Suzanne's husband lived in Michigan the longest. He attended Saugatuck Elementary School and Saugatuck High School—in fact, last year he attended his high school class reunion, and everyone was there! Bruce's mother and grandmother lived there for at least 40 years, and Suzanne remembers Bruce's mother, Marjorie, entering her famous dill pickles in the local county fair.

So with these ties and fond remembrances of Michigan, we thought a cookbook featuring some of the best this state has to offer would be appreciated. We hope you agree.

Marjorie Snyder
Suzanne Breckenridge
March 2001

ॐ

Acknowledgments

We'd like to thank Mary Erwin of the University of Michigan Press for supporting us as we put together this book. She let us choose our pace and style and trusted our decisions about content.

Thanks to Jerry Minnich, the publisher of *The Wisconsin Herb Cookbook*, who suggested us for this project.

Thanks to our students throughout the many years of cooking classes and from wherever we took our road show for giving us honest feedback.

Thanks to Ann McNitt, who first introduced us to cooking with herbs and let her class be our stage.

Thanks to our many friends and relatives who shared meals, mostly experimental, over the years and gave us praise and polite criticism.

Last, but certainly not least, we thank our families—Suzanne's husband Bruce, their daughter, Sarah, and son, Ethan; and Marjorie's husband, Charles, their two daughters, Ryan and Dana, and their great-chef son-in-law, Chris. During our intense recipe development they put up with some unusual meals—sometimes consisting only of desserts or side dishes—all in our pursuit of the perfect recipe! A special thanks to them for their love and encouragement.

Contents

Introduction

"Where did you and Suzanne meet?" This is the question our students always are curious to know. I guess they think we're going to say "at LaVarenne in France or the Culinary Institute in New York." Then we tell them, and they seem somewhat disillusioned—maybe I'm reading into it. Actually, I thought our chance meeting was rather unique—we met on the beach. Why, that's the way romance novels begin! I'm afraid our husbands didn't think much about it when we both came home and said we had met a new neighbor who also had a daughter the same age as ours. This was a big deal. Wheels started turning and visions of new playmates spun through our heads since we both lived in a neighborhood where there weren't many kids.

I don't particularly like sun, and I like sand and water even less, at least being out in them, so when I discovered that another Mom was willing to take my daughter to swimming lessons in exchange for playtime and baby-sitting, I jumped at the chance. Suzanne is a sun-worshipper and I am not; in that respect we are exact opposites and over the years of being friends and partners, this is probably the only thing we don't agree on. Not bad.

In the process of our daughter-exchanges, we did what most mothers do when watching their kids play. We talked and eventually our talk got around to what we both did. At that time we were both full-time Moms on part-time schedules . . . isn't that the case for everyone? Suzanne was teaching at our local Junior-Technical College in the Art Department. Her specialty was ceramics. I was teaching at the same place but in the Business Department.

It was summer and Suzanne and I both had interests in gardening. She had a beautiful flower garden, growing things that aren't supposed to grow but somehow did. I tried to play Earth Mother and grow organic vegetables and chickens for future free-range dinners; thankfully, city ordinances prohibited the latter. We also discovered in our talks that we lived around the block from one another—a fact that proved very handy in later years.

As the first summer continued, Suzanne and I would talk about recipes, not uncommon even today. We were really interested in trying all kinds of foods since neither of us had much background in ethnic cuisine, or herbs for that matter.

One day a brochure of noncredit classes was stuck in our mail and we noticed that a local woman was offering a class on Herbs. Just Herbs. So when fall arrived and our daughters started kindergarten we signed up for the class. I hadn't taken a class since college and I don't think Suzanne had either. The class was taught by a delightful and very knowledgeable woman named Anne McNitt. The class was in the evening and it had about six or seven equally herbally challenged people! It met in a smelly chemistry lab of a high school. Try and counteract the scent of sulfuric acid with herbs! Anne was filled with information. In fact, I still have her handouts (done on a mimeograph machine no less) and my notes, which I actually consulted while writing this book. It was her enthusiasm that sparked something in both Suzanne and me. She lived and breathed herbs and she made it seem like that's just the way life should be. It didn't take long for us to get just as interested.

Anne asked if any of us would be interested in bringing in some herbal treats. Suzanne and I volunteered to make a few of our favorites and work on a few together. It was at this moment we knew we shared more than a common interest; we shared a common taste. As we talked we found out we both had a wonderful gift. We can talk about a flavor and we both know what the other is tasting. Not many people in the food business can say that. We prepared several things. One was a lovely dill-flavored salmon mousse with scales made from slivered almonds tinted pale orange-pink! The class enjoyed it and they asked that we teach them how it was made.

We decided to take their advice and teach exactly what they wanted. Herb Cooking. That spring we worked on a schedule. Suzanne, with her graphic arts background, designed beautiful brochures; with my English background, I did the writing. We sent them out to our former classmates, who passed them along to friends, and pretty soon we had a full enrollment. We met at my house since the kitchen was bigger than Suzanne's. (Suzanne, after all these years, still miraculously turns out wedding banquet feasts in a kitchen the size of a dining room table!) The classes were successful. We continued for many years offering classes on Cooking with Herbs. They were both fun and exhausting.

We called ourselves The Herb Forum. Word of mouth kept our classes filled; eventually some of our students got us interested in sharing our knowledge publicly. They asked that we write for a local newspaper and a local magazine and eventually we became the Food Editors for *Wisconsin Trails Magazine*. During that time Suzanne increased her family. Her son was born. We began experimenting with herbal products. We started selling herbal sauces, pestos, mustards, and vinegars at our local Farmers Market.

We like to think of ourselves as front-runners in the condiment craze. We bought gigantic stainless steel stockpots and began cranking out vinegars. During those summers we never experienced sinus problems; cauldrons of vinegar and mustard pretty much cleared our heads! We were quite successful at this condiment venture, but eventually it became too much and the Farmers Market rules for homemade products changed. We had to decide to expand into a full-time job or venture in another direction. We chose the latter. We started catering, another adventure that almost broke our backs.

We also tried to get the public to learn what we had found so fascinating—herbs. We and six others started the Madison, Wisconsin, Herb Society, an organization that today boasts over 200 members. We helped design Madison's first public herb garden at Olbrich Park, gave many public lectures there, and sponsored local chefs who did programs for us.

Finally, it was time for us to put some of our recipes to the test, so we wrote our first book, *The Wisconsin Country Gourmet*, a beautiful full-color cookbook published by Wisconsin Trails. We are still very proud of that work. Recipes in it were based on our earlier magazine articles and we still find them good enough that we use them ourselves. Now there's an endorsement!

We continued to teach classes. But after a rather untimely accident in one of our classes that involved my cat we decided to move on.

Well, that was 19 years ago. Since then we opened and closed a catering business and joined two other women for another cooking school adventure. I had another daughter, and we have taken our Herb Cooking Show on the road—in the style of Laverne and Shirley. That brings us to today. After all the classes and all the articles we've written, we finally decided to put together an updated version of Cooking with Herbs *à la* Suzanne and Marge. We hope you enjoy it.

Marjorie A. Snyder
Madison, Wisconsin
March 2001

ﾞ

History, Growing Ideas & Uses of Herbs

History

Herbs have a sneaky way of becoming an obsession when given half a chance. Once you start learning about them and begin using them you'll find out what a fascinating part they've played in antiquity and still play in our personal lives. They're a delight to the touch, smell, and taste and are the subject of countless stories from history, mythology, literature, medicine, and witchcraft. They become part of your life. But for those of you not yet bitten by the herb bug, where do you begin? How do you go about using herbs? Where do you start? Can you start out small? What if your family doesn't like them? Whew. There are a lot of questions to answer.

Fortunately, as herbalists who have done our share of trial and error, we thought we'd better start at the real beginning before swamping you with details about herbs, cooking, and gardening. First things first. Just exactly what is an herb? After much thinking and consulting botanicals and herbals, we only became more confused ourselves. Then we decided to do the scholarly thing and consult a real source: the dictionary. We discovered that our trusted Webster's dictionary didn't offer as much help as we thought. The definition we found was . . . "an herb is a seed plant of which the stem does not become woody or persist (as a shrub or tree) but remains more or less soft and succulent and dies to the ground (or entirely) after flowering. . . ." This definition covers a great deal, includes more plants than we can name, and excludes some plants we know are herbs. Using Webster's definition, even tomatoes and snapdragons are classified as herbs, but rosemary is not! So we continued our search and came across a few local herbalists who found their answer years ago. Simply, we discovered, they narrow the field down considerably with an easy "litmus" test. An herb or spice to them is a plant that falls into one of five categories. It should either be decorative, fragrant, medicinal, culinary, or used in dyeing. This seemed a logical approach, and being cooks, we decided to concentrate only on the culinary plants.

Most herbs are native to the Mediterranean region and can tolerate poor soil, light watering, and very little fertilizer. The part of the herb used for cooking is mainly the green leaves and in some cases the seeds or flowers. Spices are a little different. By definition, they resemble herbs, but instead of growing in mild climates, they prefer tropical areas. They're almost always brown or yellow in color and the roots, pods, seeds, and bark are their prized features.

Herbs were not used in cooking at first; rather, they were used in religion and medicine. There is no real documented date when most herbs were discovered. Legend tells us that people learned about herbs by observing animals and how they reacted to various plants. If eating a particular plant resulted in a certain behavioral or physical change, such as lethargy, then it was thought the plants had caused it. This, of course, is also how poisonous plants were discovered!

Centuries later, specific plants that produced known effects were confined to a Physic Garden. They were grown in monasteries and studied by both the clergy and doctors. One of the theories that explained the medicinal properties of herbs was the Doctrine of Signatures. In essence it was thought that the appearance of a plant, its color, scent, and shape, indicated the disease for which a cure was provided. For instance, red flowering burdock was used to purify the blood. This is not now a widely accepted theory, but it is the origin of many herbal names. The study of herbs continued but still mostly by the medical profession. Somewhere along the way witchcraft emerged. Herbs were used to cast spells—a few berries from Deadly Nightshade would cause mild delirium. Herbs were given in varying degrees for specific spells, so witchcraft was now linked to medicine and herbs.

Eventually herbs started to become familiar in everyone's home. Women became keepers of the herbs. Wives and mothers were in charge of the household and this included the health of the family. They often had to administer simple herbal remedies. Then the real breakthrough occurred. More and more people began living in cities. Their food was not as fresh, and they needed some way to preserve it. People began to use the same plants they used for medicine to preserve meats and vegetables—in reality to disguise the sometimes rancid foods. Herbs now were being used for cooking. Fortunately things have evolved even further and herbs are now used to enhance the best flavors of food rather than masking the worst.

Growing Ideas

To help you explore the world of herbs and see how flavors improve, we've chosen a basic culinary sample of 12 easy-to-grow and widely used herbs. Following their in-depth descriptions, we've briefly outlined another group of 24 herbs that we couldn't do without. They're not as common in every garden, but eventually you'll probably want to include some of them, too. They all grow successfully in Michigan's climate.

After deciding to plant an herb garden and before plowing up the back forty, there are other things to consider. How many plants do you want? Which plants do you want? How many are needed for a family? What kind of space do you have? And how much time and money do you want to spend on this adventure?

Ideally, you should have your backyard soil or your chosen garden site tested. And don't forget the orientation of your site—is it sunny, partially sunny, or all in the shade? It's better to have this decided and analyzed now than to undo all your good intentions later.

Design

One of the most exciting things about growing herbs is the actual design of the garden. An herb garden is a place of enchantment—no matter what size. And here is your chance to be truly creative—even more than in a flower garden. Throughout history herb gardens were designed around a theme. Of course you can intersperse them in border gardens, in vegetable gardens, in perennial gardens, or in annual beds, but making them a focal point in your overall garden scheme is more fun.

There are hundreds of books that will give you precise guidelines. (We've included several designs at the end of this chapter.) Some use age-old designs like the knot garden—an old Elizabethan idea of intermingling plants to form a maze. Those, like the ones in castle courtyards, were intricate and large enough to actually walk through. Today many of these still exist in England, Italy, and France. Many public gardens in this country have reproduced them but in much smaller scale. You can do this yourself in your own backyard in miniature form.

There are other traditional herb garden designs you could use as inspiration. Some of these possibilities are: a lemon garden, silver garden, blue-, white-, or pink-flowering herb garden, Shakespeare garden, Biblical garden, Italian garden, and the list goes on. Besides a specific theme garden, you can choose a garden that fits a specific landscape feature—water element, small driveway garden, hillside garden, the old Colonial backdoor kitchen garden, even an all-container garden. You're limited only by your imagination. Once you've decided on a theme and a design, the plants to be included must be given some thought, along with the site orientation—sun, shade, or partial shade. The following page offers some ideas:

Ground Cover Herbs:
> Sweet Woodruff, Mints, Creeping Thyme, Creeping Oregano, Winter Savory

Rock Garden Herbs:
> Rosemary, Thyme, Dwarf Sages, Savory, Corsican Mint

Bee Garden Herbs:
> Hyssop, Marjoram, Mint, Lemon Balm, Savories, Thyme

Container Herbs:
> Chives, Common Thyme, Corsican Mint, Scented Geraniums, Lemon Verbena, Ginger, Marjoram, Pineapple Sage, Rosemary, Nasturtiums, Calendula, Salad Burnet

Hanging Basket Herbs:
> Creeping Thyme, Creeping Rosemary, Nasturtiums, Mint, Scented Geraniums, Creeping Savory

Tea Plant Herbs:
> Chamomile, Lemon Balm, Sage, Mint, Rosemary, Lemon Verbena, Bee Balm, Pineapple Sage, Thyme

Partial Shade Herbs:
> Chives, Basil, French Tarragon, Lovage, Sweet Woodruff, Mint, Chervil, Parsley, Lemon Balm

You need patience the first year of your herb garden. It's a learning experience! You'll quickly discover what plants do well and which you'll want to remove. You'll also discover which plants need more or less sun and more or less water. This is true even for container and hanging basket herb gardens.

Planting
It's been said that sowing seeds directly into the soil will result in the strongest and hardiest

plant specimens. But if you choose to buy plants rather than starting them from seeds, select large, bright green, bushy, bug-free plants for a good start and a burst of show in a short time. Know the plant dimensions before you begin to plant. What are the adult height and width of your plant? Does it spread slowly or grow more upright? Does it reseed itself or must you plant new ones each year? Plan this out on paper and label your plants as they are placed in the garden. Don't rely on your memory to pick out your tiny plants from a weed once they start growing!

Most of the perennial plants can be put into the ground in Michigan as soon as the soil is warm enough to be worked. In new beds, dig 10"-12" deep and remove as much clay and stone as possible. If the soil has too much clay or is too full of rocks, you may need to remove all of it and start over with good top soil and a light mix of manure. No matter what our soil is like, we always add a little lime to sweeten the herbs and a little peat moss to loosen the soil. Each year after that we work compost around the beds and supplement with more lime. We keep our herbs mulched with either cocoa hulls or leaves and grass clippings and work them in the following spring. This cuts down on weeds and means less watering.

Because herb gardens are generally more formal in design than other gardens, it's nice to frame them either with bricks (which is traditional), railroad ties, wattle fences (an old Colonial-designed fence that's woven out of willow branches), decorative wooden fences, or hedge plants like boxwood, germander, or santolina. Paths should also be carefully planned. Use bricks, flagstone, cedar bark, or finely crushed stone. Choose a texture to balance your design.

Once your herb garden is planted, maintaining it is very easy. Herbs are virtually maintenance-free, pest resistant, and with their sweet fragrance, a pure pleasure to weed. It only takes a few minutes each day to care for your garden, unless you have acres! In the beginning you'll probably spend more time weeding since vigorous weeds can overcrowd young plants, but by the middle of the summer your plants will have established themselves and after that it's only fun.

Using Herbs

Using your garden is the next step. Fresh is best. Pick the fragrant leaves and flowers and use them in your recipes. From experience, we suggest you take it slow. Don't use too many herbs at one meal or in one dish; they can be overpowering. Like the chocolate chip cookies made with curry powder produced when I once told my class to experiment with spices and their favorite recipe! In the recipe section of this book we've included sample menus to get you on your way to successfully combining and using herbs. Almost all of them contain herbs but not so many as to be overwhelming.

As the season grows on, so will your herbs and you will be faced with another dilemma—a rather nice one. What are you going to do with all these herbs? Preserve them. The two most common methods are freezing and drying. Dried herbs are fine to use in recipes, in some cases even better than fresh. Dried herbs are more concentrated than fresh ones, so in recipes you'll use less of them. The ratio is three to one; that is, 1 tsp. dried is equal to 1 tbl. fresh.

Freezing Herbs

Some herbs freeze better than others, but in any case, thawed frozen herbs become soggy (aromatic but soggy). They don't look as appealing in salads or as garnishes and are best used in soups, stews, or other cooked dishes. Basil, tarragon, dill, Italian parsley, and chives are most commonly frozen. Rinse the fresh leaves, shake them dry, and for everything but chives, strip the leaves from the stem and place on a cookie sheet. Freeze for a few hours. When completely frozen, remove from sheets and place in plastic boxes with lids. Label and freeze. For chives, simply mince the stalks and place in a small freezer container. Some people make purees of their herbs and freeze them into ice cubes. Just be sure you label the containers!

Drying Herbs

To dry herbs you have four choices: hang drying, quick drying, decorative drying, and tray drying. One is sure to fit your needs. For any method, pick the fresh herbs in the late morning, after the dew has dried off and shortly before the afternoon heat sets in. Wash them under cool running water and dry with paper or cloth towels.

Hang Drying: Gather the herbs into small bunches and tie with string or rubber bands. Hang them upside down in a well-ventilated room, attic, or kitchen. If the room is dusty, place the bunch in a paper bag that's been perforated with holes and tie the bag around the stems. It's not particularly attractive, so place it in a dark or infrequently used room. Basil should be dried like this because exposure to light causes the leaves to turn black.

Quick Drying: Spread the herb leaves, whole or stripped from the stalks, on a cheesecloth or parchment-paper-covered rack in the oven at its lowest setting. Leave the door ajar and stir occasionally until they are crisp. You'll be surprised that this will only take a few minutes.

Decorative Drying: You need a deep cardboard box with a lid. Pour in 2" of a drying medium, like borax powder, extra fine sand, silica gel, or equal parts of cornmeal and borax. Lay the flowers (stems removed) or leaves in the medium and pour more on top to completely cover. The flowers and leaves will dry in five to seven days. Use these only for decoration.

Tray Drying: This method requires a few building supplies. Use a wooden frame, such as an old window, or make one any size you want. Cover it with very fine screening and staple securely to the frame. You can make several; they're very good for drying flowers for decoration. Place the leaves on top and let dry in the summer air or in a well-ventilated warm room. Stir the leaves daily. They'll dry in about seven to ten days.

The newest method for drying and preserving your herbs is with a microwave or dehydrator. They're just as effective as the natural methods. Because appliances vary so much in power, we suggest you follow your manufacturer's directions for exact times and methods.

Storing Herbs

When your herbs are completely dry, strip them from their stalks if this hasn't been done already and place in containers with tight-fitting lids (mason jars, old jelly jars, tin containers, and ceramic jars all work well). Label and store in a dark place away from direct sunlight. Many people store herbs on a shelf above a stove, but this causes the herbs to dry out too quickly and lose their aroma. Freshly dried herbs will keep their fragrance for a year or longer. Smell for flavor. If the herbs smell musty or have no scent, it's time to toss them on your compost pile! We find most herbs dry well, with the exception of parsley, cilantro, and chervil. Their dried flavor is similar to shredded green construction paper!

On the following pages you'll find specific information about growing each culinary herb. It's best to start from seeds or plants and we've included the growing conditions, varieties, and uses for herbs in your kitchen. For more detailed information, see *The Michigan Gardening Guide* by Jerry Minnich.

A Basic Kitchen Garden

	Type	Light	Height	Start From	Uses
BASIL *Ocimum basilicum*	A	S & FS	1 1/2'	seed	Pasta, tomatoes, soups, zucchini, salads
CHIVES *Allium schoenoprasum*	P	S	2'	plants	Breads, soup, fish, omelets, salads
CILANTRO *Coriandrum sativum*	A	FS	1'	seed	Salsas, tomatoes, Asian, Thai, Mexican foods
DILL *Anethum graveolens*	A	FS	3-4'	seed	Pickles, fish, salads, cheese dips, soups
MARJORAM *Origanum marjorana*	A	FS	12-18"	plant	Pasta sauces, eggs, salads
MINT *Mentha species*	P	S	1"-3'	plant	Tea, fruit dishes, salads, desserts
OREGANO *Origanum vulgare*	P	FS	4"-1'	plant	Salads, pasta sauces, pizza, meats
PARSLEY *Petroselinum crispum*	A	S	8-18"	plants	Everything
ROSEMARY *Rosmarinus officinalis*	TP	FS & S	6"-3'	plant	Dressings, potatoes, lamb, fish, bread
SAGE *Salvia officinalis*	P/A	FS	2-3'	plant	Dressings, bread, pork
TARRAGON *Artemisia dracunculus*	P	S & FS	2-3'	plant	Poultry, vinegars, salads, chicken
THYME *Thymus vulgaris*	P	FS	2"-12"	plant	Beef, chicken, soup, salads

A = Annual   P = Perennial   TP = Tender Perennial   FS = Full Sun   S = Sun, but can tolerate some shade

12 Easy-to-Grow Kitchen Herbs

Basil (*Ocimum basilicum*)

Type: Annual

Light Conditions: Full sun to partial shade

Moisture & Soil: Prefers moderately rich soil; don't overwater

Varieties: Over 20 types: we suggest purple or opal, lemon, cinnamon, Thai, ruffled, sweet or Italian, bush, holy, and camphor

Propagation: Seeds, plants

Growth Habit: 18"-24", grows upright and bushes out about 10" per plant. Easy and quick to grow from seed. Sow directly into the ground after all danger of frost is gone. It's the first herb to succumb to frost. Leaves are bright green, except the opal, and should be pinched back as soon as it flowers.

Suggestions: We suggest one package of seed for average kitchen use, plus one of each plant variety for experimenting. The bush variety makes a wonderful border plant.

Historical, Mythological & Medicinal Lore: In Greek, basil means king. It represents love, honor, and devotion. During the Middle Ages newlyweds had sprigs of basil scattered around their doors and windows to insure marital fidelity. It was one of the Elizabethan strewing herbs—herbs that are scattered on the floor to create a pleasant smell when crushed underfoot. In India the plant is used in aromatherapy and brings enlightenment and harmony, plus it is used as a disinfectant against malaria.

Not all associations are pleasant. The name basil was derived from "basilisk," a serpent-like creature that could kill with a look, and for many years was linked with poisonous beasts. In Salem, Massachusetts, a pot of basil was strong evidence of the presence of a witch.

Culinary Uses: A pot of basil is said to keep flies away. The scent of the leaves is "perfumey," a combination of clove and pepper with a hint of licorice. It's often used in Italian cooking and is closely associated with tomato-based dishes. It goes well with eggplant, zucchini, mushrooms, eggs, meat, and poultry dishes. It's most well known for pesto, a sauce made from basil leaves, oil, cheese, and nuts.

9

Pesto is used on pasta, over tomato salad, in salad dressing, soups, and for purists as a dip for crusty bread.

Chives (*Allium schoenoprasum*)

Type: Perennial

Light Conditions: Sun to partial sun

Moisture & Soil: Rich garden soil, average watering

Varieties: Garlic or Chinese

Propagation: Division, plants, seeds

Growth Habit: Grows to about 2'. Should be clipped regularly throughout the season to about 6"-8" or it falls over and looks ragged. Grows well in pots, even indoors. Can be sown directly into the soil. Every three to four years it should be dug up and divided to promote healthy plants.

Suggestions: Chives make a good border plant, if clipped regularly. In early spring delicate purple blossoms form and can be used in salads or dried for arrangements. When added to vinegar it tints it a lovely lavender color; unfortunately if not removed soon enough the flavor is very strong and unpleasant smelling.

Historical, Mythological & Medicinal Lore: It is an old European custom to hang bunches of chives in doorways to ward off evil spirits. In Chinese medical history the volatile oil in chives is said to have a tonic effect and helps control high blood pressure.

Culinary Uses: Use chives fresh at the end of cooking or for garnishes. Heating chives causes them to disintegrate. Its mild onion flavor is favored in egg dishes, salads, soups, marinades, and cheese. Difficult to dry successfully, most often it's commercially freeze-dried. It's one of the herbs in the French fines herbes. Whole chive stems are often used as decorative ribbons around bunches of cooked carrots, asparagus, and green beans.

Cilantro (*Coriandrum sativum*), also called Chinese Parsley or Coriander

Type: Annual

Light Conditions: Full sun

Moisture & Soil: Prefers dry soil. When it's very hot it tends to bolt, like spring lettuce.

Varieties: None

Propagation: Seeds

Growth Habit: Grows to about 12"-18". The leaves look like a ferny parsley plant.

Suggestions: Grow from seeds and sow throughout the growing season since in northern climates plants tend to go to seed quickly. It's the only plant we know that's both an herb and a spice. The leaves are the herb, but when it goes to seed, the seeds are considered to be a spice. Cilantro has an unusual taste and it's one of those herbs that you either will love, or as Suzanne says, learn to love!

Historical, Mythological & Medicinal Lore: Coriander's name is from the Greek word for "bug" because of its pungent odor. It is used in many cultures. Chinese herbalists used it in a drink as an aphrodisiac, linking it to immortality. Seeds were found in the Egyptian tombs and sprouted after thousands of years. In India the plant is said to cool hot stomachs, banish gas, and aid digestion. Early Romans crushed the seeds and inhaled the aroma to relieve dizziness; they called it "dizzycorn." And it's one of the bitter herbs mentioned in the Bible for Passover

Culinary Uses: A favorite herb of ours. Use it only in fresh form—dried has no flavor. It's found in many ethnic cuisines: Thai, Mexican, Indian, Moroccan, Spanish, and African. In Thai cooking, the roots with their nut-like flavor are used as well.

Coriander seeds are ground and used extensively in baking in northern European countries. It has a slight orange taste. We use it in poaching pears and in desserts with apples, gingerbreads, cooked fruits, cookies, and cakes. It's also part of the spice combination known as curry powder.

The leaves are indispensable in cooking. We use them in salsas, salads, tortilla dishes, and pasta sauces and with fish and chicken.

Dill (*Anethum graveolens*)

Type: Annual

Light Conditions: Full sun

Moisture & Soil: Poor but well drained soil. Water moderately.

Varieties: A variety sometimes called dwarf or Dukat is a new hybrid that reportedly grows only to 12" and has mostly feathery leaves

Propagation: Seeds

Growth Habit: Regular dill grows to about 3'-4' with flower head and seeds

Suggestions: We grow Dukat dill from seed in the spring and early fall.

Historical, Mythological & Medicinal Lore: Dill is the Norse word meaning "to lull" and often has a soporific effect on babies. In Colonial times the dill seed was given to church parishioners to nibble in hopes of suppressing hunger pangs that developed during long sermons.

Culinary Uses: The feathery leaves or weed with its unmistakable flavor is used as often as parsley. It's particularly good in egg and potato dishes, with cucumber, shellfish, smoked fish, poultry, cheese, carrots, peas, green beans, cabbage, cooked root vegetables, rice, mixed with cottage cheese, over lamb, veal, or chicken while roasting, and added to gravies.

The seed has more intense flavor and is mainly used in breads, chutneys, and pickles.

Marjoram (*Marjoram hortensis* or *Origanum marjorana*)

Type: Annual

Light Conditions: Full sun

Moisture & Soil: Prefers a slightly alkaline soil, needs good drainage, moderate watering

Varieties: Pot marjoram

Propagation: Plants, seeds

Growth Habit: A slender upright plant 12"-18" tall, it flowers in early summer with white and pink flowers that grow in a knot-like cluster. It needs constant pinching to promote bushiness. Slow to germinate from seeds. Easy to grow from plants or cuttings.

Suggestions: Since leaves are so small, we plant several for average consumption. Some we grow in containers. This sweet smelling herb doesn't get the recognition it deserves. We use it in many foods.

Historical, Mythological & Medicinal Lore: A symbol of happiness often woven into a bride's headpiece. Because of its sweet aroma, Venus was said to have created marjoram. It was used during Elizabethan times as a strewing herb.

American Indians used it in many ways. It was drunk as a tea and used as a gargle for sore throats, and the leaves were chewed to make the breath sweeter.

Culinary Uses: The flavor is sweet and perfume-like. Often used in vinaigrettes, salads, egg dishes, soups, with fish, sausage, onions, potatoes, tomatoes, pizza, mushrooms, and chicken.

13

Mint *(Mentha species)*

Type: Perennial

Light Conditions: Partial shade to shade

Moisture & Soil: Rich, moist soil, water more frequently than other herbs

Varieties: Many types. We suggest: apple, orange, pennyroyal, Corsican (tender perennial), chocolate, lemon, grapefruit, spearmint, peppermint, pineapple, Kentucky Colonel, Korean (anise flavored).

Propagation: Cuttings, division, plants, seeds

Growth Habit: A very invasive plant that spreads by underground runners. It grows from 1" (Corsican) to 3'. Use plants or cuttings or acquire by division. Has lavender blossoms in late summer that attract bees.

Plant in areas that you don't want anything else to grow; in containers sunk in the ground, or surround the plant with metal strips.

Suggestions: We grow peppermint, spearmint, orange, and Corsican (in pots). One plant is more than enough for a family.

Historical, Mythological & Medicinal Lore: Mint is the symbol of hospitality and wisdom. In India it was used to scent a room by hanging bunches in doorways. In medieval times it was used as a strewing herb. Hebrews sprinkled it on the floor of synagogues to freshen the air, and Greeks and Romans polished banquet tables with mint leaves to promote healthy appetites.

Today mint plays a large role in medicine as the active ingredient in most menthol flavors. It was once used to treat hiccups and its soothing effect eases nausea and vomiting. Ancient medicine men used the leaves to combat dog bites, prevent indigestion, cure mouth ailments, and heal skin diseases. It is said if you rub the leaves on your face, neck, and arms it repels mosquitoes. Planted close to the house it will discourage mice from entering.

14

Ancient Greeks believed that when Pluto, god of the underworld, fell in love with Mentha, his wife, Persephone, flew into a jealous rage and turned Mentha into this herb and left her to grow in the forest forever.

Culinary Uses: Fresh leaves are best, but it dries beautifully. You can candy the leaves for use in cake decoration. Corsican mint has the most intense mint flavor and was originally the main ingredient in crème de menthe. It's used extensively in Middle Eastern cooking and said to tame the heat of foods in Thai cuisine.

It's rich in vitamins and minerals and is particularly good in desserts, fruit salads, sauces, and lamb dishes and as a refreshing tea, hot or iced. It goes well with peas, carrots, green beans, spinach, cabbage, new potatoes, chicken, applesauce, poached pears, chocolate, fruit cocktails, and jellies.

❧

Oregano (*Origanum vulgare*)

Type: Perennial

Light Conditions: Full sun

Moisture & Soil: Needs well drained good soil. Allow for spreading. Water evenly.

Varieties: Many types. We suggest golden creeping, Greek, Mexican, Dittany of Crete, Cuban, and Puerto Rican; sometimes called wild marjoram.

Propagation: Plants, cuttings, division, seeds

Growth Habit: Sprawling plant and some varieties are suitable for hanging pots. Grows from 4" to about 1'. It flowers in mid to late summer with pink and purple blossoms. Should be replaced every three to four years as it becomes woody and bitter tasting.

Suggestions: We grow several varieties, some for ground covers, like golden, and others for culinary use, like Greek or Mexican.

Historical, Mythological & Medicinal Lore: According to legend, a Greek servant of a cruel king was carrying a large bottle of a favored perfume and accidentally dropped it. The servant was so terrified he fainted. The gods saw the unconscious boy and saved him from the king by turning him into a fragrant herb—oregano. Then they hid him deep in the forest to protect him from the king's rage.

In Latin, oregano means "joy of the mountains." Livestock that grazed oregano meadows were said to have tasty meat. Early herbalists combined the leaves with honey and applied it to scrapes, bruises, insect bites, and aching muscles. American pioneers used it as snuff and rolled the leaves into cigarettes.

Culinary Uses: It's called the pizza plant. It has a sharp taste, a little like thyme. Found extensively in Italian cooking and Mexican and Spanish recipes. Use fresh or dried with beef, pork, lamb, salad dressings, marinades, with beans, lentils, eggplant, summer squash, stews, pasta sauces, and cheese spreads. It dries well.

Parsley (*Petroselinum crispum*)

Type: Biennial, treated in this climate as an annual. Second year growth tends to be bitter tasting.

Light Conditions: Partial sun

Moisture & Soil: Grows in moderately rich soil, water evenly

Varieties: Italian, curly, and Hamburg (grown for the root)

Propagation: Plants, seeds

Growth Habit: Grows 8"-18" depending on variety. Very, very slow to germinate from seed. Soaking seeds in water overnight helps. Plants are preferred. Curly parsley is more compact and used as an edging plant. Italian gets quite tall and full. Once it flowers, the flavor becomes bitter tasting. Doesn't make a good potted plant because of the long tap root.

Suggestions: We plant three to four Italian parsley plants for our kitchen use—it has more flavor than the curly variety. Parsley is so good for you it should be a staple in any kitchen. It contains incredibly high amounts of vitamins A and C and large quantities of iron, calcium, and iodine and more beta carotene than a large carrot. It's the most universal herb.

Historical, Mythological & Medicinal Lore: Early Greeks fed it to chariot horses to make them run faster and wove it into wreaths for athletes to ensure speed and victory. The early Romans used it as a breath cleanser, especially after orgies to mask alcoholic odors. The custom of placing parsley on dinner plates probably has its basis in that old tale.

Culinary Uses: A universal herb that can be used with any food or in combination with any herb, except desserts. Italian parsley has the favored taste, curly parsley is often used as garnish. It keeps fresh in the refrigerator if stored in a glass of water. Combined with garlic and lemon zest it's called gremolata, an Italian garnish added to stews and risottos. It's the main ingredient in bouquet garni and fines herbes. Only use it fresh—it loses its flavor when dried.

Rosemary (*Rosmarinus officinalis*)

Type: Tender perennial in our climate

Light Conditions: Full sun

Moisture & Soil: Grows in light, dry, and slightly alkaline soil. Add lime for sweetness. Indoors in winter it must be watered two to three times weekly.

Varieties: Many varieties. Some we use are creeping or trailing, pink, golden, white, and Tuscan blue

Propagation: Cuttings, layering, plants, seeds

Growth Habit: Grows to 3' or more. Can be easily trained as a topiary or bonsai plant. Some varieties (the trailing and creeping ones) are used in hanging baskets. Slow growing and best started with plants or cuttings. Keep your rosemary in good-sized clay pots and sink in the ground during the summer. Must be brought inside in winter. Keep in a cool, very sunny room and water very frequently.

Suggestions: We suggest two plants per household or more. One that's upright and trained like a small tree, the other in a hanging basket.

Historical, Mythological & Medicinal Lore: The name rosemary is Latin for "dew of the sea" because it grows along the craggy cliffs of the Mediterranean. It is also called the herb of remembrance as in Shakespeare's *Hamlet*: "There's Rosemary, that's for Remembrance. . . ." Greek scholars tucked rosemary sprigs in their hair when studying to help them remember what they learned. Some stories say that rosemary was used to try to awaken Sleeping Beauty.

In Elizabethan days, rosemary sprigs were tied with colored ribbons, then the tips dipped in gold and given to wedding guests to symbolize love and faithfulness. Brides would give sprigs of rosemary to their grooms on the wedding morning to ensure love, wisdom, and loyalty.

In the Middle Ages it was also used as a strewing herb. The strong, pungent, resinous oil of rosemary is used in perfumes, toiletries, insect repellents, furniture polish, disinfectants, moth repellents, mouthwashes, headache medicine, and sleeping powders and as a hair rinse for blondes.

Culinary Uses: It has a pine-camphor-citrus aroma and is used fresh or dried. Dried rosemary is like hard

17

pine needles and should be crushed with a mortar and pestle before adding to food. Avoid ground rosemary; it has almost no flavor. Rosemary makes a refreshing tea when mixed with sage and mint.

Great in rich dishes like pork or lamb and blends well with potatoes, egg dishes, rice, apples, oranges, poultry stuffing, venison, eggplant, squash, grilled fish, mushrooms, lentils, vinegars, and marinades.

❧

Sage *(Salvia officinalis)*

Type: Perennial/annual

Light Conditions: Full sun

Moisture & Soil: Likes well-drained alkaline soil; don't overwater

Varieties: Hundreds of varieties, perennial and annual. We use dwarf sage, purple, tricolor, honeydew melon, pineapple sage, common sage

Propagation: Cutting, layering, plants, seeds

Growth Habit: Grows 2' to 3' and very bushy. Best started with plants. Common or garden sage has beautiful violet, blue, and magenta flowers. Renew plants every five to six years. Prune old growth in the spring after flowering. Makes a good background or hedge plant because of its lovely gray-green foliage.

Suggestions: One common or garden sage plant is enough for general kitchen use. The others are more for decoration. We use pineapple sage as a container plant.

Historical, Mythological & Medicinal Lore: Salvia in Latin means "I am well" and was called the longevity herb. In medieval times sage was thought to impart wisdom and improve the memory. It was first used as a tonic or cure-all tea in the spring after a long winter. Superstition says that when all is well, sage will flourish.

Today, some North American Indians use bundles of a certain type of sage for "smudge sticks."

They dry it and light it to produce smoke. It is then waved around rooms, houses, and cars to disperse and remove any gloomy spirits.

As a cosmetic, it's a popular hair rinse for brunettes and also whitens teeth!

Culinary Uses: Sage dries well but has sharp sticks—often referred to as rubbed sage. Chopping in a mortar and pestle will help.

Sage is said to counteract the fatty tastes of certain foods like pork, veal, goose, pheasant, duck, and sausage. It's used to flavor cheese (English sage derby), fish chowders, and winter squash and, of course, in poultry stuffing. In Italian cooking it's often used in desserts with apples and pears. Avoid ground sage; it has very little flavor.

Tarragon *(Artemisia dracunculus)*

Type: Perennial

Light Conditions: Full sun, tolerates a little shade

Moisture & Soil: Soil should be light and loamy; needs good drainage

Varieties: French and Russian

Propagation: Cuttings and plants

Growth Habit: Grows 2' to 3' tall and spreads 15"-18". Shelter it from cold winds. French tarragon does not flower or set seeds.

Suggestions: Only buy French tarragon for cooking. Russian tarragon looks similar and grows a little larger with white flowers, but the leaves taste like a blade of grass! French tarragon has the characteristic licorice taste. One plant is enough for kitchen use.

Historical, Mythological & Medicinal Lore: Tarragon is called the herb of virtue, yet it's considered an aphrodisiac. Tonics were given to restore romantic feelings in married couples, and brides chewed fresh leaves before their weddings to freshen breath and ensure a blissful marriage.

The French call tarragon "esdragon," or little dragon. Its dragon-like root system can strangle the plant if it is not divided every few years. And it was thought to have powers to heal bites of snakes, serpents, and other venomous creatures.

Marie Antoinette established the herb's exotic reputation. The queen loved the licorice flavor of tarragon and assigned one lady-in-waiting the sole duty of picking perfect fresh leaves each day for her salad. She insisted the girl wear new white leather gloves each day and crush the leaves only slightly so no juice would stain them. The task was performed with such precision and attention that the phrase "handle with kid gloves" evolved.

Culinary Uses: Probably the least well known herb to beginning cooks. Most popular in French cuisine in dishes like Béarnaise sauce or in fines herbes. It's prized in vinegars, great with fish, peas, spinach, asparagus, chicken, shellfish, cauliflower, eggs, cheese, tomatoes, mushrooms, sauces, butters, and fresh in salads.

It dries very well but can turn brown if left too long.

20

Thyme (*Thymus vulgaris*)

Type: Perennial

Light Conditions: Full sun

Moisture & Soil: Soil should not be acidic but can be stony or contain a little sand. Water regularly

Varieties: Hundreds of types; some we suggest are Doone Valley, English, silver, woolly, caraway, coconut, creeping, English, golden lemon—upright and creeping, Mother of Thyme, nutmeg, and oregano. It has beautiful flowers, ranging in color from white to red, that bees love. Good in landscapes because of its texture and growth habits.

Propagation: Cuttings, layering, plants, seeds

Growth Habit: Grows from 2"-12". Can be grown from seeds but purchasing plants is preferred and allows for more variety. Great in rock gardens, in between flagstones, or in wall gardens. The upright varieties are good in containers, and the creeping varieties make fine hanging basket plants. Can be brought indoors in the winter. Shelter from strong winds when outdoors.

Suggestions: We have many varieties in our gardens. Great as container plants. We particularly like the lemon varieties and oregano-flavored thyme.

Historical, Mythological & Medicinal Lore: In Greek history it was the symbol of strength and bravery. Soldiers were given an infusion made from it to renew their strength. Sprigs of it were added to their uniforms and often it was sewn into scarves. Shakespeare referred to it in *A Midsummer Night's Dream*: "I know a bank where the wild thyme grows. . . ."

It was one of the strewing herbs in castles and the early colonists used it as a moth repellent.

The noted herbalist Nicholas Culpepper used it as a remedy for shortness of breath, and today it's a principal ingredient in cough medicines and some antiseptic salves.

Culinary Uses: Use fresh or dried. It dries very well and keeps its flavor longer than most herbs. A universal herb with a strong pungent flavor. Used in meat sauces, soups, with onions, tomatoes, peas, eggs, poultry stuffing, lamb, beef, pork, rice, carrots, onions, and biscuits. One of the main herbs in bouquet garni and in some fines herbes. Avoid ground thyme. It has very little flavor.

21

Secondary Kitchen Herbs

The following 24 herbs we use frequently in our cooking, but they are not as often found in Michigan gardens. Some are indispensable, some are less familiar, others you may not have heard of. All will add flavor and fun to your cooking. All can be grown in Michigan, though some take more pampering than others.

❧

Anise Hyssop (*Agastache foeniculum*)

Type: Perennial

Propagation: Plants

Growing Conditions: Full sun, grows to 3', prefers well-drained soil

Facts: Sometimes called "anise mint." The seed and the purple flower are used in cooking. Imparts a sweet licorice taste of anise seed. Used to sweeten food sometimes without the addition of sugar. Makes a delightful tea. Add leaves to fruit salads.

❧

Borage (*Borago officinalis*)

Type: Annual

Propagation: Seeds, reseeds freely

Growing Conditions: Full sun, grows 1'-3', prefers dry, poor, light soil

Facts: Soft furry-like leaves taste like cucumber and are added to salads and vegetable dishes. The beautiful pink-blue starry blossoms are used in summer drinks, ice cubes, and ice rings and dried for decoration.

❧

Calendula (*Calendula officinalis*)

Type: Annual

Propagation: Seeds, plants

Growing Conditions: Full sun, grows to 1', prefers light, sandy, moderately rich soil

Facts: Can be grown in pots. Also known as "pot marigold." Prized for its lovely yellow-orange flowers which are used as a saffron substitute, only for the color. Add to green salads, rice dishes, creamy soups, cheese spreads, sandwich spreads, and dips. Petals are slightly peppery and when mixed with garlic and dill make a good herb seasoning for tossing on steamed vegetables.

❧

Caraway (*Carum carvi*)

Type: Biennial, treated as an annual in Michigan

23

Propagation: Seeds, sow in late summer for next spring, reseeds freely

Growing Conditions: Full sun, grows 12"-18", prefers average soil, good drainage

Facts: Spicy seeds are traditionally added to rye breads, cabbage dishes, coleslaw, seed cakes, soups, stews, and sauerkraut. Carrot-like leaves are used as garnish. The edible root tastes something like parsnips.

🌿

Chamomile (Matricaria recutita)

Type: Annual

Propagation: Seeds, reseeds freely

Growing Conditions: Full sun, grows 2"-12", average soil

Facts: Also called German chamomile. The flowers are used for tea to aid in digestion and to soothe stomachaches. Roman and English chamomiles are perennial ground covers. Sometimes chamomile is added to fruit salads and desserts. Can be grown in a container.

🌿

Chervil (Anthriscus cereifolium)

Type: Annual

Propagation: Seeds, reseeds freely

Growing Conditions: Semi-shade, grows to 9"-10", prefers moist, rich, light soil

Facts: Chervil resembles parsley in appearance but is more ferny. It is best used fresh and doesn't dry well. Add to cooked foods at the last minute. Has a mild anise-like taste. Great added to steamed spring vegetables like peas, potatoes, asparagus, and carrots. Goes well with chicken, fish, egg dishes, and vichyssoise and is sometimes added to fines herbes, bouquet garni, and Béarnaise sauce.

🌿

Cumin (Cuminum cyminum)

Type: Annual

Propagation: Seeds

Growing Conditions: Full sun, lots of warm days, grows about 10", average soil with good drainage

Facts: Member of the parsley family. Has a very strong pungent odor and used in Middle Eastern, Mexican, Indian, and North African cuisines. Seeds are most flavorful and should be crushed in a mortar and pestle before adding to chili, tomato sauces, beans, beef dishes, breads, cauliflower, carrot dishes, couscous, sausages, and some cheeses.

🌿

24

Fennel (*Foeniculum vulgare*)

Type: Perennial/annual

Propagation: Seeds

Growing Conditions: Full sun, grows 1-1 1/2', prefers rich, moist soil

Facts: There are two varieties, Florence and common. Florence is harvested as a vegetable and common for seeds. Prized by the Italians for its globe-like edible bulb. Possesses a sweet anise-celery flavor. Baked in cream sauces, braised, eaten raw in salads, pasta sauces, marinated, and makes a delicious creamy soup. To use the bulb for cooking, harvest before plant flowers.

ஜ

Garlic (*Allium sativum*)

Type: Perennial

Propagation: Bulbs

Growing Conditions: Full sun, grows to 12"-24", prefers rich, moist garden soil

Facts: Needs a long growing season to harvest large bulbs. It may be necessary to leave in the ground until the following season. Varieties include elephant and Rocambole. Plant cloves of garlic bulb. Can eat leaves, like chives. When tops fall over and die down it can be harvested. Uses are extensive and defined by personal taste. Eat raw in salads, vinaigrettes, marinades or make into sauces and mayonnaises (aioli).

ஜ

Ginger (*Zingiber officinale*)

Type: Tender perennial

Propagation: Bulbs

Growing Conditions: Full sun, grows 1'-3', prefers moist, well drained soil

Facts: A tropical plant that can be grown in containers and brought in during the winter. After one year dig up roots from young sprouts. Has bamboo-like stems and leaves. Mist occasionally when brought indoors. Like garlic, ginger has infinite uses. Available candied or crystallized for cakes, tarts, confections, cookies, jellies; also found in ground form and used fresh in marinades, salsas, curry dishes, Thai, Mexican, Caribbean, and Asian foods.

ஜ

Lavender (*Lavandula species*)

Type: Perennial

Propagation: Plants, seeds

Growing Conditions: Full sun, grows to 18"-24",

average soil and good drainage

Facts: Called the king of fragrant herbs. The seed, flowers, and leaves are edible. Used in desserts like cakes and cookies, and in salads, it is one of the herbs in Herbes de Provence (see Index).

❧

Leeks (*Allium ampeloprasum*)

Type: Biennial

Propagation: Seeds or transplants

Growing Conditions: Full to filtered sun, grows 18"-20", needs moist soil

Facts: Leeks are treated as an annual and should be planted in trenches 4"-6" deep. Pile the soil around the stems as they grow to produce long white edible stalks. Mulch well. Some gardeners overwinter leeks for spring harvesting.

Leeks should be washed well before using; the inner leaves usually hide dirt and stones because of mounding. Leeks have a more delicate flavor than onions. Called the king of the soup onions—vichyssoise is the most famous soup with leeks. Leeks are often included in soup stocks. An excellent vegetable-herb used a great deal in Italian cooking, in salads, or cooked in quiches and braised dishes.

Lemon Balm (*Melissa officinalis*)

Type: Perennial

Propagation: Seeds, root division, cuttings, layering, plants

Growing Conditions: Sun to partial sun, grows 2'-3' and about 24" wide, prefers moist, rich soil. Self sows.

Facts: From the mint family, hardy, and spreads. Can become invasive. Lemon balm has a mild citrus scent, more in its fragrance than flavor. Makes wonderful tea—hot or iced. Reminds you of lemon peel with a minty sweet accent. Used in fruit salads, jellies, tarts, tea breads, and rice and with chicken and fish.

❧

Lemon Verbena (*Aloysia triphylla*)

Type: Tender perennial

Propagation: Root cuttings, plants

Growing Conditions: Full sun, grows from 2'-8', prefers well drained soil; perfect in containers

Facts: More of a tropical plant. Has white flowers in late summer. The flavor has an intense citrus taste, making it a favorite in cooking or in teas and punch. Add to berries for sweetness without much sugar. Dries well. Use in rice, muffins, tea cakes, salad, jellies, and sorbets.

❦

Lovage (*Levisticum officinale*)

Type: Perennial

Propagation: Plants, seeds

Growing Conditions: Sun to partial shade, grows 6"-10", average garden soil

Facts: Looks like a giant celery stalk with an even more pronounced flavor. Sometimes called the Bloody Mary plant because the stalks are hollow and make a good straw for the famous drink. Leaves can be dried but lose their fragrance quickly. To preserve it for winter use, it can be pureed with a little water and frozen in ice cube trays. Very good in soups, stocks, stews, and poultry dishes and in bouquet garnis. Use sparingly.

❦

Nasturtium (*Tropaeolum majus*)

Type: Annual

Propagation: Seeds, plants

Growing Conditions: Sun, grows to 6", average garden soil

Facts: The brilliant orange, yellow, and red flowers are prized for adding to salads and decorating

desserts. The flowers are edible and so are the peppery-tasting leaves. The buds are pickled and make a mock caper.

❦

Perilla (*Perilla frutescens*)

Type: Annual

Propagation: Seeds, plants

Growing Conditions: Full sun, grows to about 3', average garden soil

Facts: Reseeds itself with abandon. Often mistaken in our climate for a perennial opal basil. There are two varieties—one with green jagged leaves, the other with dark opal jagged leaves. The flavor is similar to cinnamon basil. A popular Japanese herb, called "shisho." It's a common ingredient in gourmet or mesclun salad mixes. Beautiful foliage—can be grown in large containers.

❦

Pineapple Sage (*Salvia elegans*)

Type: Annual

Propagation: Cuttings, plants

Growing Conditions: Full sun, grows to about 3', prefers loamy soil

Facts: Part of the large salvia family. Has beautiful

red blossoms. The leaves with their beautiful pronounced pineapple flavor are used in salads, fruit dishes, and teas.

❧

Salad Burnet (Sanguisorba minor)

Type: Perennial

Propagation: Seeds, plants, cuttings

Growing Conditions: Full sun to partial shade, grows to about 12", average to moist garden soil, with good drainage

Facts: Beautiful lacy-looking plant that is often overlooked in the garden. Remove flowers as they develop to promote vigorous growth. Has a delicate cucumber flavor, making it great for people who have trouble digesting cucumbers. Used in salads, vinegars, tea sandwiches, vinaigrettes, soups, and sauces and added to cream cheese.

❧

Savory (Winter: Satureja montana or Summer: Satureja hortensis)

Type: Winter is a perennial; summer is an annual.

Propagation: Seeds, cuttings, or plants

Growing Conditions: Sun to partial shade. Winter grows to 12"; Summer grows to 2'. Prefers light,

well drained soil.

Facts: The flavor of summer savory hints of basil-lavender. The winter is more pungent, like thyme-marjoram. It's popular in German cooking, particularly with beans and sausage dishes. Also good in soups, with lentils, pork, veal, and sauces. Winter savory makes a nice evergreen-type plant in your landscape. Summer savory is often planted in hanging baskets. Both have a slight peppery taste.

❧

Scented Geraniums (Pelargonium species)

Type: Annual

Propagation: Cuttings, plants

Growing Conditions: Full sun, grows to about 1 1/2'-2' tall, prefers average garden soil

Facts: Makes a great container plant. Hundreds of varieties with aromatic foliage. The flowers are secondary to the leaves. Typical scents are rose, with many varieties—lemon, apple, chocolate mint, ginger, cinnamon, nutmeg, orange, peppermint, strawberry, coconut, etc. The leaves are used in jams and jellies, pound cakes, muffins, cookies, cakes, tea, sugars, and tarts.

❧

28

Shallots (*Allium ascalonicum*)

Type: Annual/perennial

Propagation: Bulbs

Growing Conditions: Full sun, grows to about 1', prefers well drained rich soil

Facts: Another member of the onion family. Planted by separating bulbs. Grows like spring onions. Planted in fall for harvesting the next year, like garlic—it will then be larger than if planted in the spring. Has a mild, delicate onion flavor prized by cooks. Use in any recipe calling for a little onion taste. Great roasted with other vegetables—it caramelizes and becomes sweet.

✣

Sorrel (*Rumex species*)

Type: Perennial

Propagation: Seeds, self sows, root division, plants

Growing Conditions: Full sun, grows to about 1'-3', prefers rich, moist soil

Facts: Easy to grow. Prized for its lemon-spinach flavor. Leaves are best used in early spring and late fall. Cut down the seed-flower heads to promote new growth for the fall. Used in French cooking. Heat of the summer turns the leaves bitter. Add leaves to salads and coleslaw and use instead of lettuce in sandwiches. Makes great cream soups, especially with potato. Add to stuffings for trout and other fish.

✣

Sweet Woodruff (*Galium odoratum*)

Type: Perennial

Propagation: Seeds, root division, plants

Growing Conditions: Shade, grows to about 4"-6", prefers acid, moist soil

Facts: A beautiful ground cover that grows well in partial or all-shade areas. Has deep green leaves and white flowers in the early spring. Unusual herb in that it has very little flavor when fresh but when dried has a faint vanilla scent. Used in many wines, punches, vinegars, and cobblers.

✣

There are many other culinary herbs that can be added to your garden. As you become more acquainted with cuisines from around the world, you may decide to include them in your repertoire. Some may take some tender loving, and some may just be relegated to attractive house plants. No matter what, we're sure whichever plants you decide to include in your garden, you will be pleased.

Herb Garden Designs

With the following four garden designs we tried to provide a variety of ideas and materials to work with. Our *Formal Garden* is divided into four sections with an intersecting path. The path could be made from brick (our first choice), crushed rock, gravel, etc. The four squares need not all be herbs. If you like, plant the two rear squares with flowering perennials or vegetables.

The *Pizza Garden* was designed as fun for the whole family, especially children. It helps them learn the relationship between growing and using produce and herbs in a familiar food—pizza!

Our *Kitchen Garden* was designed so you can step out your door and snip fresh herbs for any dish you are preparing. It can be adapted to any size and expanded as your interests grow. Remember there are no rules, so feel free to add annual or perennial flowers.

Our *Salad Garden* will keep your salad bowl, plus your neighbors', full all summer and well into autumn. This is an easy design to reduce or expand. Remember: this is your garden, so be creative and enjoy!

FORMAL HERB GARDEN

Plant List: basil (bush, garden & lemon) bay, boxwood, calendula, chives, dianthus, garlic, germander, lavender, lemon verbena, marjoram, Corsican mint, nasturtium, oregano, shrub rose, rosemary, sage (garden, pineapple, purple, tri-colored & variegated), salad burnet, santolina, savory (winter & summer), scented geranium, tarragon, thyme (garden, lemon & silver).

32

KIDS' PIZZA GARDEN

Herb & Vegetable Plant List: basil (bush & sweet), Japanese eggplant, garlic, marjoram, onions, oregano, parsley, peppers (banana, green, Hungarian & jalapeno), scallions, tomatoes (plum, red & yellow pear).

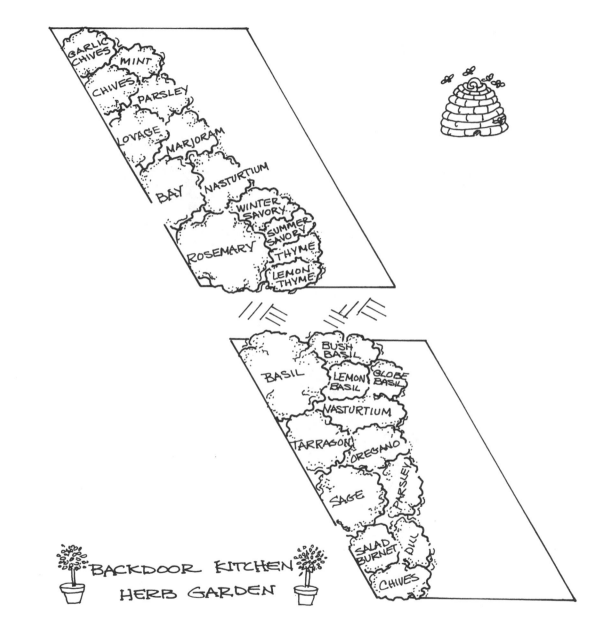

GARLIC CHIVES
MINT
CHIVES
PARSLEY
LOVAGE
MARJORAM
BAY
NASTURTIUM
WINTER SAVORY
SUMMER SAVORY
ROSEMARY
THYME
LEMON THYME

BASIL
BUSH BASIL
LEMON BASIL
GLOBE BASIL
NASTURTIUM
TARRAGON
OREGANO
SAGE
PARSLEY
SALAD BURNET
DILL
CHIVES

BACKDOOR KITCHEN HERB GARDEN

33

Plant List: basil (bush, globe & lemon), bay, chives (garden & garlic), dill, lovage, marjoram, mint, nasturtium, oregano, parsley, sage, salad burnet, savory (winter & summer), thyme (garden & lemon).

34

Herb & Vegetable Plant List: basil (bush & sweet), carrots, garlic, lettuce (arugula & mesclun), marjoram, oregano, parsley, peppers (banana, green & jalapeno), radish, rosemary, sage, spinach, thyme, tomatoes.

Appetizers & First Courses

An appetizer or first course acts as a dramatic entrance to a meal. It should tease the diner and set the mood for what's to come. Appetizers can be served informally around the kitchen stove, at the dining room table with the candles lit, or in a separate room for a more elegant feel.

The flavors should sparkle and the presentation should be thorough—cheese spreads served out of yogurt containers may be environmentally friendly but miss the mark on style! Suzanne and I both feel that visual appeal is as important as wonderfully prepared food. Always provide plates, napkins, and small utensils, even if your dish is considered "finger food."

When choosing your appetizers, consider them in relation to the whole meal. Pleasing contrasts are the rule. If your entrée is rich and heavy, your first course should be light and simple. If your main course is simple, like pasta, or light fish or chicken dishes, then this is your chance to begin with an elaborate appetizer—something you've always wanted to try but never got around to doing—a pâté, for instance.

Suzanne and I often go to restaurants and order only appetizers. We find that small samples of several things are just enough; they give us a fairly accurate indication of what a restaurant is really like, and besides we like to try all kinds of foods.

In the following pages of appetizers and first courses, we've included a wide range of flavorful dishes. Some are very simple and use only a few ingredients; some are more elaborate and may need last minute attention; others can be made ahead and frozen until just before serving. Remember, unless your appetizers are the entire meal, keep the portions small. You don't want your guests filling up before the main course is served!

35

Corn

We love the summer for the wonderful corn in Michigan. Try grilling it.

Just pull back husks and remove the silk. Tear several outside husks into 1/4" strips to use as ties. Replace husks around cobs and tie with the reserved strips. Soak corn in salted water for 5-15 minutes. Drain well. Roast on grill over hot fire 15-20 minutes, turning frequently. Remove husks and serve with plain or herb butter and salt and pepper.

For ease in preparation, mix dry ingredients and seafood ingredients in separate bowls and set aside until ready to fry.

Coriander, Shrimp & Corn Fritters
makes about 2 dozen

10 oz. frozen corn, thawed
2 jalapenos, chopped
2 scallions, chopped
2 garlic cloves, chopped
1/4 c. cilantro, chopped
1/2 c. onions, chopped
1 egg, lightly beaten
1/2 lb. raw shrimp, peeled and deveined
3/4 c. flour
1/4 c. coarse cornmeal
1 1/2 tsp. salt
1 tbl. baking powder
1 tbl. ground coriander
1/4 tsp. pepper
vegetable oil

Place all but 1/4 c. corn in a food processor and whirl till smooth. Add jalapenos, scallions, garlic, cilantro, onions, and egg and whirl until smooth. Place in a large bowl and mix in shrimp (cut in small pieces) and reserved corn. (Mixture can be refrigerated overnight at this point.)

Combine the flour, cornmeal, salt, baking powder, coriander, and pepper. Add to corn mixture and blend well.

36

Heat 1" of oil in a deep skillet and add fritters by heaping tablespoons. Don't crowd or add too many at a time (that causes them to become greasy). Turn and fry till golden. Drain on paper towels and serve with cucumber relish or any chutney, aioli, salsa, or pesto. Fritters can be kept warm in a 200° oven covered with foil.

Cucumber Relish

1 tsp. salt
2 cucumbers, peeled, seeded and chopped into small dice
2 bunches fresh cilantro, chopped
2 tbl. green chilies (mild) canned or fresh
2 limes, juiced
2 tbl. minced onion
2 tbl. fresh chives
salt and freshly ground pepper

Salt the cucumbers and place in a colander for 30 minutes. Rinse and drain and pat very dry. Add remaining ingredients and season. Chill 30 minutes.

Shrimp

We prefer shrimp with shells on. Since almost all shrimp come to the Midwest frozen, we believe shrimp with their shells on are superior in flavor and texture to those which have been shelled and precooked.

Depending upon the use, size is important. For grilling, use large or extra large shrimp; for salads, soups, and sauced entrées, use large to medium shrimp.

Shrimp is labeled by the number of shrimp per pound.

Jumbo: 5-15
Extra Large: 16-20
Large: 21-30
Medium: 31-40

37

When we picnic at outdoor theater events, we enjoy a glass of wine with friends and serve this tart while waiting for the meat to grill.

Rosemary, Caramelized Onion & Goat Cheese Tart
serves 10

Pastry
1 1/4 c. flour
1 stick unsalted butter, cut in pieces (should be very cold)
1 tsp. salt
1 egg yolk
3 tbl. ice water

In a food processor or bowl with a pastry blender, combine flour, butter, salt, and egg yolk until it resembles coarse meal. Add the ice water, 1 tbl. at a time, using on-off motion with the food processor. Do not allow pastry to form into a ball.

Place on counter and knead with the heel of your hand. Form into a flat ball and chill. Roll out to fit a 10" flan pan. Prick bottom with fork and freeze. Bake at 425° for 5-10 minutes until lightly golden brown.

Filling
2 large onions, cut in half and sliced thinly
2 tbl. butter
2 tbl. oil
1 tsp. sugar

38

1/2 tsp. salt
freshly ground pepper
1/8 tsp. cayenne
7 oz. goat cheese
4 oz. (1/2 c.) sour cream (regular or low fat)
2 eggs
2 tbl. fresh rosemary, chopped
1 sweet red pepper, roasted, seeded and chopped

In a skillet, sauté onions in butter and oil, tossing until very soft. Turn heat to low and add sugar, cover, and continue to cook an additional 10-15 minutes. Add salt and ground black pepper and cayenne. In an electric mixer or food processor thoroughly blend goat cheese, sour cream, eggs, and 1 tbl. rosemary. By hand, mix in red pepper and pour into prepared tart shell. Place onions and remaining rosemary on cheese mixture evenly. Grind fresh black pepper on top. Bake at 350° for 40-50 minutes.

Tart Pans

We always use a removable flan pan—usually 10". Check to make sure the pan is made of heavy metal and won't bend while twisting in opposite directions with your hands. The black coated pans are not a good choice, since they seem to rust.

39

Avocados

Remember to purchase the fruit one to two days in advance, which gives it time to ripen. The skin should be uniform in color, without cracks, bruises, or punctures. Make sure the skin yields to light pressure. To remove the skin, try Suzanne's method:

Cut the avocado in quarters, just cutting through the skin. Peel.

Or use Marge's method:

Cut avocado in half lengthwise and twist; pull halves apart. Remove pit with a knife. Scrape out avocado with knife or spoon. To keep the fruit from turning brown, sprinkle with fresh lemon or lime juice.

❧

Be creative with this crowd-pleasing appetizer. Roll in sliced smoked turkey or smoked salmon for a unique flavor.

Tortilla Pinwheels with Green Chilies
serves 8-10

8 oz. cream cheese, room temperature
3.5 oz. goat cheese (or substitute additional cream cheese)
2 tbl. horseradish mustard (if watery, drain well)
4-5 large flour tortillas (11")
1 c. fresh cilantro, stems removed
1 c. sliced black olives
1 1/2 c. red onions, thinly sliced
1 4-oz. can mild green chilies, drained
1 7-oz. jar roasted red peppers, drained and sliced thin
1-2 avocados, peeled and sliced (sprinkle with lemon juice)
2-3 hot fresh chilies: jalapenos, serranos, Hungarian banana, etc.

In a food processor or with a hand mixer, combine cheeses and horseradish. Blend well. Taste and adjust seasonings. Set aside.

To Assemble:

Lay tortillas on work surface and spread each tortilla with the cream cheese mixture almost to the edge. Sprinkle on each tortilla an equal portion of remaining ingredients and roll up very tightly. Wrap each in plastic wrap. Chill. Can be made up to 1 day in advance. Just before serving cut into 3/4" slices.

Besides the toppings listed here, let your imagination go wild—try other marinated vegetables or smoked fish.

Crostini
serves 6

1 loaf French bread, preferably baguettes, cut into 1/2" slices
1/4 c. butter, melted
1/4 c. olive oil
2-3 large garlic cloves, finely minced

Combine butter and oil with garlic; brush mixture on bread slices. Toast in a 350° oven or under a broiler until just lightly brown.

Gorgonzola Cheese Spread

6 oz. goat cheese
8 oz. cream cheese (regular or low fat)
4 oz. Gorgonzola cheese
cream (if needed)

Combine all cheeses (at room temperature) in a food processor until smooth and creamy. Add a little cream to thin if mixture is too thick. Chill covered up to 3 weeks. Spread on Crostini slices and top with Marinated Roasted Peppers, Fresh Tomato & Basil, or Shrimp topping.

Crostini

Crostini can be prepared in advance and stored in metal tins for up to several days. Use as a quick appetizer with assorted toppings.

41

This simple cheese is best made 1-2 days ahead of serving. It allows the herbs to blend and mellow. Fines herbes is a French term referring to finely minced herbs, usually tarragon, chives, parsley, and chervil.

Fines Herbes Cheese

8 oz. cream cheese (regular or low fat), softened
3 tbl. blue cheese
1 tbl. fresh parsley, finely minced
1 1/2 tbl. fresh tarragon, finely minced
1 small garlic clove, minced
2 tbl. cream or half-and-half (if necessary)

Soften cream cheese and blue cheese. Add herbs and garlic. Mix well. Thin with cream, if necessary. Cover with plastic wrap and chill several hours to develop flavors. Serve with French bread, pumpernickel bread, or apple slices.

Herbed Goat Cheese

4-6 oz. goat cheese (chèvre), softened
8 oz. cream cheese (regular or low fat), room temperature
1 tbl. mixed fresh herbs or 1 tsp. dried (basil, marjoram, thyme, parsley, chives)
milk (if needed)

Combine all in a food processor or in a bowl. Add milk to make a spreading consistency. Spread on Crostini slices and top with Marinated Roasted Peppers, Fresh Tomato Basil, or Shrimp topping.

Sun-Dried Tomato & Green Olive Tapenade

1/2 c. boiling water
1 1/2-2 c. sun-dried tomatoes
1/3 c. olive oil
1/3 c. pitted hot green olives
2-3 garlic cloves, coarsely chopped
1 tbl. capers
1 tbl. lemon juice
1 1/2 tsp. dried basil
freshly ground pepper
salt
2 tbl. fresh Italian parsley, chopped
1 recipe Herbed Goat Cheese

Pour boiling water over tomatoes and let soak for at least 10 minutes or until soft. When pliable, drain and set aside. In a food processor combine tomatoes and soaking liquid, olive oil, olives, and garlic. Process until a semi-smooth texture. Add capers and remaining ingredients and whirl gently, pulsing once or twice to combine. Taste and season. Keeps refrigerated and covered for several weeks. To serve, spread Crostini with Herbed Goat Cheese and a small amount of topping.

Shrimp Topping

2 large tomatoes, red, yellow, or combination, seeded, drained, and chopped
1 red pepper, seeded and chopped
1/2 c. red onion, chopped
1/2 tsp. dried oregano
1/4 c. fresh cilantro, chopped
1 jalapeno, seeded and chopped
dash sherry vinegar
olive oil
freshly grated black pepper
1/2 lb. cooked shrimp, cut in large pieces

Combine the tomatoes, pepper, onion, herbs, jalapeno, and a dash of vinegar in a bowl. Add a small amount of oil, just to bind. Taste and adjust seasonings. Gently mix in shrimp. Place a small amount of the mixture on Crostini.

Quick Appetizer 1

To a 4- or 6-oz. package of room temperature goat cheese, add 3-4 finely chopped sun-dried tomatoes (packed in oil). Mix by hand. Season with black pepper. Serve on crackers.

Quick Appetizer 2

Make small balls of the Herbed Goat Cheese and roll in toasted sesame seeds, finely minced fresh herbs, or toasted crushed nuts and spear with toothpicks.

43

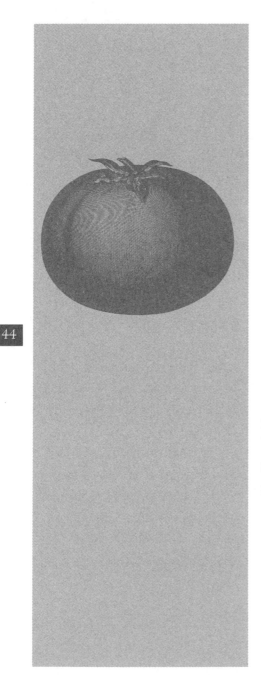

44

Fresh Tomato & Basil Topping

4 fresh Italian tomatoes, seeded, drained well, and chopped coarsely
2 tbl. olive oil
salt and freshly ground pepper
2 tbl. fresh basil, chopped
1 tbl. small red onion, minced
1 tbl. balsamic vinegar
1-2 tbl. Asiago cheese, crumbled
1 recipe Gorgonzola Cheese Spread, or
1 recipe Herbed Goat Cheese

Combine tomatoes, oil, salt, pepper, half the basil, red onion, and vinegar. Gently mix and taste. Season. Just before serving, spread Crostini with a cheese mixture and spoon Tomato & Basil topping on top. Sprinkle with remaining basil and cheese.

Here's what to do with all of those red bell peppers at the end of the season when they're finally reasonably priced! We usually double or triple this recipe.

Marinated Roasted Pepper Topping
makes 2 cups

6 large red and green bell peppers, mixed (or use all red peppers)*
1/2 c. olive oil
1/4 c. red wine vinegar
2 tbl. sherry vinegar
2-3 garlic cloves, minced
1 tbl. fresh basil, minced
salt and freshly ground pepper

Roast peppers in broiler. Cut into 1/2" strips. Combine with other ingredients and chill. Bring to room temperature to serve. To serve, spread Crostini with desired cheese mixture and top with a little of this topping.

Can also use a 12-oz. jar of roasted red peppers (not pimentos). Add 1 tbl. honey if flavors are too acidic.

Roasting Peppers

Roasting any variety of peppers eliminates the bitter skin and gives the flesh a mellow sweet flavor. There are several ways to roast peppers. The oldest method is to skewer a pepper with a long-handled fork and hold it directly over a gas flame. An easier method is to use your broiler (gas or electric). Place the peppers on a foil-lined baking sheet as close to the heat source as possible. As the pepper blackens (blisters), turn often until it is uniformly charred. With either method, place the peppers in a plastic bag after roasting and let sit at room temperature until they are cool enough to handle—usually about 30 minutes. Peel off the softened skin and clean the pepper of any seeds or membrane. You're now ready to use the peppers in any dish. Covered with olive oil and stored in the refrigerator, they will last several weeks.

This dainty appetizer can be made ahead, refrigerated, and reheated—be sure to keep it covered with foil to prevent it from drying out. It's such a popular appetizer, we usually double the recipe.

Wild Rice Blinis
serves 4

1 1/2 c. wild rice, slightly overcooked
1 egg
4 tbl. flour
2/3 c. milk
1/2 tsp. salt
1/2 tsp. baking powder
1 tbl. sugar
1 tbl. minced scallions
2 tbl. butter, melted
oil

Place wild rice, egg, flour, milk, salt, baking powder, sugar, scallions, and melted butter in a blender or food processor. Blend until well-combined and a semi-coarse consistency. Add 1 tbl. oil to a large nonstick skillet set on medium heat. For each pancake, add 1 1/2-2 tbl. batter. Pancakes should be 1 1/2-2" in diameter. Fry 2 minutes per side or until golden and done. Add oil as needed.

Serve immediately with one of the following toppings (see toppings below). Blinis can be made ahead, covered, and refrigerated. To reheat, cover with aluminum foil and heat in a 325° oven until warm.

Blinis

We're taking liberties here by calling these tiny pancakes blinis. Actually a blini is of Russian origin—a yeast-raised buckwheat pancake with a slightly sour taste. With wild rice the texture is coarser, but the flavors are similar.

46

Toppings:

1 1/2 c. sour cream (regular or low fat)
1 jar EACH black and red caviar

1 1/2 c. sour cream (regular or low fat)
1/2 tbl. prepared horseradish
1 tbl. minced fresh dill (extra sprigs for garnish)
6 oz. lox, cut in matchsticks

1 1/2 c. Herbed Goat Cheese
2 c. Marinated Roasted Peppers

1 1/2 c. sour cream (regular or low fat)
1 1/2 -2 tbl. minced fresh herbs (tarragon, dill, marjoram, basil)
1/2 lb. cooked shrimp, cut in half lengthwise

1 c. sour cream (regular or low fat)
2 tbl. fresh cilantro, minced
1 ripe avocado, diced
1/2 lb. cooked shrimp, cut in half lengthwise

Quick Appetizer 3

Mince finely chopped dill, parsley, and chives into softened cream cheese. Add a little olive oil and season with salt and lots of freshly ground black pepper. Use to stuff raw mushrooms or hollowed out cherry tomatoes for a quick hors d'oeuvre.

47

Phyllo Triangles

Flat sheets of phyllo dough are available in 2 sizes, 1 lb. (14" x 18") or 8 oz. (9" x 13"). Either will work for appetizer triangles. Cut the smaller sheets into 4 strips and the larger sheets into 6. Once the filling is added and the triangles are folded, place on baking sheets in a single layer and freeze. When completely frozen, remove to plastic boxes with sides and store between sheets of wax paper. Then, any time you want to make a quick appetizer, pull out a few, place on an ungreased baking sheet, and bake until golden.

❧

Marge and I make these triangles in large quantities and freeze them. They're one of our most popular appetizers. Besides the filling below, use curried chicken, shrimp with tarragon, roasted peppers, and our Herbed Goat Cheese.

Italian Sausage Phyllo Triangles
serves 15

1 lb. hot Italian sausage
1/4 c. Dijon mustard (herbed with basil or other Italian seasonings)
1/2 c. heavy cream
2 tsp. dried basil (reduce amount if mustard contains herbs)
1/4 tsp. freshly grated nutmeg
1/2 c. chopped red bell pepper
phyllo sheets (about 10)
melted butter (about 1 stick)

Remove casing from link-style sausage. Crumble and place in a skillet and brown. Remove and drain on paper towels. Return to pan and add mustard, cream, basil, and nutmeg. Cook and reduce until thick and creamy. Add red peppers; taste and adjust seasonings. Chill.

To Assemble:

Using a pastry brush, butter one sheet of phyllo, place another sheet on top, and butter lightly. With longest side facing you, cut into 6 long strips, about 2 1/2" wide. Place a small amount of the chilled mixture on bottom and

48

roll up flag-style. Place on baking sheets and bake at 350° for 15-20 minutes. They can be frozen before cooking.

Another method of folding is to use one sheet of phyllo, short side facing you. Butter and fold sheet over toward you. Cut into 4 or 5 strips. Place a small portion of the sausage mixture on the bottom and roll up like a flag.

This recipe makes an attractive and tasty gift at holiday time. Place in a hinged French canning jar and tie with raffia strands. Be sure to include a note saying to store in the refrigerator.

Herbed Feta
serves 4

1 tbl. dried rosemary or
   1 1/2 tsp. fresh, minced
1 garlic clove, minced
1 tbl. lemon juice
2 tbl. olive oil
1/2 lb. feta cheese cut into
   1/2" cubes
Greek olives

In a mortar, grind rosemary. In a small bowl combine garlic, lemon juice, and rosemary and beat in oil slowly. Place feta in bowl and gently toss. Cover and chill. Keeps several weeks in refrigerator. Serve with olives.

49

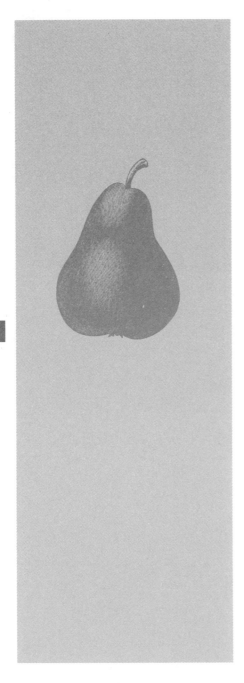

Marge loves making pâtés, particularly during the holidays. Often she'll make several small ones from one basic recipe and vary the textured ingredients, such as apricots instead of pears, golden raisins instead of currants, and different spice and herb combinations.

Pear, Garlic & Ham Pâté
serves 10-12

2 lb. pork steak (should have some fat)
1/2 c. currants
1/4 c. sautéed, diced red onion
1/4 c. port
1 lb. ground turkey or chicken
1/2 c. shelled natural pistachios
1 1/2 tsp. freshly ground nutmeg
1 1/2 tsp. ground allspice
1/3 c. dried apricots, cut into large pieces
1/2 lb. smoked ham or pork chops, cut into large chunks
6 large cloves garlic, minced
2 eggs
1/2-1 tsp. pâté seasoning (See Index)
2 pears, peeled and cut into small dice
salt and freshly ground pepper
1 lb. bacon

Grind pork in food processor in batches. Mixture should be very smooth but not too fluid. Remove to a large bowl. Soak currants in port for 30 minutes. Combine all ingredients, except bacon, and mix well

50

with hands. Fry 1 tbl. of the mixture for a taste test. Adjust seasonings at this point.

In the bottom of a loaf pan or pâté pan arrange bacon strips in a staggered pattern with every other row draped over the side of the pan. When observed from above, every other strip should extend beyond the side of the pan about 3" on both the right and left sides of the pan. Spoon in pâté mixture; rap pan on surface to eliminate any air pockets. Fold bacon strips over pâté mixture. Cover with more bacon and top with foil or lid (poke air holes in foil).

Place pâté pan or loaf pan in a bain marie (larger pan filled with hot water halfway up sides of pan). Bake in a 325° oven for 2 hours or until temperature registers 160° internally. Remove and pour off excess fat. Let sit 10-15 minutes and pour more fat off. Cool to room temperature and place foil on top and weight with cans or bricks and refrigerate overnight. (The bricks compress the meat mixture making it easier to slice.)

Serve with herbed Dijon mustard and small sour pickles and French bread. The pâté can be stored in the refrigerator for up to 2 1/2 weeks.

Pâtés vs. Terrines

These two words are often used interchangeably but historically were different. A pâté was the savory mixture, and the terrine was the container used to hold it. Either word is acceptable now. Pâtés are easy to make and are impressive first courses. Use well-marbled meats—you need some fat to keep the mixture moist during cooking. After the long cooking times (usually 1 1/2-2 hours) pour off the accumulated liquid. Use interesting food in the mixture: diced apricots, pistachios, smoked ham, turkey, pears, apples, currants, dark and golden raisins, sliced blanched leeks, or asparagus, to name a few. When you cut your pâté slices, you'll see a mosaic of colors and textures.

Be sure to season your pâtés generously. Make a sample patty and fry it to check. Remember, pâtés are served cold, and chilling foods tends to dilute flavors, especially salt.

Cooking Wines & Liqueurs

Don't be tempted to buy grocery store cooking wine when a recipe calls for it. They are so full of chemicals and salt they contain little flavor. Use wines and liqueurs to add unique flavors to simple recipes. Remember that the alcohol is burned off once the liqueur is heated. Buy good quality brands and store them in dark, dry cupboards away from direct sun. Many wines and liqueurs have a long shelflife, including sherry, brandy, Madeira, Marsala, dry white vermouth (used whenever a recipe calls for white wine), crème de menthe, crème de cassis (black currant), Amaretto, etc.

This old-fashioned spreadable pâté is made with chicken livers. Relax, though, it's so delicious, rich, and meaty tasting, you'll be a convert!

Sage & Calvados Pâté
serves 10-12

2 tbl. butter
1/2 lb. chicken livers
1/4 lb. fresh mushrooms, chopped coarsely
1/4 c. scallions, sliced
2 tbl. chopped chives
1/3 c. Calvados (apple brandy) or sherry
2 cloves garlic, minced
1/4 tsp. dry mustard
1 tbl. fresh sage, minced
1/2 tsp. dried thyme, minced
1/4 c. soft butter
salt and freshly ground pepper

Melt butter in skillet and sauté livers and mushrooms, scallions, and chives for five minutes. Add wine, garlic, mustard, sage, and thyme. Cover and simmer 10 minutes or until livers and mushrooms are very tender. Uncover and continue cooking until liquids are almost evaporated. Whirl in a blender and add butter. Taste and adjust seasonings. Store up to two weeks in the refrigerator. Serve with French bread or crackers.

Here's something to do with all of the zucchini that mysteriously appears in the garden.

Zucchini, Leek &
Roasted Red Pepper Quiche
serves 10

1 Pâté Brisée (pastry shell; see next page)
1 tbl. Dijon mustard
3 c. grated zucchini, unpeeled
salt
1 leek, chopped
2 tbl. butter
3/4 c. heavy cream
1 c. grated Gruyère or aged Swiss cheese
3 eggs, lightly beaten
1 roasted red pepper, julienned
1 tsp. freshly grated nutmeg
1 1/2 tsp. dried marjoram
salt and freshly ground pepper

Prebake pastry in a preheated 400° oven for 10 minutes. Cool. Spread bottom of pastry with Dijon mustard. Set aside.

Reduce heat to 350°. Place zucchini in a colander and sprinkle with a little salt and drain 5 minutes. Rinse well and squeeze very dry.

Sauté leeks in the butter until soft. Remove and set aside. Combine the cream, cheese, and eggs and beat very

Pastry Shells

Pastry shells can be prepared ahead and frozen for up to 6 months. Be sure to seal tightly in plastic or foil. No need to thaw to prebake.

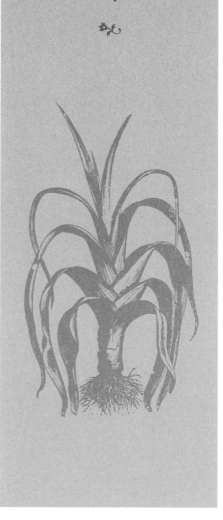

53

Tailgate Picnic Menu

Zucchini, Leek & Roasted
Red Pepper Quiche

❧

Saltimbocca (Pork Scallops
with Prosciutto & Sage)

❧

Italian White Bean Salad

❧

Almond Ginger Torte with Fresh
Raspberry Sauce

❧

Serve with California Chardonnay,
Valpolicella, or Chianti Classico wine

well. Add the pepper, herbs, leeks, salt, and freshly ground pepper to taste. Mix. Place the zucchini on bottom of the pastry shell. Spread evenly. Pour cheese-egg mixture over top and sprinkle with additional cheese, if desired. Bake 35 minutes or until top is puffed and golden and a knife inserted in the center comes out clean. Let stand 5 minutes before slicing. Can be made ahead and stored at room temperature.

Pâté Brisée

1 1/4 c. flour
1/4 tsp. salt
6 tbl. cold butter, cut into bits
2 tbl. solid shortening
2-3 tbl. ice water

In a bowl mix flour and salt with a pastry blender or food processor. Add shortening and butter with quick on-off pulses. Mixture should resemble coarse meal. Add ice water in small amounts. Toss gently. Remove and knead on a lightly floured surface a few seconds. Flatten into a circle, cover with plastic wrap, and chill 30 minutes. Roll out to fit a 10" removable-bottom flan pan. Prick bottom with a fork several times and place in freezer for at least 30 minutes. Partially bake in a 400° oven for 10 minutes or until lightly golden.

❧

This is a great appetizer to prepare ahead of time; in fact we like to double this recipe. Serve by itself or with French bread as part of an antipasto platter.

Lemon Basil & Pear Caponata
serves 6

2 large eggplants, peeled and cut into 1/2" dice (about 8 c.)
2 large onions, chopped
4 garlic cloves, finely chopped
3 tbl. olive oil
1 28-oz. can Italian tomatoes, chopped, undrained
1 tbl. sugar
3 tbl. EACH fresh thyme and Italian parsley, chopped
1/4 c. fresh lemon basil (or regular basil), minced
2 tbl. capers
1/4 c. currants or golden raisins
1/4 c. balsamic vinegar
2 large pears, unpeeled, cut in 1/2" dice
salt and freshly ground pepper
2 tbl. toasted pine nuts (optional)

Place eggplants in a colander and sprinkle with salt. Let drain for 30 minutes. Rinse well and pat dry. Heat oven to 425°. Place eggplants on baking sheets with 2 tbl. olive oil and roast for 20-25 minutes or until tender. Toss occasionally.

In a large skillet add remaining oil and sauté onions and garlic over low heat. Cover to develop some moisture. Cook until golden, about 5-7 minutes. Add eggplants,

Antipasto

A great Italian invention to tide you over until dinner or to serve as a delicious picnic or appetizer meal.

Antipasto literally means "before the pasta course." Today it's usually a small assortment of little surprises: marinated vegetables, cheeses, thinly sliced sausages, and crusty bread. It's very easy to make, especially if you keep a well stocked pantry.

Have on hand canned marinated artichokes, olives, hard cheeses, tuna in oil, roasted peppers, and frozen focaccia. Place each in separate small bowls and spice them up with a sprinkling of herbs, such as fresh or dried basil, oregano, rosemary, good olive oil, and freshly ground pepper.

Eggplants

When choosing eggplants remember to look for shiny dark purple skins without any soft spots, dents, or brown areas. Peel the skin with a vegetable peeler, slice, and salt. The salt removes the bitter taste. Let sit a half hour and rinse. Don't forget this step, or the eggplant will be very salty!

56

tomatoes, sugar, herbs, capers, currants, and vinegar. Cook over medium heat for 10 minutes. Add pears and cook until just soft. Taste and adjust seasonings. Chill several hours. To serve, sprinkle with pine nuts and accompany with warmed, sliced bread.

Suzanne's daughter, Sarah, has become a pro at making pizzas for her friends. Never mind the pepperoni and tomato sauce; she experiments with favorite food combinations like spicy chicken and salsa or portabella mushrooms with brie.

Quick Food Processor Pizza Dough

1 c. water
2 tbl. olive oil
3 1/4 c. flour (can substitute 1/2-3/4 c. whole wheat flour)
2 tbl. sugar
1 tsp. salt (increase if using whole wheat flour)
1 pkg. dry yeast
1 egg

Heat water and oil until it reaches 110° (we find an instant-read thermometer handy for this). Place 1 1/2 c. flour, sugar, salt, and yeast in food processor. With motor running, add water and oil and whirl 2-3 seconds. Add egg, process again. Sprinkle 1 1/2 c. flour and process until it forms a ball. Knead on a floured surface for 3-4 minutes. Divide into thirds and stretch or roll thin and fit in pizza pans, or cover with plastic and let rest 30 minutes (this eliminates elasticity).

Recipe makes 1 12" x 18" cookie sheet + 1 pizza pan or 3 12" pizza pans.

Pizza Dough Variations

While the dough is in the food processor, add one of the following additions or use your imagination and add some of your favorite herbs or other savory ingredients.

Pepperoni
3 oz. finely minced pepperoni
1/4 tsp. red pepper flakes
dash cayenne pepper

Basil & Black Pepper
1 tbl. dried basil
2 tsp. coarsely ground black pepper

Rosemary
1 tbl. fresh rosemary

58

Mushrooms, Basil & Pancetta Pizza
(makes enough for 2 10" x 15" baking pans)

1 oz. dried assorted mushrooms and 1 c. boiling water
1 tbl. butter
1 tbl. oil
3-4 oz. pancetta, cut in 1/4" dice
1-1 1/2 lb. fresh mushrooms, assorted varieties
juice of 1/2 lemon
1 medium onion, halved and sliced
6 cloves garlic, minced
1 tsp. fennel seeds
2 tbl. sherry
1 tbl. fresh basil, minced
1/2 c. Parmesan cheese
2 c. shredded Asiago cheese
salt and coarsely ground black pepper
olive oil

Prebake pizza crust for 5-7 minutes at 400°. Soak mushrooms 30 minutes. Remove and discard tough stems. Slice mushroom caps and reserve. Strain liquid. Reserve and set aside. Melt butter and oil and sauté pancetta 1-2 minutes until done. Remove to a bowl. Sprinkle fresh mushrooms with lemon juice and add to pan with onion, garlic, fennel seeds, sherry, dried mushrooms, and reserved soaking liquid. Cover, reduce heat to low, and cook until mushrooms are soft. Remove mushroom mixture to pancetta bowl with a slotted spoon. Raise heat and reduce liquid till slightly thick. Stir often. Pour over mushrooms and add basil. Taste and adjust with seasonings.

To Assemble:

For one pizza, spread half the mushroom mixture over pizza dough and sprinkle on half the Parmesan and half the Asiago cheese. Season and bake in preheated 400° oven for 10-15 minutes or until brown and cheese is melted.

Caramelized Onion, Gorgonzola & Fresh Rosemary Pizza
(makes enough filling for 2 10" x 15" baking sheets)

2 tbl. butter
2 tbl. oil
4 very large onions, halved and thinly sliced
3/4 c. Gorgonzola cheese, crumbled
2 tbl. fresh rosemary, chopped coarsely
salt and freshly ground pepper

Melt butter and oil in large skillet. Add onions and cook over low heat until light brown and caramelized. Stir often to prevent burning.

To Assemble:

Spread onion mixture over pizza dough. Dot with cheese and sprinkle with rosemary. Season. Bake at 400° for 15 minutes or until dough is slightly brown and cheese is melted.

Pizza Parties

Hosting a pizza party is fun and different from years gone by. To begin with, the pizza toppings are unusual. Dough making is the same, but we've included some variations that you'll want to try.

Prepare the dough a few days ahead and keep it refrigerated. The day of your party, roll out the dough to fit your largest baking sheets (10" x 15" works well). Prebake them for about 5-7 minutes at 400°. Cover dough with plastic wrap and stack up until ready to use—this can be done early in the day.

Next, assemble your ingredients on trays for each type of pizza. When guests arrive, get them to join in assembling pizzas. Round out the meal with a salad, wine or a good Michigan beer, and a simple fruit dessert.

Thai Shrimp & Cilantro Pizza
(makes enough for 2 10" x 15" baking pans)

8 oz. raw shrimp, peeled and deveined

Marinade
1/3 c. bottled Thai sweet chili sauce
2 tbl. oil
1 tbl. vinegar
1 tsp. gingerroot, minced
1 garlic clove, minced

Topping
1 tbl. sesame oil
1 c. mozzarella cheese
2 carrots, peeled and finely julienned, parboil 2 minutes
4-6 scallions, finely julienned
2/3 c. fresh cilantro, chopped
2 tbl. fresh basil, shredded
2 jalapeno peppers, seeded and julienned
1/4 c. Parmesan cheese

Marinate shrimp in chili sauce, oil, vinegar, gingerroot, and garlic. Toss well and chill for 30 minutes.

To Assemble:

Cook pizza crust for 5-7 minutes at 400°. Remove and brush with sesame oil and place topping ingredients in the following order: 1/2 c. mozzarella, shrimp (removed from marinade), carrots, scallions, cilantro, basil, peppers, 1/2 c. mozzarella, and Parmesan. Bake at 400° for 10 minutes or until shrimp are done.

Delicate and fanciful in appearance, these phyllo hors d'oeuvres are much quicker and easier to make than the triangle shapes. They can be made ahead and frozen but do not stack in layers, as the ends will break.

Shrimp Phyllo Purses
serves 15

1 16-oz. pkg. phyllo dough
melted butter

Filling
3 slices bacon, chopped
2 garlic cloves, minced
3 tbl. jalapeno, minced (or to taste)
1/2 c. scallions, chopped
1/2 lb. shrimp, peeled, deveined, and chopped
1 tbl. curry powder or homemade (or to taste)
1/2 c. currants
7-8 oz. herbed cheese
1/3 c. coarsely chopped salted peanuts
1 tbl. chutney

Sauté bacon 2 minutes; add garlic and jalapenos. Continue cooking and add scallions, shrimp, and curry powder. Cook until shrimp are just done and have turned pink-orange. Remove from heat and mix in currants, cheese, peanuts, and chutney. Taste and adjust flavors. Cool.
To Assemble:
Place one sheet of phyllo dough on a counter. Brush

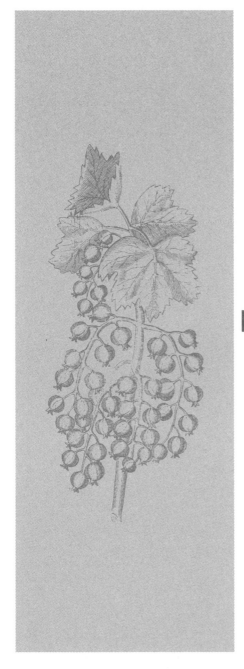

Prosciutto

Prosciutto (Italian ham) is slightly smoky and salty, a cross between Canadian bacon and country-cured ham.

It's served as an antipasto wrapped around fresh melon pieces or blanched asparagus and lends an assertive taste to cooking. Prosciutto must be sliced very thin, almost transparent. Most Italian specialty food stores carry both domestic and imported prosciutto. Prices and quality vary; ask for a sample to determine your favorite.

62

lightly with butter; repeat until there are 3 layers. Cut into 3"-4" squares. Place 1-2 tbl. of the filling in the center of each square. Gather the four corners together and squeeze halfway down to form a pouch. Place in ungreased mini-muffin tins and bake at 375° for 15-20 minutes or until golden. Serve immediately with Jalapeno, Chipotle, or Red Chili Aioli (see Index).

Turn this dish into a hot or cold entrée by cutting the slices larger or leaving the rolls whole. It's great at picnics or buffets in the summer.

Chicken Giardiniera

serves 12 as an appetizer or 8 as an entrée

4 whole chicken breasts, halved, skinned, boned, and pounded to
    1/8"-1/4" thick
24 very thin slices of Genoa salami
1 tbl. EACH butter and olive oil

Filling

2/3 c. hot Giardiniera, well drained
1 egg yolk
4 oz. plain or herbed goat cheese
8 oz. cream cheese (regular or low fat), room temperature
1 garlic clove, minced
3 tbl. toasted walnut halves, coarsely chopped
3 tbl. fresh Italian parsley, minced
1 tsp. dried basil
1 tsp. dried marjoram
salt and freshly ground pepper

Place Giardiniera, egg yolk, cheeses, and garlic in a food processor and whirl until just combined. Mixture should have some texture. Remove to a bowl and mix in walnuts, parsley, herbs, salt, and pepper. Taste and adjust seasonings. Can be set aside to chill in the refrigerator overnight.

Giardiniera

Giardiniera is an Italian condiment of mixed pickled vegetables. It's often part of an antipasto platter or a garnish with boiled dinners. In some neighborhood Italian restaurants it's used as a pizza topping.

The marinade is made of wine vinegar and herbs. It's rather tart and slightly acidic but great with crusty bread and robust red wine.

Unlike the usual American pickled vegetables, Giardiniera is not sweet and doesn't contain dill. Many vegetables are used—carrots, celery, pearl onions, small cucumbers, cauliflower, and peppers. In some gourmet shops you'll find it displayed on counters—beautifully layered in large designer canning jars.

63

To Assemble:

Cover the work surface with wax paper and lay out the pounded chicken breasts in a row—shiny side of breast down. Place 3 slices of Genoa salami on each and spread with 2-3 tbl. of the Giardiniera mixture on top. Roll chicken up like a jelly roll, and place seam side down on a plate. Cover with plastic wrap and chill 2 hours or overnight. This helps to set the shape.

Melt butter and oil in a large skillet. Dredge chicken rolls with a little flour. Sauté in pan, turning to brown on each side. Add more oil if necessary. Remove rolls to a baking dish that will hold the chicken snugly together. Cover with foil and bake for 25 minutes or until done in a 350° oven. Cool. Cover each roll with plastic wrap and chill 8-10 hours or overnight. Cut off ends and save for munching! Slice rolls 1/2" thick and arrange on a platter. Serve cold with an aioli (see the recipe that follows and the Index).

Sun-Dried Tomato Aioli

2 garlic cloves, chopped
1/4 c. sun-dried tomatoes
2 tbl. seasoned rice vinegar
1 egg
3/4 c. oil
salt and freshly ground pepper

With motor running, add the garlic to a food processor or blender. Whirl till finely chopped. Add sun-dried tomatoes, vinegar, and egg and whirl until smooth. With motor running, very slowly add the oil until all is used up. Taste and adjust flavors. Store up to 3 weeks in the refrigerator.

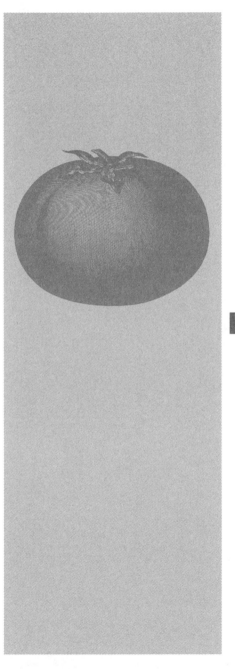

One summer Suzanne and I and two good friends, Tomi Gutterman and Lucy Ito, formed a group called the Jaguar School of Cooking. We gave classes on barbecues, grilling, and picnics. One of the students' favorite dishes was this flavorful appetizer/side dish/vegetarian entrée of Lucy's. See if you don't agree.

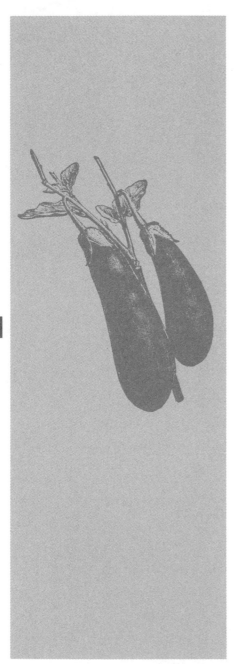

Marinated Eggplant Rolls
serves 8-10 as an appetizer

2 eggplants, unpeeled, cut into rounds, 3/8" slices
salt
6 oz. goat cheese, room temperature
4 oz. cream cheese (regular or low fat), room temperature

Marinade
2 garlic cloves, chopped
1/4 c. EACH fresh Italian parsley and basil, chopped
1/3 c. red wine vinegar
2/3 c. olive oil
salt and freshly ground pepper

Place eggplant slices on a baking sheet with sides; lightly salt and allow to sit for 30 minutes. Preheat oven to 400°. Combine cheeses and set aside.

Rinse eggplant with water and return to baking sheet. Add a little more water to just lightly cover the bottom of the baking sheet. Cover tightly with foil and place in oven. Cook-steam until soft, about 5-8 minutes. Turn once. Add more water to keep eggplant from sticking to pan.

When cool enough to handle, spread each eggplant slice with a little cheese and roll into "cigars." Place in a glass or ceramic shallow dish, seam side down.

To make marinade, in a food processor with motor running, put in garlic and mince. Add parsley and basil; mince again. Transfer to a bowl and add vinegar. Whisk in olive oil; season with salt and pepper. Taste and adjust seasonings. Pour marinade over eggplant rolls. Cover with plastic wrap and chill overnight. Serve at room temperature.

Appetizer Cocktail Party

Crostini with Shrimp Topping
Sun-Dried Tomato
& Green Olive Tapenade

❧

Rosemary, Caramelized Onion
& Goat Cheese Tart

❧

Italian Sausage Phyllo Triangles

❧

Marinated Eggplant Rolls

❧

Pear, Garlic & Ham Pâté

❧

Rosemary Walnuts

❧

Serve with a California or Italian
brut sparkling wine,
champagne cocktail, or Kir Royale

67

Quesadillas can be prepared ahead. Cook as below and place on a foil-lined baking sheet. Cover with more foil and keep warm in a 350° oven.

Chive Quesadillas with Brie & Pears
serves 10-12

2 tbl. butter
1/4 c. vegetable oil
1 pkg. flour tortillas, medium to large size
8 oz. Brie, white rind removed, room temperature
1-2 pears, unpeeled, cored and very thinly sliced
1/2 c. fresh chives, whole stems
Salsa (Cranberry-Jalapeno Salsa) (See Index)

Melt butter and oil, adding about 1/2 tsp. to a large hot non-stick skillet. Place one tortilla into pan and arrange several pear slices over half. Dot with crumbled Brie (about 2 tbl.). Add 2-3 chive stems. Fold tortillas in half and brush with a little melted butter-oil mixture. Turn several times until tortillas are golden and cheese begins to melt. Add melted butter-oil mixture only as needed. Remove, cut in wedges, and serve with a favorite salsa, such as Cranberry-Jalapeno Salsa.

Brie

Originally from France, Brie is known as the Queen of Cheeses. Today it's produced throughout the world.

Brie comes in wedges or rounds. It's characterized by a soft white edible crust and a creamy, buttery center. For the best flavor, purchase fresh cut wedges, rather than pre-cut. Once Brie is cut, it no longer ripens and begins to diminish in flavor. Remember to serve at room temperature for maximum taste.

68

Serve this attractive hors d'oeuvre with toast points or a good quality water cracker.

Goat Cheese Torta with Sun-Dried Tomato Pesto
serves 6-8

5 oz. goat cheese, room temperature
3 oz. cream cheese (regular or low fat), room temperature
3 oz. feta cheese
1/2 recipe Sun-Dried Tomato Pesto
2-3 sun-dried tomatoes, finely julienned
2 tbl. fresh basil, chopped

In a bowl combine the goat cheese and cream cheese. Add feta and combine lightly, creating a coarse texture. Line a 1 1/2 c. ramekin (or straight sided bowl) with plastic wrap. Place half of the cheese mixture in the bottom of the ramekin; press down smoothly. Spread 2-3 tbl. pesto on top of cheese mixture; smooth evenly. Refrigerate overnight or at least 4 hours.

When ready to serve, invert torta on serving platter. Remove plastic wrap. Place some pesto around bottom of torta. Decoratively sprinkle julienne strips of sun-dried tomato and basil on top.

This is a very versatile snack. Other flavor combinations are possible by adding different herbs to the original recipe, such as 1 tsp. homemade or commercial chili powder, 1 1/2 tsp. Italian seasoning, or 1 1/2 tsp. dill weed. Experiment and add your own favorite herb or mix.

Pita Chips

1 pkg. pita bread
1/2 c. butter, room temperature
3 tbl. fresh parsley, finely minced
1 garlic clove, finely minced
salt and freshly ground pepper

Mix butter with parsley, garlic, salt, and pepper. Cut pita bread into eighths and separate. Spread the inside portion with the butter mixture. Place on a baking sheet and bake in a 375° oven for 15-25 minutes or until crisp. Remove and cool on a rack. Store in airtight containers until ready to use. Serve with soups and chili or with herbed cheese and dipping sauces.

Feta Cheese

Feta is a fresh Greek cheese made of goat or sheep's milk. Unlike chèvre, feta is shaped without a rind, packed in brine or salt, and allowed to ripen.

The texture is soft and crumbly with a tangy, salty flavor. Feta has many uses—crumbled into salads, minced with tomatoes, melted in pasta sauces, marinated, or just enjoyed as an appetizer with cured olives.

Sun-Dried Tomato Pesto

3-4 large garlic cloves
1 c. sun-dried tomatoes (if not pliable, reconstitute in hot water, omitting the 2 tbl. hot water)
2 tbl. hot water
4 tbl. Parmesan cheese, grated
1/2 c. olive oil
1/2 c. walnuts or pine nuts
freshly ground pepper

In a blender or food processor, while motor is running, add garlic. Next add tomatoes and water and combine well. Slowly add Parmesan cheese and oil, then walnuts. Season to taste with pepper.

These are great fun to make once you get the hang of it. Count the first couple rolls as trial runs as you learn the following technique. Add or subtract ingredients; all that is required is fresh produce.

Fresh Spring Rolls with Rice Paper
makes 10 rolls

20 rice papers, 8" diameter
1/3 c. hoisin sauce
1/2 lb. shrimp, cooked and sliced lengthwise, or
    cooked marinated chicken or pork, sliced thin
1 large carrot, julienned (use a mandoline)
5 romaine lettuce leaves, shredded thin
2 scallions, thinly sliced
2 1-oz. bunches dried cellophane noodles cooked until soft or
    cooked soba noodles*
2 small zucchini, julienned
1 small bunch cilantro, thick stems removed
1/4 c. fresh basil, thinly sliced
1/2 c. peanuts, coarsely chopped

Fill large bowl with hot water. Dip two rice papers in water until slightly softened, 10-20 seconds. Remove and pat dry. Place on top of each other. Spread 2 tsp. hoisin sauce on lower third of rice paper, 1" from edges. On the lower third of rice paper place shrimp in a horizontal row. Top with a small amount of carrots, lettuce, scallions, noodles, zucchini, and cilantro, then sprinkle with basil and peanuts.

Mandoline

This European tool, traditionally only available in restaurants, slices, shreds, waffle cuts, and juliennes vegetables with great speed and precision. It is now a staple in serious cooks' kitchens. It will cut your prep time in half, but it is not child's play. You must pay utmost attention while using this utensil so as not to injure your fingers.

The heavy-duty European models are quite expensive and found only in specialty or gourmet cookware shops. Less expensive but very effective plastic versions are available in Asian grocery stores and some mail-order catalogs.

Fold rice paper over just enough to cover filling, then fold in both sides, ensuring a snug fit. Roll up into a compact cylinder about 6" long. Repeat with remaining rice paper and fillings. Rolls can be made a day ahead but when refrigerating, separate each roll with plastic wrap. Serve with Dipping Sauce.

*available in Asian grocery stores

Dipping Sauce
1/2 c. soy sauce
1/4 c. rice vinegar
2 scallions, minced
2 tbl. fresh lemon juice
2 tsp. sesame oil
4 large garlic cloves, finely minced

Combine all ingredients; stir well. Cover and let stand 15 minutes before serving.

This is a fun, interactive cooking recipe for dinner parties. It has the added advantage of being quick and easy to make.

Asian Chicken in Lettuce Cups
serves 6-8

2 chicken breasts, halved, boned, skinned, and finely chopped

2 tsp. cornstarch

1/2 whole egg, beaten

2 tbl. sesame oil

1 tbl. soy sauce

2 tsp. Chile Paste with Garlic*

2 garlic cloves, minced

1 1/2 tsp. fresh ginger, minced

1/4 c. EACH fresh red pepper and carrot, minced

8 fresh pea pods, julienned

1 c. pine nuts, toasted

1 small head of leaf lettuce

3 wonton skins, cut into thin strips and fried until crisp

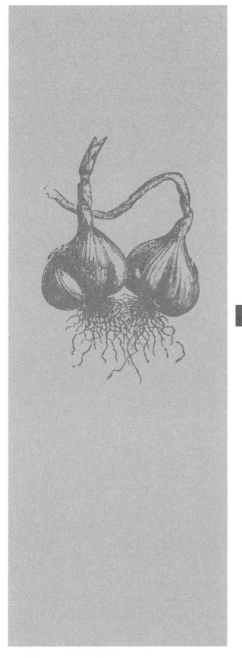

In a bowl combine chicken, cornstarch, egg, sesame oil, soy sauce, and Chile Paste. Sauté mixture in a hot sauté pan for 2 minutes. Remove chicken from pan and set aside. Add garlic, ginger, red pepper, carrot, and pea pods. Continue to sauté while stirring an additional 1-2 minutes. Add chicken mixture; combine with vegetables and pine nuts. Place lettuce leaves on outside of platter and chicken mixture in center. Sprinkle with wonton strips.

To serve, place the chicken mixture on a lettuce

73.

leaf and fold lettuce over chicken. Roll up and serve with Dipping Sauce.

available in Asian grocery stores

Dipping Sauce

1/3 c. rice vinegar
2 tbl. sugar
1 tsp. salt
1 tsp. Chile Paste with Garlic
2 tbl. green onion, chopped
2 tbl. soy sauce
1/4 c. white wine
1 tbl. sesame oil

Combine all ingredients and mix well.

Salads: Side Dishes & Main Dishes

This was one of the most difficult chapters for us to do. Not because herb salads are hard to make but because in the course of writing this book, we had developed many more recipes than we needed. Working around the size constraints of the book was more of a challenge than inventing recipes!

We have tried to provide our readers with a selection of simple green salads to accompany dinner, such as our Boston Lettuce & Goat Cheese Salad with Honey Vinaigrette or the intriguing Fennel & Lychee Nut Salad. Side dish salads are exemplified by the colorful Dried Blueberry Couscous Salad. Also included are salads for picnics and buffets. Those are the hearty main dish varieties like Black Bean, Corn & Cilantro Salad or the spicy Asian Noodle Salad. We hope you have as much fun preparing these recipes as we did.

A tart-sweet salad that goes especially well with spicy food like our Southwest Chicken with Chipotle Chili Sauce or Shrimp in Black Bean Pasta Sauce (see Index).

Spinach, Red Onion & Orange Salad with Poppyseed Vinaigrette
serves 4

10-12 oz. fresh spinach, trimmed and washed
1 small red onion, halved and thinly sliced
2 oranges, peeled and sliced
1 c. blue cheese, crumbled

Vinaigrette
3 tbl. honey
1 1/2 tsp. dry mustard
1 tsp. salt
1/3 c. flavored vinegar (raspberry, blueberry, red wine, etc.)
2 tbl. minced scallions
1 tbl. grated onion
3/4 c. oil
1 1/2 tsp. poppy seeds
1/4 c. fresh chives, minced

Place spinach, red onion, and oranges on a large platter. Combine vinaigrette ingredients and taste. Add more honey if needed. Just before serving pour a little on salad and toss lightly. Sprinkle on cheese and serve.

Michigan Winter Dinner

Butternut Squash Thyme Soup

❦

Pork Tenderloin with Calvados-Lingonberry Sauce

❦

Wild Rice Pilaf with Hazelnuts & Michigan Dried Cherries

❦

Spinach, Red Onion & Orange Salad with Poppyseed Vinaigrette

❦

Glazed Pear Tart

❦

Serve with a California Merlot wine

After a weekend of outdoor events or any busy weekend, we serve this nutritious dish on Sunday nights with hot homemade bran muffins.

Winter Fruit Salad with Dried Cherries & Mint
serves 4

2-3 Granny Smith apples, cored, unpeeled, and diced in
   1/2" chunks
1 orange, peeled and chopped in large pieces
1 c. seedless grapes
1 banana, sliced (optional)
2-3 pears, unpeeled, cored, and diced in 1/2" chunks
1/3 c. dried cherries
1 c. Swiss cheese, cut in 1/2" chunks
1 c. sharp aged cheddar cheese, cut in 1/2" chunks
1/2 c. toasted whole almonds
1/2 c. toasted whole pecans
2 tbl. minced fresh mint
3 tbl. honey

Combine all ingredients and refrigerate 30 minutes before serving.

Toasting Nuts

If you toast nuts (pecans, almonds, walnuts, pine nuts) before adding them to recipes the flavors are heightened. It's such a simple step but often overlooked. Even if a recipe doesn't call for this process, we generally do it—particularly for salads, garnishes, or tarts. The procedure is simple. Place the quantity of nuts called for in a recipe on a baking sheet and put into a preheated 400° oven. Toast for 4-5 minutes. Remove and toss gently and continue toasting for another 2-3 minutes. Be sure to check often, since nuts burn quickly. The general rule is, if you can smell them toasting, it's probably too late!

Sun-Dried Tomatoes

When purchasing sun-dried tomatoes look for Romas; they're meatier and more intensely flavored than regular tomatoes. They're available packed in oil or in cellophane bags. If the dried tomatoes are not pliable, reconstitute them in boiling water.

We keep a large canning jar in the refrigerator filled with good olive oil and tomatoes. As the supply gets low, we simply add more sun-dried tomatoes.

The oil is great added to pasta sauces, for quick sautés, or mixed with cream cheese for an appetizer.

Marge's husband, Chuck, serves this salad when he makes Cajun food—a specialty of his. He finds the "element of danger" involved in making a Cajun roux a real challenge. It can also be served as part of an antipasto platter.

Artichoke Salad with Sun-Dried Tomatoes
serves 6-8

Vinaigrette
> 6-7 tbl. olive oil
> juice of 1 lemon (about 1/3 c.)
> 1 tbl. EACH Dijon mustard and horseradish
> 1 tsp. paprika
> 3 tbl. fresh Italian parsley, minced
> 1 tsp. EACH dried thyme and tarragon
> 1/2 c. scallions, minced
> 1-1 1/2 tbl. honey
> salt and freshly ground pepper

Salad Mixings
> 2 13-oz. cans artichoke hearts, drained and quartered
> 1 head escarole or endive, shredded
> 4 sun-dried tomatoes, sliced
> 2/3 c. black olives, halved

Combine all vinaigrette ingredients in a covered jar. Shake well. Season to taste. Pour over artichoke pieces and marinate 1 hour in refrigerator.

On a large platter toss together lettuce, artichokes, sundried tomatoes, and olives just before serving.

When your garden is filled with sweet tomatoes, this simple dish will show them off.

Tomato & Sweet Onion Salad
serves 6-8

4 large tomatoes
1 large sweet onion, very thinly sliced
2 tbl. fresh basil, chopped, or 1 tsp. dried + 1 tbl. fresh parsley
1/4 c. good olive oil
2 tbl. red wine vinegar
salt and freshly ground pepper

Cut tomatoes in 1/4" slices. Arrange in a single layer on a serving platter. Separate onion into rings and scatter over tomatoes. Sprinkle with salt, pepper, and basil. Combine oil and vinegar and drizzle over salad. Cover with plastic wrap and chill 2-4 hours. Return to room temperature to serve.

Tomatoes

Besides growing the old reliable tomatoes like Better Boy, Early Girl, and Big Boy, venture out and add a few heirlooms to your garden.

Try sunny yellow Chello Cherry, rosy-pink Japanese Odorike, golden-orange Mandarin Cross, bi-colored Old Flame, or the sweet French varieties. Look for them in gourmet seed catalogs. They'll not only add color to your garden, but a plate of these sliced tomatoes will look like a rainbow.

79

Salad Fruit

When cutting up fruit, make sure you leave strawberries for the very end, since they are very fragile and tend to break down sooner than melons and pineapples. We also keep cut pineapples away from other fruits until the last minute—the acid in pineapple causes other fruits to deteriorate more quickly.

This is another creative salad. The fruit can also be kiwi, mango, banana, or raspberries. For variety, use more than one flavor of mint.

Summer Fruit Salad with Yogurt-Mint Dressing
serves 4-6

1 8-oz. carton plain or vanilla yogurt
2 tbl. honey
1 tsp. grated orange rind
1/2 tsp. grated fresh ginger
3 tbl. minced fresh mint
6-8 c. assorted sliced and cut up fruit (strawberries, melons, pineapple, grapes, cherries, or blueberries)
lettuce leaves (optional)

Combine the yogurt, honey, orange rind, ginger, and mint. Mix well. Chill several hours. Just before serving, line individual plates with lettuce. Place about 1 cup of assorted fruits on top of lettuce. Spoon a generous dollop of the yogurt mixture on top of the fruit on each plate and serve with a mint sprig.

We must admit this is a strange combination of ingredients, but they work brilliantly together!

Boston Lettuce & Goat Cheese Salad with Honey Vinaigrette
serves 6-8

1 head Boston lettuce
1 small head radicchio
1 small bulb fennel, thinly sliced and chopped (about 1/3 c.)
1/2 c. goat cheese, crumbled
1/2 pt. strawberries, whole or sliced
1/2 c. toasted whole pecans*
freshly ground pepper

Arrange torn lettuce and radicchio on individual plates or a large platter and sprinkle with fennel, goat cheese, and strawberries. Drizzle dressing over and toss gently. Add pecans, more strawberries, if needed, and a grinding of pepper.

Honey Vinaigrette
1/2 c. olive oil
3 tbl. fruit flavored or tarragon vinegar
2 tsp. balsamic vinegar
1 1/2 tsp. dried marjoram
2 1/2 tbl. honey (or to taste)
3/4 tsp. salt

Place all ingredients in a jar and shake well.
*Toast whole pecans in a 400° oven for 8-10 minutes.

Radicchio

The current popularity of radicchio (pronounced RA-DEEK-E-O) is evident in restaurants across the country. Although a common sight in Italian grocery stores, this chicory is relatively new to most Americans. It can be grown locally but does take some pampering. Its distinctive ruby-red color adds a bright spot to salads, but if not properly shaded during the growing process, it will turn a green or deep copper color.

Radicchio has a slightly bitter taste that goes well with other assertive greens, like escarole or endive, and benefits from strong-flavored vinaigrettes.

Spinach

When choosing spinach make sure the leaves are fresh and not bruised. If leaves are large, fold in half and tear with stem side up, pulling the stem back toward leaf to remove. Submerge in water and wash twice, making sure sand and dirt have been removed.

82

An unusual but very tasty salad; it happens to be a favorite of both of our brothers: John (Suzanne's brother) and Fred (Marge's brother).

Fennel & Lychee Nut Salad
serves 8-10

Vinaigrette

9 tbl. vegetable oil
1/3 c. flavored vinegar (raspberry, pear, blueberry, etc.)
2 tbl. orange juice
1 1/2 tbl. honey (or to taste)
2 tsp. sesame oil
salt and freshly ground pepper

Combine the vinaigrette ingredients in a jar or bowl and mix well. Taste and adjust the seasonings. Set aside or store in the refrigerator.

Salad Mixings

2 c. mixed baby lettuces
1 small head Bibb, Boston, or leaf lettuce
3 c. fresh spinach, washed and deribbed
1 c. Daikon radish or peeled jicama, julienned
1 small fennel bulb, sliced in thin rings
10-12 fresh snow peas, blanched 7-10 seconds
2/3 c. canned lychee nuts, quartered
1 c. toasted walnut halves

To Assemble:

Place lettuce greens on a large platter. Sprinkle with radish or jicama, fennel, snow peas, and lychee nuts. Add half the vinaigrette and toss to coat evenly. Add more if needed. Sprinkle salad with walnuts and serve.

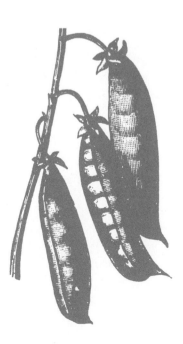

Lychee Nuts

A unique ingredient in this salad is lychee nuts, a Chinese fruit that's small and oval-shaped, with a red outer shell-like skin. The pulp is sweet, milky-white, and translucent. The fresh variety is expensive and difficult to find. We use the canned type that is available in almost every grocery store. It's already peeled, pitted, and packed in a light sugar syrup. Kids find it a great snack to eat right out of the can.

Couscous

Couscous is a staple in North African cooking, especially Morocco. It's made of semolina (durum wheat), the same grain used in imported pasta. It's usually sold in this country precooked and instant. The traditional long cooking process uses semolina grains that are flour coated.

It has a cereal-like smell and taste, but with simple additions it becomes a sophisticated side dish to almost any grilled meat, poultry, or seafood. It's a bright change from rice when mixed with butter and freshly grated Parmesan.

Marge's older daughter, Ryan, requests this salad whenever she visits home. Its unique flavor goes especially well with grilled beef, pork, or lamb and tastes great even several days later. Vary the colorful vegetables with whatever you have on hand.

Dried Blueberry Couscous Salad
serves 8-10

3 c. chicken stock
7 tbl. vegetable or olive oil
1/4 tsp. EACH turmeric, ground allspice, ground cloves, and
    ground ginger
1 1/2 c. or 1 10-oz. box couscous
1/3 c. EACH diced dried apricots, golden raisins, and
    dried blueberries
2 c. zucchini, unpeeled and chopped
1-1 1/2 c. carrots, chopped
1/4 c. fresh lemon juice
1/3 c. red onion, chopped
1 1/2 tsp. salt (or to taste)
3 tbl. EACH minced fresh chives and fresh mint
2 tsp. honey (or to taste)
1/3 c. toasted slivered almonds

Bring stock, 3 tbl. oil, and spices to a boil. Add couscous and boil over moderate heat 2 minutes or until liquid is absorbed. Add apricots, golden raisins, and dried blueberries. Cover and let stand 15 minutes. Chill.

Break up couscous till each grain is separate and

add rest of ingredients, including remaining oil. Taste and adjust seasonings. Chill 4 hours. Taste before serving. If too dry, add more oil and lemon juice. Garnish with toasted almonds.

Zucchini

When growing zucchini, 2 or 3 plants are enough for an average family. Small, baby zucchini are prized for their tender, delicate flavor. Middle-sized zucchini are great shredded and sautéed with olive oil, garlic, and a sprinkling of fresh herbs.

Left unattended, baby zucchini soon become blimp-size but are still good when grated into soups, in quick breads, or stuffed with other vegetables.

85

Jalapenos

When chopping or mincing jalapenos make sure they are seeded first. The veins in the membranes holding the seeds are the receptacles for the "real heat." The seeds growing next to the veins are also extra hot. If you have sensitive hands, wear rubber gloves during the procedure.

This is a nice combination of fruit, jalapenos, and peppers. It is exotic but very refreshing.

Tropical Melon Salsa Salad
serves 6

1 cantaloupe, seeded and cut in 1/2" chunks
2-3 jalapenos, finely minced
1 1/2 c. bell peppers (use an assortment of colors—red, yellow, orange, green) cut into 1/2" chunks
1/2 c. red onions, chopped
1 1/2 c. jicama or Daikon radish, chopped
3-4 scallions, chopped
1/2 c. cilantro, chopped
3 tbl. lime juice
3 tbl. oil
3 tbl. herbed vinegar
honey (to taste)

Combine all ingredients in a bowl and toss. Adjust sweetness and chill several hours.

This is Marge's 90-year-old German Aunt Elfriede's recipe. She's always received compliments for this simple but delicious salad in every restaurant she's owned.

Tante Friedel's Potato Salad
serves 6-8

3 lb. red potatoes, with or without skins
1 c. chopped onion
1/2 c. fresh parsley, minced
1/4 c. olive oil
2 tbl. Dijon mustard (or herbed)
1c. homemade or good quality mayonnaise
salt and freshly ground pepper

Boil potatoes until fork-tender. Drain and run under cold water. Chop into large chunks and put in a large bowl. Add onions, parsley, and half the olive oil. In a small bowl mix the remaining oil, mustard, and mayonnaise. Add to potatoes and blend well. Season to taste. Garnish with additional parsley before serving. Flavors improve the second day, but serve cold.

Homemade Mayonnaise

Making your own mayonnaise is fun and the end product is delicious. There's no comparison to the store-bought variety, and it can be varied in so many ways. All you need are a blender and good olive oil (but not extra virgin, because the flavor is too intense). The secret to thick, fluffy mayonnaise is the slow addition of oil.

Other recipes can include roasted red peppers, garlic, jalapenos, sesame oil, chili powder, and any flavor that fits your culinary needs.

87

Asparagus

When purchasing asparagus make sure the spears are crisp and bright green without shriveled skin. Break off the white "root" end where it naturally snaps and boil in a sauté pan with 2" of water for no more than 2 minutes. Start thicker asparagus before thin ones for even cooking. Immediately rinse in cold water. To transform this salad into a main dish add 1 1/2 c. smoked ham cubes.

This spring salad can also be a late summer salad with the substitution of green beans for asparagus.

Tuscan Spring Salad
serves 8

10-12 small new potatoes (unpeeled)
1 lb. fresh asparagus or green beans
3-4 carrots, sliced thin or on the diagonal
1 tsp. sugar

Vinaigrette

2 garlic cloves, minced
1/4 c. fresh parsley, minced
1 tbl. dried basil or 3 tbl. fresh, minced
2/3 c. olive oil
6 tbl. red wine vinegar
1 tsp. salt and freshly ground pepper
1/3 c. chopped scallions

Cook potatoes in salted water 15-20 minutes or until tender. Drain and chill. Cook asparagus in boiling water until barely tender. Drain and chill. Slice into 2" pieces. Put sugar in boiling water; add carrots and blanch until barely tender. Drain and chill. Set aside.

To prepare Vinaigrette, in a blender or food processor with motor running put garlic and whirl. Add the parsley, basil, oil, and vinegar. Whirl until smooth. Season with salt and pepper. Mix in scallions. Pour over vegetables. Lightly toss. Chill and reseason before serving.

As with many salads, the ingredients and amounts are flexible with the season and your pantry. Feel free to add other vegetables like cauliflower, yellow summer squash, whole baby squash, and sliced baby carrots, as well as other types of hard cheese and salami.

Italian Rosemary Rice Salad
serves 10

Vinaigrette
> 1/2 lemon, juiced
> 5 tbl. red wine vinegar
> 2 tsp. dried basil
> 1 1/2 tbl. fresh rosemary, chopped
> 2/3 c. olive oil
> salt and freshly ground pepper
> 2 tsp. honey (or to taste)

Salad Mixings
> 4 c. cooked cold rice
> 2 c. cooked garbanzo beans (1 15-oz. can, well drained)
> 10 oz. artichoke hearts, chopped
> 1/4 c. Kalamata or other oil-cured olives
> 1 1/2 c. celery, sliced or on the diagonal
> 5-8 oz. salami, cubed
> 1/2 c. red onion, chopped
> 1/2 c. fontinella or mozzarella cheese, chopped
> 1 zucchini, chopped (1 1/2 c.)
> 10-12 sun-dried tomatoes, sliced (softened or reconstituted)
> 1/2 c. fresh Italian parsley, minced

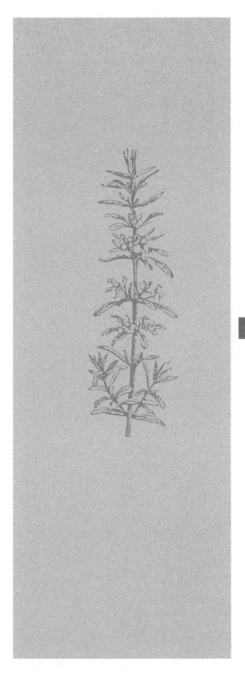

89

Beach Picnic Menu

Seafood Gazpacho

❦

*Chicken Giardiniera with Sun-Dried
Tomato Aioli*

❦

Italian Rosemary Rice Salad

❦

Triple Ginger Tart

❦

*Serve with a Johannisberg Riesling
or Spanish Rioja wine*

Combine vinaigrette ingredients in a jar and mix. Taste and adjust seasonings.

Combine salad ingredients in a large bowl; add vinaigrette and toss gently. Taste and adjust flavors. Chill overnight. Bring to room temperature to serve.

Michigan is the nation's leader in dried bean production. Here's a recipe that uses just one of many beans grown in Michigan.

Italian White Bean Salad
serves 8

3 12-oz. cans white beans (or homemade equivalent)
1/4 c. EACH olive oil and red wine vinegar
2 tomatoes, seeded, drained, and chopped
1/2 c. fresh parsley, minced
1 1/2 tsp. EACH dried marjoram and dried oregano
2 tsp. dried basil
1 tsp. fennel seeds
1/2 c. sliced black olives
1 c. celery, sliced
1 c. chopped red pepper
3 scallions, minced
2 garlic cloves, minced
1 tsp. honey (or to taste)
lettuce leaves (optional)

Drain and rinse beans. Combine and mix. Taste and adjust seasonings. Chill. Serve cold on lettuce leaves.

Dried Beans

Beans, lentils, and peas—known as legumes—are more versatile than their humble culinary beginnings. A menu mainstay for thousands of years, beans provide nutritious simple meals for pennies. Most dried beans require soaking in water for 8-10 hours before cooking. When in a hurry, substitute canned beans for dried. Remember this easy conversion: 1 lb. of dried beans = approximately 6 c. canned beans.

Scoville Unit

Scoville units, developed in 1902 by Wilbur Scoville, offer a way to measure the power of the capsicum (pepper). Scoville needed to measure the heat of peppers used in making the muscle salve "Heet."

Scoville based his units on how much he had to dilute the chili before he could not taste any heat. The scale ranges from 0 for bell peppers to 200,000 for the hottest habaneros. On a scale 0 to 10, bell peppers are 0, jalapenos are 7, serranos are 8, and habaneros are 10.

92

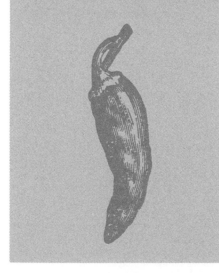

We especially like this salad for a festive warm summer night buffet. Add sliced cooked chicken or turkey for a hearty buffet entrée.

Black Bean, Corn & Cilantro Salad
serves 8-10

2 15-oz. cans black beans, rinsed well and drained
   (or homemade equivalent)
2 c. cooked corn, cooled or 1 10-oz. frozen package, thawed
   and drained
1 c. green and red bell peppers, cut in 1/4"-1/2" pieces
1-2 jalapenos, seeded and finely minced
3/4 c. red onion, finely chopped
1/2 c. fresh cilantro, coarsely chopped
1/2 c. Daikon radish,* peeled, cut in 1/4" cubes
6 medium flour tortillas
vegetable oil
salt

Vinaigrette

1 1/2 tbl. honey
2 cloves garlic, minced
3 tbl. sherry vinegar or spicy herb vinegar
1/3 c. vegetable oil
1/8 tsp. cayenne pepper
1/2 tsp. ground cloves
2 tsp. dried oregano
1 1/2 tsp. ground cumin (See Index)
2 tsp. salt
freshly ground black pepper

In a large bowl combine beans, corn, peppers, onions, and cilantro. In a jar combine vinaigrette ingredients and pour over bean mixture. Toss well and season to taste. Chill until serving time. Mix in radish before serving.

For garnish: cut tortillas into wedges or strips. Fry in 1/2" hot oil until light golden brown. Turn once. Drain on paper towels and salt lightly. Store in metal cookie tins until ready to use.

Place bean salad on a large platter and place tortilla chips around edges of the platter.

If unavailable, you can substitute with jicama—or omit. Daikon radishes are white and very long (like a huge carrot) and mild in taste. They may be found in Asian food markets and large specialty food stores. Don't add the Daikon until just before serving or it will turn gray from the black beans.

Tortilla Chips

Fresh flour tortilla chips are an easy and special treat. The shapes can vary between the standard strips or wedges, or you can be as creative as you like. Cut flour tortillas into wedge shapes with a knife or scissors. Fry in small batches in a heavy deep pan with 1/2" of very hot vegetable oil, until golden on both sides. For removing chips, we find using a Chinese wok strainer is easiest. The chips cook very quickly, so watch carefully. Place chips on paper towels to cool and absorb any excess oil. Then put chips into a large paper bag, add salt, and toss carefully. Store in a covered metal tin until ready to use (within 2-3 days).

93

Coconut

When curry dishes and other Indian foods are served, small bowls of condiments are included: toasted nuts, minced fresh herbs, chutneys, relishes, raisins, yogurt, and coconut. The condiments provide another dimension to the food—some are hot, others crunchy, mild, salty, sour, or sweet. Coconut combines two: sweet and crunchy—but must be toasted first.

This simple process takes just a few minutes. Begin with a preheated 400° oven. Spread the sweetened, raw, or unsweetened coconut on large baking sheets and place in the oven. Bake for about 2 minutes, remove, and gently toss. You will notice that the coconut browns on the outer edges first. Return to the oven for another minute or two and remove to a bowl. Coconut burns even faster than nuts, so watch carefully.

94

If you are making this salad ahead of time, wait until just before serving to mix in the peanuts and coconut—it keeps them from becoming mushy. This can become a vegetarian dish by omitting the chicken, or transform it into a party dish by substituting 1 lb. cooked shrimp for the chicken.

Curry Chicken & Rice Salad
serves 8

Vinaigrette
> 2/3 c. vegetable oil
> 1/4 c. vinegar
> 2 tsp. Dijon mustard
> 1 1/2 tbl. honey
> 1 1/2 tsp. curry powder, commercial or homemade (or to taste) (See Index)
> 1 1/2 tsp. salt
> freshly ground pepper

Salad Mixings
> 1 1/2 c. chopped onions
> 3 cloves garlic
> 2 tbl. vegetable oil
> 1 1/2 tsp. curry powder, commercial or homemade (See Index)
> 1 1/2 whole cooked chicken breasts, skinned, boned, and cut into 1/2" cubes or shreds
> 1 c. chopped scallions
> 1 c. currants or golden raisins
> 2 green peppers, cut into thin strips (1/3" x 2")
> 1 1/2 c. celery, cut diagonally

1 c. *salted peanut halves*
1 c. *toasted coconut*
2 *Granny Smith apples, halved, cored, and cut into 1/2" cubes*
4 c. *cooked rice*
salt and freshly ground pepper

In a jar, make the vinaigrette by combining oil, vinegar, mustard, honey, 1 1/2 tsp. curry powder, salt, and pepper; then set aside.

Sauté onions and garlic in 2 tbl. vegetable oil; add 1 1/2 tsp. curry powder and continue to sauté 2-3 minutes, until onions are transparent. Add cooked onion mixture to a large bowl; combine with remaining ingredients, reserving 1/2 c. peanuts and coconut. Toss salad ingredients with vinaigrette, season to taste, and sprinkle with reserved peanuts and coconut just before serving.

Poaching Chicken

When cooking chicken for salads we like to poach it in water with thyme, bay leaves, onion, and parsley stems. Simmer slowly until just done. The chicken becomes flavorful yet moist with this method. Remove the chicken and keep the liquid as a tasty stock.

95

Rice Vinegar

We use seasoned or unseasoned rice vinegar for many of our vinaigrettes, salsas, aiolis, and marinades.

It's made from fermented rice and imparts a delicate, mild, and less acidic flavor than most vinegars. Substitute it in any salad dressing but cut down on the honey or sugar if using the seasoned vinegar.

We like this salad for ladies' luncheons, served with small flavorful muffins or quick breads such as zucchini or cherry.

Wild Rice, Smoked Turkey & Dried Cherry Salad
serves 4

Vinaigrette
　　1 tbl. EACH orange juice and grated rind
　　1/4 c. vegetable oil
　　2 tbl. EACH rice vinegar and honey
　　2 tsp. dried tarragon
　　salt and freshly ground pepper

Salad Mixings
　　2 c. cooked wild rice
　　1 c. smoked turkey, cut into cubes
　　1/2 c. EACH scallions and celery, chopped
　　2 tbl. fresh chives, chopped
　　1/3 c. dried cherries
　　1-2 oranges, chopped (rind grated)
　　1/2 c. pea pods, blanched
　　3 oz. chèvre (goat cheese)
　　1 c. toasted pecans
　　Bibb or leaf lettuce

Combine vinaigrette ingredients in a large bowl and whisk. Add rice, turkey, scallions, celery, chives, dried cherries, and oranges. Toss and season to taste. Chill. Just before serving add pea pods, goat cheese, and pecans. Mix gently and serve on a platter lined with lettuce.

We like to prepare large buffet dinners featuring at least 3 salads of differing ethnic groups, such as Asian Noodle, Black Bean, Corn & Cilantro, *and* Curry Chicken & Rice Salad.

Asian Noodle Salad
serves 6

Marinade
    2 tbl. Thai chili sauce
    1 tbl. oil
    1/4 c. water
    3/4-1 lb. fresh shrimp, peeled and deveined*

Vinaigrette
    1 1/2-2 tbl. fresh ginger, finely minced
    1/4 c. soy sauce
    3 1/2-4 tbl. sesame oil
    dash chili oil
    1/2 tsp. Chile Paste with Garlic (*Available at Asian food stores*)
    juice of 1/2 lime
    6 tbl. oil
    2 tbl. sugar
    1/4 c. rice vinegar

Salad Mixings
    1 lb. Asian noodles, cooked
    4 oz. pea pods, blanched
    10 oz. mini corn, drained, cut in half lengths
    3 tbl. fresh basil, chopped

Asian Noodles

There are as many Asian noodles as Italian pastas, each with a specific use and unique flavor. Soba (made from buckwheat) is a Japanese noodle—thin, round, and tan-colored (some are flavored with green tea). Udon, also a round noodle, is much thicker and requires a longer cooking time.

                    ら

The popular ramen, or somen, is precooked and makes a quick lunch—you'll find it with a variety of seasonings in almost every grocery store.

                    ら

Chinese noodles, called mein, are available fresh or dried and come in a variety of shapes, sizes, and flavors.

                    ら

97

Asian Noodles, continued

Cellophane noodles, which look like transparent fishing line, are made from mung beans. Tasteless by themselves, they absorb the flavor of the liquid they are cooked in.

§

Last on our list are rice sticks, or mai fun—a vermicelli made from rice. When deep fried, they puff up to twice their original size. Fun to serve and great to eat as a salad topping or with stir-fried vegetables.

§

98

1/2 c. red onion, chopped
1/4 c. scallions, chopped
1 yellow or red pepper, julienned
2 large carrots (1 1/2 c.), julienned and blanched
1 yellow squash, unpeeled, julienned
1/2 c. chopped cilantro
chopped scallions for garnish
basil for garnish
*Omit shrimp for a tasty vegetarian dish.

Combine Thai chili sauce, oil, and water. Mix well and add raw shrimp. Let marinate 30 minutes. Remove from marinade and grill or sauté in a skillet until shrimp turn pink-orange. Place cooked shrimp in a bowl and set aside.

To make the vinaigrette, combine all ingredients in a jar or small bowl and whisk. Taste and adjust seasonings. Add half of the vinaigrette to the shrimp and toss. Cover bowl with plastic wrap and chill 30 minutes to overnight.

Place the remaining vinaigrette in another bowl and add the cooked noodles, pea pods, corn, basil, onion, scallions, pepper, carrots, squash, and cilantro. Toss gently and taste and adjust seasonings.

To serve, place noodle mixture on a large platter. Scatter shrimp on top and garnish with additional scallions and fresh basil. Serve cold or at room temperature.

When grilling tenderloin for dinner, make extra to use in this next-day salad. You can substitute sirloin or other tender beef.

Beef Tenderloin Salad with Thyme Balsamic Vinaigrette
serves 6

1 lb. beef tenderloin
oil for sautéing

Marinade

1/4 c. oil
2 tbl. lemon juice
2 tsp. freshly ground black pepper
salt
1/4 tsp. hot pepper sauce
1/4 tsp. hot chili oil

Vinaigrette

3-4 tbl. balsamic vinegar
2 cloves garlic, minced
1 tbl. Dijon or herbed mustard
4 tbl. fresh parsley, minced
1 1/2 tsp. dried thyme
1/4 c. olive oil

Salad Mixings

3/4 lb. green beans, partially blanched, or asparagus
1 large red pepper, julienned

99

4 scallions, sliced in 1" lengths
2 small heads of Belgian endive, cleaned
1 small head of romaine or radicchio
1/2 red onion, thinly sliced
2 tomatoes, sliced, or 8-10 patio tomatoes, halved

Basic Vinaigrette

1/2 c. olive oil
3 tbl. vinegar
1-2 tbl. honey
1 tsp. Dijon mustard
1 tsp. dried herbs or 1 tbl. fresh
herbs*

Combine all ingredients in a jar and mix well. Taste and adjust seasonings. Store in refrigerator if using fresh herbs.

*basil, oregano, marjoram, thyme, rosemary, tarragon, Italian parsley, salad burnet, or a preferred combination of herbs

❦

Place the whole trimmed tenderloin in a shallow bowl. Combine all the marinade ingredients in a bowl and mix well. Pour over tenderloin. Marinate at room temperature 1 hour or overnight in the refrigerator.

Make the vinaigrette by combining the vinegar, garlic, mustard, thyme, and parsley. Gradually whisk in olive oil. Taste and adjust seasonings.

Sauté beef in a small amount of oil for 15-20 minutes or until done. It should be slightly pink inside. The meat can also be grilled. With either method, let beef rest 5-10 minutes to set juices before slicing. Cut into strips and add with green beans to vinaigrette. Let both marinate in refrigerator for 15 minutes. Add peppers and scallions.

To serve, arrange endive, romaine, or radicchio on a large serving platter—tear into bite-size pieces. Add red onions and beef and toss gently. Decorate with tomatoes.

This colorful and very flavorful salad is great to take to potlucks and summer buffets—add the salmon and the salsa at the last minute to prevent the mixture from becoming too soggy.

Santa Fe Salmon Salad
serves 4

1 lb. salmon fillets (not steaks)

Vinaigrette
1 garlic clove, minced
1 jalapeno, minced
1/2 c. EACH fresh lime juice, orange juice, and oil
2 tsp. Dijon mustard
1 tsp. salt
3/4 tsp. EACH sugar and ground cumin

Salad Mixings
2 bunches watercress, picked over and cleaned
1 head romaine, cleaned and shredded
1/2 c. cilantro, chopped
1/2 c. EACH red and green pepper, julienned
1 jicama, peeled and chopped (optional)

Salsa
4 scallions, chopped
2 tomatillos, husks removed and minced
2 Italian tomatoes, seeded and chopped

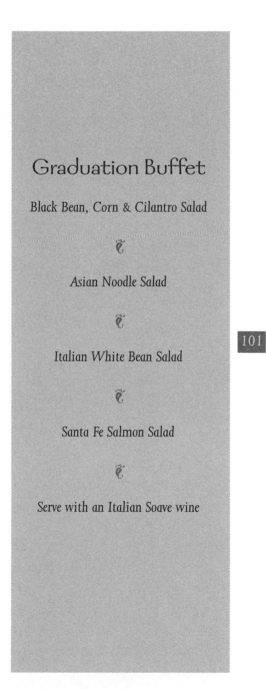

Graduation Buffet

Black Bean, Corn & Cilantro Salad

❦

Asian Noodle Salad

❦

Italian White Bean Salad

❦

Santa Fe Salmon Salad

❦

Serve with an Italian Soave wine

101

Vinaigrette Hints

To make vinaigrettes creamy, slowly whisk the olive oil in by hand. A miniature metal or wire whisk is especially handy for this procedure.

Combine leftover vinaigrettes to make marinades for chicken, pork, beef, and vegetables.

Combine vinaigrette ingredients and pour about 1/4 c. over salmon and place in a resealable plastic food-storage bag and refrigerate for 1 hour. Combine salsa ingredients and set aside.

Grill or broil salmon till done. Salmon can be served cold or warm. On a large platter place the salad mixings and toss with a little of the vinaigrette. Place salmon around salad mixings and top with salsa.

Use whatever smoked fish is available to you—whitefish, salmon, trout, etc. This is an elegant salad that is best served as a first course or even as an appetizer with a fresh fruit platter, a variety of blue cheeses, and wine.

Blueberry Smoked Fish Salad with Dill
serves 4

3 c. tender greens (mesclun, etc.)
8 oz. smoked fish, cut in small pieces
1 c. fresh blueberries (not frozen)
2 tbl. fresh chives, chopped
2 scallions, including green tops, sliced on the diagonal
1-2 tbl. extra virgin olive oil
1/4 lemon, juiced
1 1/2 tbl. fresh dill, chopped
freshly ground pepper

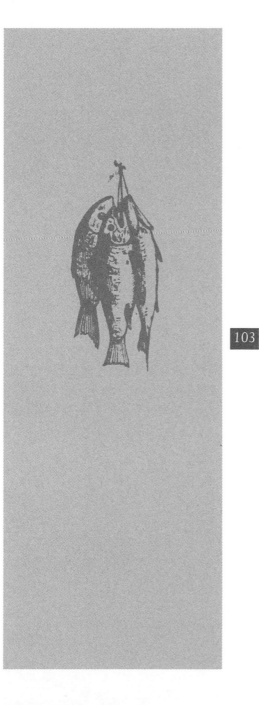

Place the greens on a platter and scatter on the fish, blueberries, chives, scallions, and dill. Sprinkle with lemon juice and oil; add a generous amount of freshly grated black pepper. Taste and adjust seasonings. Salad can sit out 30 minutes before serving. Garnish with additional dill sprigs.

103

104

Vinaigrette Hints

If using fresh herbs or prepared mustard, store vinaigrettes in the refrigerator. They will keep 4-5 weeks.

Don't be tempted to discard the vinaigrette when you see that the oil has congealed. Oil hardens in cold temperatures. Simply bring it to room temperature or place in a pan of lukewarm water for 3-4 minutes.

A beautiful summer salad to serve when bell peppers are in season and reasonably priced. Use all one color or combine several for a festive dish. The vinaigrette is unique and slightly sweet because of the fruit. If plums aren't available, substitute peaches or nectarines.

Sweet Pepper Salad with Plum Vinaigrette
serves 4

Vinaigrette
2 plums, cut in half and skins removed
3 tbl. fruity vinegar or red wine vinegar
1/2 c. regular or extra virgin olive oil
1 1/2 tsp. coarse-ground Dijon mustard
1 tbl. fresh marjoram, chopped
honey (to taste)
salt and freshly ground pepper

Salad Mixings
1/3 c. toasted walnut halves
1 1/2 qt. assorted salad greens (mesclun)
3 fresh bell peppers, julienned

In a blender, place plums, vinegar, mustard, and marjoram; whirl till smooth. Add olive oil and blend well. Taste and add honey, if needed; season with salt and pepper. Keep refrigerated until ready to serve.

Place washed and dried greens on a large serving platter. Toss on peppers and half of the vinaigrette. Mix well, adding more vinaigrette if needed. Sprinkle on walnuts and a few grindings of pepper.

Vinaigrette Hints

Use good quality olive oils. Bottles labeled extra virgin oil are darker green, strongly flavored, and more expensive. Use sparingly in vinaigrettes, even cutting the total oil with regular olive oil for a milder flavor. Extra virgin olive oil is wonderful with assertive greens.

105

Summer Picnic
Menu

Curried Cream of Red Pepper Soup

❧

Beef Tenderloin Salad with Thyme
Balsamic Vinaigrette

❧

Grilled Vegetable Salad with
Basil Pesto Vinaigrette

❧

Cinnamon Caramel Nut Tart

❧

Serve with a dry Rose
or Valpolicella wine

For interesting variations on this simple summer salad use different pestos, such as Sun-Dried Tomato, Cilantro, or Dill Pesto (see Index).

Grilled Vegetable Salad with Basil Pesto Vinaigrette
serves 4

Pesto Vinaigrette
2 tbl. balsamic vinegar
1 tbl. red wine vinegar
1 tbl. prepared Basil pesto (See Index)
1/2 tsp. salt
1/4 tsp. freshly ground pepper
3/4 c. olive oil

Salad Mixings
1 medium eggplant, cut crosswise into 1/2" diagonal slices
salt and freshly ground pepper
2 medium zucchini, cut into 1/2" diagonal slices
2 medium yellow summer squash, cut into
    1/2" diagonal slices
4 c. mixed baby lettuces (mesclun)

Make vinaigrette in a small bowl by combining vinegars, pesto, salt, and pepper and whisking in oil. Set aside.
Place eggplant slices in a colander and sprinkle with salt. Let drain for 30 minutes. Rinse with water and pat dry.
Brush all vegetables with a little vinaigrette and

arrange on medium-hot grill (an indoor grill works well, or a hibachi can be used). Grill vegetables until slightly soft but still a little firm. Turn once.

Toss lettuces with 1/4 c. of the vinaigrette and arrange on a platter or individual plates. Place grilled vegetables on top and drizzle with additional vinaigrette, if needed.

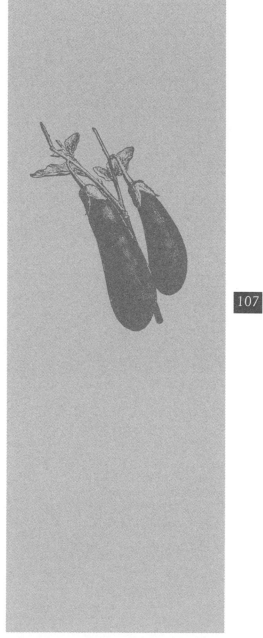

Suzanne uses an inexpensive Japanese mandoline she loves. It makes fast, easy, and beautiful julienned vegetables, which add a special touch to salads.

Three Cabbage Coleslaw with Roasted Peanuts
serves 8

Dressing

1/2 c. EACH plain yogurt and mayonnaise (regular or low fat)
2 tsp. sesame oil
3 tbl. apple cider or rice vinegar
1/2 medium red onion, coarsely chopped
1 tsp. celery seeds
1/2 tsp. freshly ground pepper
1 tsp. salt
1 tbl. sugar

Salad Mixings

1/2 small head napa cabbage, thinly sliced
1/4 head EACH green and red cabbage, thinly sliced
3 carrots, shredded or julienned
3 scallions, thinly sliced
1/2 bunch fresh cilantro, chopped
1 c. roasted peanuts, coarsely chopped

In a blender combine yogurt, mayonnaise, sesame oil, vinegar, and red onion. Mix in celery seeds, pepper, salt, and sugar and set aside. In a large bowl combine cabbage and carrots. Add dressing, scallions, and cilantro, mixing well. Just before serving sprinkle with chopped peanuts.

In this salad we find that flank steak that has been grilled and marinated in a little soy sauce and sesame oil has the best flavor.

Ginger Beef Salad with Bok Choy
serves 4

Vinaigrette
2 tbl. orange juice
1 tsp. hoisin sauce
1/2 tsp. sesame oil
1/4 c. vegetable oil
honey (if needed)

Salad Mixings
1 lb. cooked flank steak, thinly sliced across the grain
4 c. chopped bok choy
1 c. Daikon radish, julienned
4 oz. cooked, sliced asparagus
2 tbl. pickled ginger (optional)*
1/4 c. cilantro, chopped
1 tbl. toasted sesame seeds

Mix vinaigrette ingredients and taste for seasonings. Combine salad mixings on a large platter. Pour some vinaigrette over the flank steak mixture and toss. If too dry, add more vinaigrette.

*available in Asian grocery stores

109

If you double the marinade and double the amount of pork, you can have one meal of grilled pork chops and the next day make the salad with the leftovers.

Bourbon Salad with Pork & Yams
serves 4

3 tbl. bourbon
3 tbl. Dijon mustard
3 tbl. molasses
1 tbl. chili powder, commercial or homemade
4 butterflied, boneless pork chops, 1/2" thick
1/2 lb. yams, peeled and cut in 1/2" slices
1/4 c. fresh lime juice
3 tbl. scallions, chopped
1 tbl. fresh parsley, chopped
salt and freshly ground pepper
6 tbl. olive oil
1 head chicory, endive, or escarole, chopped
2 c. shredded red cabbage
2 Granny Smith apples, unpeeled, cored and cut in chunks
honey (if needed)

Mix 1 1/2 tbl. each of bourbon, mustard, and molasses and 1 tsp. chili powder in a resealable food-storage bag. Add pork chops and yams and refrigerate in marinade 4 hours.

Broil or grill pork until browned but white and moist inside, about 4 minutes per side. Let cool to room temperature and cut into 1/2" cubes. Broil or grill yams until soft and browned.

Mix remaining bourbon, mustard, molasses, and chili powder with lime juice, scallions, parsley, salt, pepper, and olive oil. Taste and adjust seasonings.

Combine lettuce, cabbage, and apples with a little of the vinaigrette. Arrange attractively on a platter. Mix pork and yams with remaining vinaigrette. Place on top of the vegetables. Serve at room temperature.

Middle Eastern Spices

Middle Eastern cuisine is fresh and colorful. It depends a great deal on perfectly ripe fruits and vegetables, and often recipes are variations on themes. What makes them distinctive are some of the unusual spices.

Zaa'tar and sumac are Middle Eastern spices, readily available to American cooks. Zaa'tar is a combination of sesame seeds, oregano, and sumac. It's a salty/sour blend used in soups, marinades, and rice dishes. The sumac is not the same poisonous variety grown in North America but a sour red-colored tasty herb.

This is a good way to use the bumper crop of zucchini that seems to appear overnight in our gardens. If you only have large-sized zucchini, remove some of the soft, mealy center and reserve it for stuffing or breads.

Italian Herbed Zucchini Salad
serves 4

Vinaigrette

2 garlic cloves, minced
2 tbl. herbed vinegar
6 tbl. extra virgin olive oil
1 tbl. fresh Italian parsley, minced
1/4 c. fresh mint, minced
1 tbl. EACH fresh basil, oregano, and marjoram
   (or 1 tsp. each, dried)
1/4 tsp. dried red pepper flakes
salt
honey (if needed)

Salad Mixings

4 large zucchini, unpeeled and cut into julienne strips
   (3" x 1/4")
3 c. assorted greens (romaine, escarole, endive)

Combine vinaigrette ingredients and taste.
About 30 minutes before serving, place greens and zucchini on a large serving platter. Drizzle on some of the vinaigrette and toss well. Just before serving, taste and add more vinaigrette if the salad is too dry.

Soups

We have divided our Soup chapter into three areas: Cold, Dinner or First Course, and Hearty Whole Meal Soups and Chilis. Some are cream soups that are light yet rich tasting, perfect in the most elegant of menus, such as our Cream of Five Onion Soup, Butternut Thyme Squash Soup, and the spicy Curried Cream of Red Pepper Soup.

The hearty soups are meant to be entrées. A soup such as Lentil, Leek & Ham may be served as dinner. Coriander Chicken Chili can make a fine Sunday night potluck supper. Minestrone can serve as a quick one-dish meal on a busy weekday. We're sure you're going to find them unique and satisfying.

Fresh vs. Dried Bread Crumbs

There is a difference! Dried crumbs refers to bread or rolls that are dried out and whirled in a food processor or blender. Fresh bread crumbs are made from fresh bread or rolls, whirled in a blender till soft and fluffy. Their uses are different. Dried bread crumbs give a hard coating to foods like fried chicken or fish. Fresh bread crumbs give a light coating or thicken foods. When a soup or stew is a little watery you can add a handful of fresh bread crumbs to the base without cooking it. This replaces the often used white sauce or roux.

114

This soup is so flavorful and fresh tasting, even those people who aren't fond of cold soups ask for seconds.

Seafood Gazpacho
serves 8

2 cloves garlic, minced
1 small cucumber, peeled, seeded, and cut into 1/4" pieces
1 sweet red pepper, cored, seeded, and finely minced
1/2 medium red onion, finely chopped
1 1/2 c. EACH chicken stock and tomato juice
1 14-oz. can Italian tomatoes, chopped with liquid
  (or the equivalent fresh)
1/4 c. EACH fresh lime juice and olive oil
1 c. fresh bread crumbs (2-3 slices of fresh bread, any kind,
  whirled in a blender or food processor)
1 1/2 tsp. cumin seed, crushed
1 tsp. dried oregano
1 sprig salad burnet (optional)
3 tbl. fresh cilantro, chopped
1 sprig thyme
salt and freshly ground pepper
1/2 lb. cooked shrimp, cut in large pieces, chilled

In a large bowl mix garlic, cucumber, red pepper, onion, stock, tomatoes, and tomato juice. Stir in lime juice, oil, bread crumbs, and herbs. Puree half of the soup in a blender; add to bowl. Season with salt and pepper. Chill 8 hours or overnight. Stir in shrimp just before serving.

Suzanne's family takes this comforting soup on ski trips. The combination of the smoky bacon and nutty flavored rice makes it a hit.

Cream of Wild Rice Soup
serves 6

2/3 c. wild rice
1/2 c. onion, diced
1/2 c. celery, diced
1/2 c. carrots, diced
3 strips bacon, diced
4 1/2 c. chicken stock
1/2 tsp. dried thyme
1 tsp. dried crushed rosemary
3/4 c. heavy cream
beurre manié (1 tbl. flour and 1 tbl. butter kneaded together)
salt and freshly ground pepper
fresh parsley

Sauté rice, onion, celery, carrots, and bacon until vegetables are tender and bacon is crisp, 3-4 minutes. Remove all but 1 tbl. of bacon drippings. Stir in stock and herbs, bring to a boil, reduce heat, and cover. Simmer until rice is tender, 30-40 minutes. Stir in cream; whisk in beurre manié until soup thickens. Season. Add more stock if soup appears too thick. Serve hot and garnish with chopped fresh parsley.

Wild Rice

Wild rice is a Native American grass, grown in the waters of the western Great Lakes region. It is indigenous to Wisconsin, Michigan, and Minnesota and commercially grown in California. Considered by many a luxury product, we find the price well worth the extra pennies. We use raw wild rice instead of parboiled or instant for a better flavor.

Wild rice should not be overcooked, which is easy, since it is surprisingly more delicate than the other varieties. Remember to prewash the rice in 3 or 4 changes of water to remove small stones, etc.

115

Stock—Homemade vs. Canned

All of us wish we had time to make and freeze our own chicken or beef stock. Not only is it inexpensive, but the flavor is far superior to anything you can buy. But today's busy schedules don't always permit such endeavors, so the only option is canned stock or broth.

There are many varieties of canned, powdered, paste, or liquid stocks and the final decision is up to you. We prefer the low-salt canned beef or chicken stocks or the liquid beef or chicken concentrates. A can of beef or chicken broth is approximately 1 7/8 cup of liquid. Naturally just shy of 2 cups!

116

This is another elegant soup best served as a first course with our delicate homemade crackers.

Cream of Five Onion Soup with Herbed Cheese Crackers
serves 8-10

4 heads (not cloves) garlic, unpeeled
3 tbl. olive oil
2 tbl. butter
3 leeks, white part only, chopped
1 onion, chopped
1 bunch scallions, white part only, chopped
6 tbl. flour
4 c. chicken stock
1/3 c. dry sherry
1/2 c. heavy cream
fresh lemon juice, to taste
salt and freshly ground pepper, to taste
2 tbl. fresh chives, minced

Cut off top 1/4" of each garlic head. Place heads in a small baking dish and drizzle with 1 tbl. olive oil. Turn to coat. Cover dish with foil. Bake in a preheated 350° oven for 1 hour or until cloves are very, very soft. Let cool. (Can be baked 1-2 days ahead and refrigerated.) Press individual garlic cloves to release the puree. Set aside.

Melt butter and 2 tbl. olive oil in a soup kettle or deep saucepan. Sauté leeks, onions, and scallions until soft, about 8 minutes. Reduce heat to low and add garlic puree.

Add flour and cook 8-10 minutes, stirring occasionally. Stir in stock and sherry. Simmer 20 minutes, stirring occasionally. Remove from heat and let cool slightly. Puree in batches in a blender or food processor. Return to saucepan and add cream. Simmer until slightly thick, about 7-10 minutes. Add lemon juice to taste and season with salt and pepper. Thin out with chicken stock if soup is too thick. Ladle into bowls and garnish with chives.

Herbed Cheese Crackers

1/4 c. butter, room temperature
1/2 c. flour
dash of salt
1/2 c. shredded Swiss, cheddar, or Edam cheese (2 oz.)
1-2 tbl. water, if needed
1 egg, beaten
1/4 c. poppy seeds, caraway, or sesame seeds (singly
   or in combination)

Grease a large baking sheet and set aside. Preheat oven to 375°. In a food processor or mixer combine butter, flour, salt, and cheese. Whirl or mix well. Add water in small amounts until mixture sticks to itself. Wrap in plastic wrap and chill 15 minutes.

On a floured board (or in between pieces of wax paper) roll pastry to about 14" x 10". Cut into strips with a pastry wheel or with decorative cookie cutters. Handle dough carefully; it's quite fragile. Place cutouts on prepared pan. Brush with egg and sprinkle on seeds. Bake for 10 minutes or until crisp and golden brown. Store in airtight tins.

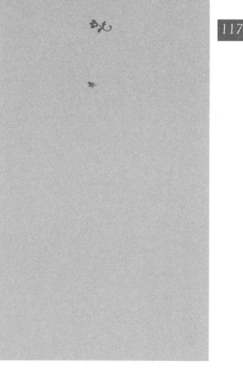

Stock, continued

So if your recipe calls for 2 cups, simply add the difference in water. The secret to picking the right stock or broth is to read the label. Make sure the first ingredient isn't salt. The product should contain chicken or beef.

If you have a little time, you can enhance commercial stocks with a few aromatic vegetables and herbs.

A great soup to make at the end of the summer when red peppers are inexpensive and plentiful.

Curried Cream of Red Pepper Soup
serves 10-12

1/2 c. onions, chopped
1 tbl. curry powder, homemade or commercial (mild)
2 tbl. butter
3 large fresh red bell peppers, chopped
2 1/2 c. chicken stock
3 tbl. raw white rice
1 c. heavy cream
salt and freshly ground pepper
1 recipe Fresh Tomato Salsa

In a large saucepan or Dutch oven sauté the onions and curry powder in the butter until soft, 2-3 minutes. Lower heat, add peppers, and cook 3-4 minutes. Add stock and rice; cover and simmer 15 minutes or until rice is cooked and peppers are very soft. Cool; puree in a blender or food processor. Add cream and season. Chill 8 hours or overnight. Taste and add more curry powder, salt, and pepper, if needed. Serve with a generous dollop of salsa in each bowl.

118

Fresh Tomato Salsa

    1 medium tomato, seeded and diced
    1 tbl. red onion, minced
    1 1/2 tsp. jalapeno pepper, minced
    1 tbl. balsamic vinegar
    1 tbl. fresh basil, minced
    1/2 tbl. olive oil
    salt and freshly ground pepper

Combine all ingredients; season. Cover with plastic wrap and chill.

Salsas

Salsas are more than the typical tomato-chili-onion mixture served with chips. Salsas are fresh relishes that can add zip to soups, grilled fish, chicken or beef, homemade tortilla chips, and even omelets.

What's nice about salsas are the varieties you can make or buy. Some commercial salsas are quite good—but check to be sure they aren't too watery. If the flavor seems flat, add some fresh minced chilis, or herbs, or even a dash of herb vinegar.

Making salsa is fun and easy. Use the freshest fruits and seasonal vegetables and don't be afraid to experiment. Cut the ingredients in small similar sizes—usually 1/4"-1/2" dice—and combine only at the last minute.

119

Quick Chicken Stock

1 tbl. oil
1 onion, unpeeled, chopped
2 carrots, unpeeled, chopped
1 celery stalk with leaves, chopped
1 stalk parsley, with stems
3 cans chicken stock, low salt

Sauté in oil the onions, carrots, and celery until slightly brown. Add stock and parsley and cook on low 30 minutes. Strain and use.

§

Winter Squash

When peeling winter squash use a vegetable parer. Cut off the underlayer of green along with skin.

Peak grocery season for butternuts is October through December. Look for squash that seem heavy for their size, smooth-skinned with hard, tough rinds. Keep in a cool place until ready to use.

§

120

A beautiful autumn orange-colored soup that would make a grand start to any dinner, at a tailgate picnic, or even a casual meal on its own, with a crusty bread and a salad of mixed greens.

Butternut Squash Thyme Soup
serves 8-10

4-4 1/2 lb. butternut squash
2 leeks, cleaned and chopped, or 2 1/2 c. chopped onion
5-5 1/2 c. chicken stock
1 tsp. dried thyme
2/3 c. sour cream (regular or low fat)
1 tsp. salt
freshly ground pepper
1/8 tsp. cayenne
4 tbl. rum (optional)
freshly minced parsley and chives
sour cream (regular or low fat)

Peel squash, cube, and remove seeds. Place squash and leeks in a stockpot; add chicken stock and thyme. Cook 20 minutes or until tender. In a blender or food processor puree squash mixture in batches, adding sour cream (if mixture becomes too thick add additional stock). Return squash to pot; season with salt, pepper, and cayenne; add rum. Reheat; mix well. Serve garnished with parsley, chives, and a dollop of sour cream in the center of each bowl.

A good way to introduce cooked beans to your family. If you don't have the varieties suggested, use any cooked, canned bean.

Vegetarian Chili with Mushroom & Eggplant
serves 10-12

1/2 oz. dried mushrooms (porcini, cepes, shiitake, etc.,
   or a combination)
1 c. boiling water
1 large eggplant, peeled and cut into 1" chunks
salt
3 tbl. oil
4-6 garlic cloves, minced
2 onions, chopped
1 large green bell pepper
10-12 oz. fresh mushrooms, trimmed and quartered
1 28-oz. can Italian tomatoes, chopped with liquid
2 tbl. chili powder, commercial or homemade (mild) (See Index)
1 tbl. EACH ground cumin and dried oregano
1 1/2 tsp. fennel seeds
salt
dash cayenne pepper
2 cans (15-16 oz. each) garbanzo beans, or homemade equivalent
1 can (15-16 oz.) EACH white or navy beans,
   small red beans, and kidney beans
sour cream (regular or low fat) or plain yogurt
cilantro
salsa

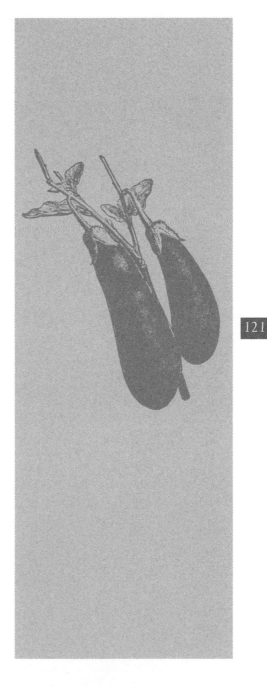

121

Dried Mushrooms

Dried mushrooms have become very popular recently and are more widely available to the home cook. They're expensive, with an intense flavor, but only a few are called for in recipes. There are many varieties and new ones are appearing on grocers' shelves all the time. Most common are the Chinese shiitakes, chanterelles, cepes, morels, and the Italian porcini. You can buy them singly or in mixes.

Once purchased, store them in a dry place, similar to where you store pasta. Dried mushrooms must be reconstituted to use—a simple process. Place the amount called for in a bowl and cover with 1" boiling water. Let stand for about 30 minutes, or until they are soft. Remove any woody stems (particularly with shiitakes) and slice. Use as your recipe calls for but don't throw away the liquid. Strain through a coffee filter to remove any grit or small particles and use in your recipe or freeze for use in other recipes.

Pour boiling water over mushrooms and soak for 30 minutes. Cut into small pieces and save soaking liquid. Place eggplant cubes in a colander and sprinkle with salt. Let drain 30 minutes. Rinse with water and dry well.

Place oil in large kettle or Dutch oven and sauté garlic, onions, and green pepper 1-2 minutes. Add fresh and dried mushrooms, eggplant, tomatoes, herbs, and strained mushroom soaking liquid. Bring to a boil, reduce heat, and simmer 30 minutes or until eggplant is tender. Add beans and a little water if too dry. Adjust seasonings and heat through, about 10-15 minutes more.

To serve, garnish each bowl with a dollop of sour cream or yogurt, cilantro leaves, and salsa and serve with Sage Corn Bread.

Chicken chili is an intriguing twist on the traditional Texas chili. Serve in the winter or summer with Sage Corn Bread and Tropical Melon Salsa Salad and top the meal off with our Pine Nut Tart (see Index).

Coriander Chicken Chili
serves 8

4 chicken thighs (1 1/2-2 lb.) boned, skinned,
   and cut up into 1/2-1" cubes
2 whole chicken breasts, boned, skinned, and cut
   into 1/2-1" cubes
1/3-1/2 c. flour
vegetable oil
2 onions, chopped (3 c.)
5 garlic cloves, minced
2 red bell peppers, chopped in 1/2" pieces
4-6 jalapeno peppers, seeded and chopped
3 tbl. medium hot chili powder, commercial or
   homemade (See Index)
1-2 tsp. cumin seed, crushed
1 1/2 tsp. ground coriander
1/8 tsp. ground cloves
salt
2 c. water
1 28-oz. can Italian tomatoes, chopped with liquid
1 1/2 oz. grated unsweetened chocolate
1 tsp. honey (or to taste)
2 cans (15-16 oz.) EACH white and navy beans
3 tbl. ground almonds

Tomatoes

When using fresh tomatoes we prefer Romas because their flavor is more intense and the texture is meatier. Remove the skin by lowering the tomatoes into boiling water 1 1/2-2 minutes; cool slightly and peel.

To remove seeds cut in quarters and scoop out with a spoon. If using canned tomatoes, choose Italian plum or Romas, and add a touch of honey to counteract the tin flavor.

123

Chili Powder

We prefer to use true chili powder, which is made from ground chili peppers. When purchasing chili powder, make sure the color is bright brick red. The aroma should be strong, intense, and earthy. Commercial chili powders are mixes, containing cumin, oregano, garlic powder, cayenne, paprika, black pepper, salt, sugar, and very little real chili powder.

2 tbl. toasted sesame seeds (toast seeds in skillet on medium heat
until seeds begin to brown and pop)
1 lb. smoked Italian turkey sausage (if unavailable,
use regular smoked turkey sausage) sliced in 1/2" rounds
sour cream (regular or low fat)
cilantro
lime wedges

Dredge chicken pieces in flour and brown in oil in a Dutch oven. Remove and set aside. Add 2 tbl. oil to pan and sauté onions, garlic, bell peppers, and jalapenos until soft (2-3 minutes). Add chili powder, herbs, water, tomatoes, chocolate, honey, beans, almonds, sesame seeds, and sausage. Cook 30 to 40 minutes at low heat to mellow flavors. Add chicken pieces; then cook 15 minutes at low heat. Adjust seasonings to taste. Add additional water if too thick. Garnish with dollop of sour cream, sprigs of fresh cilantro, and thinly sliced wedges of lime.

Sage Cornbread

2 c. coarse yellow cornmeal
1 c. flour
1/4 c. vegetable oil
1 8 3/4-oz. can creamed corn
1 c. (4 oz.) shredded aged cheddar cheese
1 c. buttermilk
2 eggs, beaten
2 tbl. chopped onions
1/3 c. canned mild or hot green chilies or fresh equivalent, minced
2 tsp. baking powder
1/4 c. sugar
1 1/2 tsp. salt
1 tbl. rubbed sage

Preheat oven to 350°. Grease a 7" x 11" pan or muffin tins. Set aside. In a large bowl combine cornmeal, flour, oil, creamed corn, and cheese; blend well. Add buttermilk, eggs, onions, chilies, baking powder, sugar, salt, and sage. Mix thoroughly. Pour into prepared pans. Bake 25-35 minutes or until done (wooden pick should come out clean). Crust should be lightly browned.

This soup is a real hit with kids, especially if you use fancy shaped pasta. To lower fat content, or for a vegetarian version, you may omit the bacon and substitute 2 tbl. canola oil.

Minestrone
serves 8-10

4-6 thick slices bacon, chopped in 1/2" pieces
1 1/2 c. onions, chopped
1 c. thinly sliced carrots
3/4 c. celery, chopped
4 cloves garlic, minced
3 14 1/2-oz. cans chicken stock
1 16-oz. can Italian tomatoes, reserve liquid
1/2 c. dry white wine or vermouth
2 tbl. fresh parsley, minced
1 bay leaf
2 tsp. dried basil
1 tsp. dried rosemary
salt and freshly ground pepper
1 c. dry macaroni or other small pasta
1 c. zucchini, unpeeled and sliced
1 20-oz. can white beans, drained, or homemade equivalent
Parmesan cheese, grated
Basil Pesto (See Index)

In a Dutch oven or large stockpot cook bacon until crisp. Remove and reserve. Save 3 tbl. pan drippings or add oil if necessary. Sauté onions, carrots, celery, and garlic until soft. Add stock, tomatoes, wine, and herbs. Cook over

Fresh vs. Dried Pasta

Just because the package says "fresh pasta" doesn't necessarily mean it's best. Dried pasta can actually be better. The secret is in using semolina flour, also called durum wheat or hard wheat. Most imported pastas are 100% semolina, but not all domestic pastas contain very much. If your dried pasta falls apart while cooking, chances are it didn't contain durum wheat.

126

low heat about 40 minutes. Add pasta and cook another 5 minutes or until pasta is al dente (almost done). Add zucchini and beans, heat through, and remove bay leaf. Stir in bacon and taste to adjust flavors. Serve with Parmesan cheese or a dollop of Basil Pesto.

Celery

Celery was first used as a medicinal herb, but the 16th-century Italians began using the stalks raw and boiling the roots as vegetables. Ever since, this vegetable has been very popular. The two varieties are "Golden Heart," a blanched white variety grown under paper to prevent chlorophyll from forming and turning it green, and "Pascal," a slower growing tall green variety. With celery's fresh, crunchy stalks, it's delicious cooked, fried, braised, or with a sauce and makes an excellent accompaniment to roast meats and poultry.

128

The Granny Smith apples and the mango chutney add a lot of texture and flavor to this soup. Serve with our *Winter Fruit Salad with Dried Cherries & Mint* (see Index) and pappadums (lentil wafers).

Chicken Curry Soup
serves 8

2 tbl. butter
1 onion (1 c. finely minced)
1 stalk celery, minced
1/2 c. carrot, finely minced
1 tbl. curry powder, commercial or homemade, or to taste
2 1/2 tbl. flour
3 c. chicken stock
2 whole chicken breasts, cooked and cut into
    1 1/2" x 1/4" strips
1 c. heavy cream
1/2 tsp. salt
freshly ground pepper
2 Granny Smith apples, coarsely chopped
3 tbl. mango chutney (fruit pieces minced)
1 tbl. water mixed with 2 tbl. flour
toasted coconut
minced scallions

Sauté in butter the onion, celery, carrot, and curry powder. Add flour; cook 2 minutes over low heat while stirring. Add stock, raise heat, and bring to a boil; reduce heat and simmer 20 minutes. Add chicken and cream; cook until it begins to thicken. Add salt, pepper, apples, and chutney and heat through. If soup is thin, add flour and water mixture and cook. Season to taste and serve. Garnish with toasted coconut and scallions.

Curry Powder

Curry powders vary considerably; grocery store powders often lack intense flavor. Instead, try curry powder from East Indian grocers.

Add curry powder slowly—you can always add more, but subtracting is difficult!

129

Lentils

Lentils come in a variety of colors: red, brown, orange, yellow, green, and gray. They're rich in protein and require much less cooking time than legumes.

The colorful red, orange, and yellow lentils (called split lentils) are a common ingredient in Indian curries. Cooked, they're used as thickeners for soups and curries. When ground into flour, they become the basis for pappadums—a spicy tortilla-shaped Indian cracker.

130

The surprise ingredient here is mustard seed. It gives this hearty winter soup a real kick—almost like peppers!

Lentil, Leek & Ham Soup
serves 12

1 oz. dried mushrooms
1 c. boiling water
2 tbl. olive oil
4 leeks, cut in half lengthwise, cleaned, and sliced in thin rings
1 1/2 c. carrots, chopped
2 c. onions, chopped
4 garlic cloves, minced
1/2 c. celery, chopped
8 c. beef stock
2 c. water
2 1/2 c. (1 lb.) lentils, washed and sorted
3 c. smoked or regular ham, chopped
4 tbl. tomato paste
1 1/2 tsp. mustard seeds, crushed
3 bay leaves
1 tsp. EACH dried thyme and tarragon

Pour boiling water over mushrooms and soak for 30 minutes. Place oil in a large, deep soup kettle. Sauté leeks, carrots, onions, garlic, and celery. Cover and cook about 30 minutes at medium heat or until vegetables are soft. Add remaining ingredients, including mushrooms and strained soaking liquid. Bring to a boil. Reduce heat, cover, and simmer 1-1 1/2 hours or until lentils are soft. Taste, adjust seasonings, and serve hot. This soup can be frozen.

The contrasting colors of black beans and a fresh salsa make this soup both attractive and flavorful.

Black Bean Soup with Mexican Herbs
serves 10

4 slices thick hickory bacon
1 1/2 c. onion, finely chopped
1 1/2 c. celery, finely chopped
1 1/2 c. carrots, finely chopped
1 bay leaf
1 tbl. garlic, finely chopped
1 1/2 tsp. dried thyme
2 tbl. ground cumin
1 tsp. freshly ground black pepper
1 tbl. dried oregano, crumbled
3 tbl. tomato paste
10 c. chicken stock
4 c. water (or as needed)
1 lb. black beans, canned (or homemade equivalent)
6 tbl. fresh lime juice
1/4 tsp. cayenne pepper
salt
salsa (See Index)
fresh cilantro, chopped
sour cream (regular or low fat)

Cube bacon. Place in heavy kettle and cook, stirring

Quick Soak Method for Dried Beans

Place beans in a heavy pot and add water to cover by 2". Bring to a boil and cook for 2 minutes. Remove from heat, cover, and let stand at room temperature for 1 hour. Discard water and proceed with your recipe as if they had soaked overnight.

131

Parsnips

This very sweet, underrated root vegetable once had the reputation of being an aphrodisiac! It's easily grown in Michigan, much like carrots. In fact, in recipes, they're interchangeable. Choose evenly sized parsnips for uniform cooking. Peel the skin and wax, if they've been dipped. Slice and remove woody stems of the larger parsnips. Steamed, baked, or sautéed, they're a great addition to soups.

often, until well browned. Drain all but 1 tbl. of bacon drippings. Add onions, celery, carrots, bay leaf, garlic, thyme, cumin, black pepper, and oregano. Stir to blend and cover. Cook about five minutes over moderately low heat. Do not burn. Add tomato paste and combine well. Add chicken stock, water, and cooked beans. Bring to a boil. Reduce heat and simmer 20-25 minutes.

Remove bay leaf and puree in a blender. Return soup to kettle and add lime juice and cayenne. Taste and adjust seasonings. Serve with salsa, cilantro, and a dollop of sour cream.

132

This soup is loosely based on an old Finnish fish stew called Solyanla. It's hearty, inexpensive, quick, and satisfying, especially on a winter's night. Toast thick slices of French bread and place one on the bottom of each bowl before adding the soup.

Dilled Whitefish Soup
serves 8

4 large yellow potatoes (Yukon Gold) cut into 3/4" cubes, about 4 c.
1 c. EACH onions and carrots, cubed
8-10 whole allspice berries
6 EACH parsley and dill sprigs (about 1 tbl. dried)
5 c. fish stock or chicken stock
1/2 c. dry white wine
1 1/2 lb. whitefish, walleye, haddock, or a combination
1/2 c. sour cream (regular or low fat)
salt and freshly ground pepper

In a large soup kettle or Dutch oven put potatoes, onions, carrots, allspice, parsley, dill, stock, and wine. Bring to a boil. Reduce heat and simmer 12-15 minutes, covered, until potatoes are just tender. Remove herb sprigs. Add fish and cook until it flakes easily, about 7-10 minutes. Add sour cream, heat through, taste, and adjust seasonings.

Fish Stock

6 lb. fish bones, heads, flesh of other fish, and shellfish trimmings

3 qts. water
2 onions, quartered
2 leeks, chopped
1 c. dry white wine
1 tsp. salt
2 tsp. fennel seeds
1 bay leaf
2 tbl. parsley stems
8-10 peppercorns
1 carrot, sliced
1 rib celery, sliced

Place in large stockpot and slowly bring to a boil, skimming often. Lower heat and simmer 45 minutes- 1 hour. Strain the stock. Chill overnight and remove fat from top. Use immediately or freeze.

133

Tree Trimming Party

Goat Cheese Torta with
Sun-Dried Tomato Pesto

❋

Pita Chips

❋

Seafood Chowder with Saffron

❋

Curry Chicken Salad

❋

Chocolate Cranberry Torte

❋

Serve with Brut champagne

This elegant chowder would be a perfect dish to serve on New Year's Eve with a combination of shellfish like lobster, shrimp, and scallops. Top each bowl with a dollop of sour cream and caviar for even more sophistication.

Seafood Chowder with Saffron
serves 6

1 1/2 c. onions, chopped
1 c. celery, sliced
2 tbl. butter
1 tbl. oil
1 lb. yellow potatoes, peeled, cut in large chunks
4 c. chicken stock
2 c. corn (fresh or thawed frozen)
1 c. milk
1/8 tsp. saffron (mixed with 1 tbl. hot water)
1 1/2 tsp. Worcestershire sauce
1/2 tsp. dry mustard
3 c. assorted fish (mahimahi, striped bass, salmon) cut in large
    chunks, and shellfish (scallops, lobster, shrimp)
1 1/2 c. sour cream (regular or low fat) mixed with 2 tbl. flour
1/2 tsp. cayenne pepper
1 tbl. fresh lemon juice
1 1/2 tbl. dry sherry
1 1/2 tsp. salt
1 tsp. freshly ground pepper

Sauté onions and celery in butter and oil until soft. Add potatoes and stock and cook 20 minutes or until potatoes are soft. Remove 2 c. of the soup and whirl the rest in a blender or food processor. Return all soup to pan and add corn, milk, saffron, Worcestershire sauce, and dry mustard and cook 15 minutes. Add fish and cook, then shellfish. Add sour cream, cayenne, lemon juice, sherry, salt, and pepper. Heat and taste to adjust seasonings.

Quick Fish Stock

2 c. clam juice (2 8-oz. bottles)
1 1/2 c. water
1 c. dry white wine (like vermouth)
1 onion, chopped
6 parsley stems
1/4 c. mushroom stems
6-8 whole peppercorns

Place all ingredients in a pan and simmer 30 minutes, allowing liquid to reduce to 2 c. Strain. Use immediately or freeze.

135

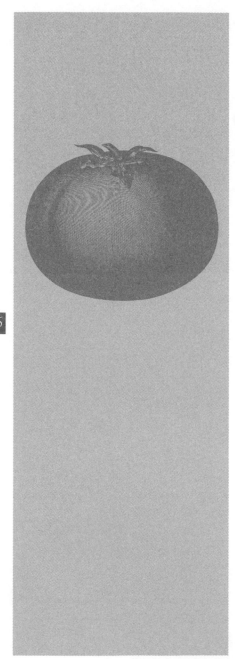

136

This soup was inspired by Marge's good friend Jim Tortorelli. Jim saves every drop of sauce, juice, or broth left over from cooked chicken dishes, then freezes it till he has enough to make his famous "scadol"—slang for escarole soup.

Italian Parsley, Escarole & White Bean Soup
serves 6-8

1 1/2 c. onions, chopped
2 tbl. extra virgin olive oil
5-6 garlic cloves, chopped
3-4 slices prosciutto, chopped
1 c. celery, chopped
1 14.5 oz. can Italian tomatoes, peeled and chopped
5 c. chicken stock
2 15-oz. cans Italian white beans (cannellini), drained
   (or homemade equivalent)
1 c. Italian parsley, chopped
1 large head escarole, tough outer leaves removed, coarsely chopped
salt and lots of freshly ground pepper
Parmesan cheese, freshly grated

Sauté the onion and garlic in the oil 2-3 minutes. Add prosciutto and celery and cook 2-3 minutes more. Add the tomatoes and stock and cook 10-15 minutes. Add the beans, parsley, and the escarole and cook until the escarole is tender, about 10 minutes. Taste and adust seasonings, adding lots of pepper. Serve in bowls with a little Parmesan cheese.

This rich, unique soup is great at picnics, beach parties, or backyard barbeques where the theme is Southwest or Mexican. Serve with any of our flavorful salsas (see Index).

Cold Tequila Avocado Soup
serves 6

3 large, firm, ripe avocados
6 tbl. fresh lime juice
1/2 c. scallions, chopped
2 garlic cloves, minced
2 tsp. chili powder, commercial or homemade (or to taste)
1/2 tsp. cumin seeds, crushed
3 c. chicken stock (not homemade)*
1/2 c. sour cream (regular or low fat)
salt and freshly ground pepper
1/2 c. cilantro, chopped
2 tbl. tequila
salsa

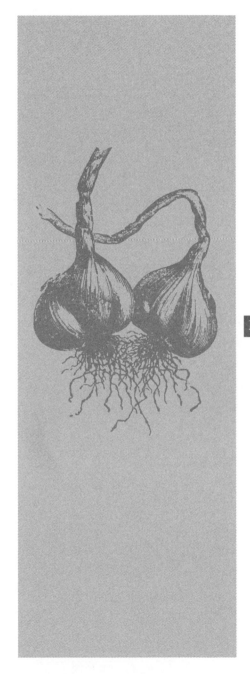

Place avocados, lime juice, scallions, garlic, and spices in a food processor and whirl till smooth. Add stock and whirl again. Place in a pitcher or deep bowl and chill several hours. Stir in sour cream. Taste and adjust seasonings; stir in cilantro. Place soup in bowls and add 1 tsp. tequila and a dollop of salsa to each bowl.

*Homemade stock is more gelatinous than commercially canned stock and not suitable for cold soup. What a shame, since homemade is far superior to canned. Yet if used the soup would be more like avocado gelatin!

138

Make this soup ahead of time—the flavor improves with age. Serve with a good hard-crusted bread and a fresh green salad.

Sweet Potato & Fennel Soup
serves 10

3 3/4 c. chicken stock
1/4 c. dry sherry
2 fennel bulbs, trimmed and chopped
2 small zucchini, cut in half lengthwise and sliced in 1/2" pieces
2 c. sweet potatoes, peeled and coarsely chopped
2 garlic cloves, chopped
6 scallions, chopped
1/2" slice fresh ginger
1 jalapeno, seeded and chopped
1 tsp. hot paprika
1 1/2 tsp. EACH ground turmeric, cumin, and ground coriander
1/3 c. fresh orange juice
1 1/2 tbl. fresh lime juice
2 13-oz. cans cannellini beans (white kidney beans)
2 tbl. rice vinegar
1 tsp. salt
1/4 tsp. freshly ground pepper
Chopped cilantro or Italian parsley for garnish

In a large saucepan or Dutch oven add stock, sherry, fennel, zucchini, sweet potatoes, garlic, scallions, ginger, jalapeno, spices, and juices. Cover and boil for 5 minutes. Remove cover and simmer until vegetables are tender. Stir

in beans and vinegar; season with salt and pepper. Ladle
1 1/2 c. of soup into a blender and whirl till smooth. Stir
blended mixture back into original mixture. Bring to a
simmer and adjust seasonings. Garnish with cilantro or
parsley before serving.

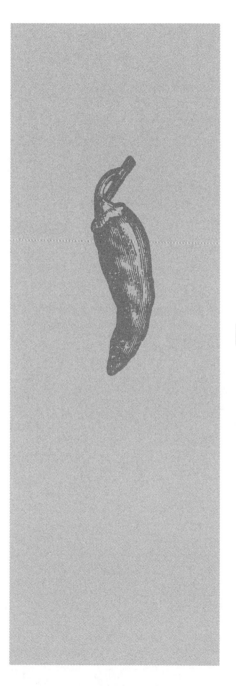

139

Thickeners

When making wine sauces for entrées, homemade mayonnaise (aioli), or soups, we often add a handful of fresh bread crumbs to thicken the mixture. Fresh crumbs are made from one slice of fresh bread whirled in a blender or food processor. This quick addition adds body without changing the flavor.

140

During the winter months this makes a wonderful, quick, and hearty Sunday night family dinner with the addition of sliced sausages, like kielbasa or one of the unique gourmet chicken sausages.

Spicy African Rice & Sweet Potato Soup
serves 6

1 tbl. oil
1 1/4 c. onions, chopped
4-5 garlic cloves, minced
2 c. sweet potatoes, peeled and cubed
5 c. chicken stock
1 tsp. dried thyme
1 1/2 tsp. cumin seed, crushed
1/4 c. rice
1 1/2 c. (approx.) hot chunky prepared salsa
1 16-oz. can garbanzo beans, drained and washed
1 zucchini, unpeeled, cut in cubes
1/3 c. peanut butter
salt & freshly ground pepper

In a large Dutch oven heat oil and sauté onions, garlic, and sweet potatoes until soft, about 5 minutes. Add stock, herbs, and rice. Bring to a boil, reduce heat, and simmer, covered, until rice is cooked and vegetables are tender, about 15-20 minutes. Add the salsa and beans and cook until sweet potatoes are tender, about 15 minutes. Add the zucchini and peanut butter and heat through. Taste and adjust seasonings. Serve hot.

Serve this soup with fresh lime wedges, our Tropical Melon Salsa Salad, and Margarita Tart for a Southwest dinner.

Fried Tortilla Soup with Pinto Beans
serves 8

1 1/2 c. onions, chopped
3 garlic cloves, chopped
2 jalapenos, seeded and minced
1/4 c. + 2 tbl. vegetable oil
1/2 tsp. ground cumin
1 tsp. dried oregano
1 1/2 tsp. hot homemade chili powder
1 14-oz. can tomatoes, including juice, chopped
2 15-oz. cans pinto beans, drained and rinsed
6 c. chicken stock
salt and freshly ground pepper
6 corn tortillas
2 oz. sharp cheddar cheese, shredded

Garnish

1/4 c. sour cream (regular or low fat)
1 3 1/2-oz. can chopped green chilies
1/3 c. cilantro, minced

In a kettle cook onions, garlic, and jalapenos in 2 tbl. oil over medium heat, stirring occasionally, for 10 minutes or until vegetables are soft. Stir in cumin, oregano, and

Growing Shelling Beans

For a real back-to-nature experience, try growing your own shelling beans. The seeds are available from most seed catalogs. One summer we successfully grew black (turtle) beans and Italian red beans with very little effort. You only need a sunny location with a trellis or fence for support and minimum care. The beans are harvested very late in the fall after they've dried out and the pods have shriveled. Then gather your harvest and shell them. That year we made gifts for the holidays of assorted dried beans and packets of herb seasonings. What a hit!

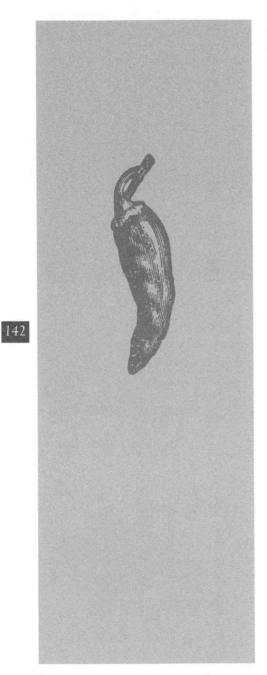

142

chili powder. Cook and combine well. Add tomatoes with juice, beans, and stock; simmer 10 minutes.

While the soup is simmering, cut the tortillas in half, stack the halves, and cut them crosswise in 1/4" strips. In a skillet heat the 1/4 c. vegetable oil until hot and sauté the tortilla strips in batches for 15 seconds or until they are crisp and pale golden. Transfer to paper towels to drain.

Add the strips to the soup and simmer for 3 minutes or until the strips just begin to soften. Divide the cheddar cheese among the bowls and ladle the soup over it.

Garnish each serving with a dollop of sour cream, a spoonful of green chilies, and some of the cilantro.

Entrées

While developing recipes for this book, Marge and I have never been at a loss for ideas. It seems as if herbs have an endless ability to adapt themselves to any food ingredients, enhancing cheese, vegetables, meat, fowl, fruit, and sweets. They can change plain chicken into a succulent dish, like Lime-Marinated Chicken with Green Sauce, or make fish come alive, like our Grilled Mahimahi with Spicy Asian Pesto. They can even make pasta jump up, like our Southwest Chicken with Chipotle Chili Sauce.

We've offered our readers quick entrées, those that take less than 30 minutes to prepare, and recipes adventuresome weekend cooks will enjoy, such as our Shrimp Ravioli made with wonton skins.

For your next dinner, thumb through the pages of our Entrée section—we're confident you'll be inspired.

143

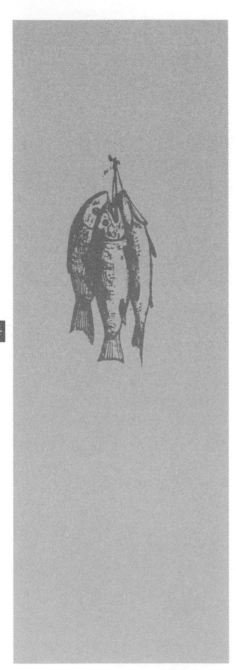

144

Marge's husband, Chuck, is a die-hard trout fisher who once used her brand new electric coffee grinder to blend fur for fly-fishing material. Consequently, they are now a two-mill family!

Trout Amandine with Fresh Chives
serves 4

1/3 c. shallots, chopped
1 tbl. butter
2 tbl. oil
juice of 1 lemon
1/4 c. toasted slivered almonds
2 tbl. fresh parsley, chopped
3 tbl. fresh chives, chopped
4 trout fillets, 4-6 oz. each
salt and freshly ground pepper
cayenne pepper

In a small skillet, sauté shallots in butter and oil for 1-2 minutes. Add 1 tbl. lemon juice and cook till shallots are soft, about 3-4 minutes. Stir in toasted almonds, parsley, and chives. Taste and adjust seasoning with more lemon juice, if needed. Set aside and keep warm.

Line a shallow baking pan with foil. Place fillets in dish and sprinkle each with salt, pepper, cayenne pepper, and 2 tbl. lemon juice. Broil till trout flakes easily. Transfer to a platter and top with almond mixture.

Friday night fish fries are a Midwest specialty—you can host your own with this recipe. Just add oven-fried potatoes, homemade coleslaw, and a juicy fruit pie. Because the breading on the fish is made from fresh bread crumbs, it will be lighter and, we think, better tasting.

Lake Perch with Rosemary
serves 4

1 c. flour
salt and freshly ground pepper
2 tsp. paprika
2 c. fresh bread crumbs (5 slices of fresh bread whirled
    in a blender or food processor)
2 tbl. dried rosemary, crushed
1-1 1/2 lb. lake perch fillets
2 eggs, beaten
1/4 c. vegetable oil (as needed)
3 tbl. butter (as needed)
lemon wedges
Remoulade Sauce

Mix flour, salt, pepper, and paprika on wax paper. Mix crumbs and rosemary and place on another sheet of wax paper. Dip each fillet in seasoned flour, in beaten egg, and then in bread crumbs, pressing with your hands to make sure crumbs adhere. (Coated fish can be covered with plastic wrap and chilled up to 1 hour.)

Heat oil and butter in a deep skillet until hot. Keep temperature consistent. Fry fillets, a few at a time, about 1

Canadian Fisheries

The Fishing Industry of Canada has come up with a simple and foolproof way of determining how long to cook fish (excluding shellfish).

Use a ruler and measure the thickest part of the fish you are cooking (even if stuffed). Calculate 10 minutes total cooking time per inch of fish. It doesn't matter if you bake, fry, or grill the fish, the time is still the same.

145

minute or until golden brown; turn to brown on both sides. Fish should begin to flake when done. Add more oil and butter as needed. Drain on paper towels and serve immediately with lemon wedges and Remoulade Sauce.

Remoulade Sauce

1 c. mayonnaise—homemade is preferable, but you can use
    commercial (regular or low fat)
1 tbl. finely chopped scallions
1 tsp. EACH dried basil, tarragon, and dill
1 large garlic clove, minced
1 tbl. minced fresh parsley
1 tbl. Dijon mustard
1 tsp. capers, chopped coarsely
1 large dill pickle, finely chopped
anchovy paste (optional)
salt and freshly ground pepper

Combine all ingredients in a bowl or blender, adding anchovy paste to your taste. Adjust seasonings and add more herbs or scallions, if needed. Refrigerate 2-4 hours to blend flavors. Serve cold.

146

Remember, when cooking any type of fish, either grilling, broiling or pan-frying, cook your fish 10 minutes for every inch of thickness (measuring the thickest part).

Tuna with Garlic Mustard Sauce
serves 2

1-1 1/2 lb. fresh tuna
1/2 c. Dijon mustard
6 cloves garlic, minced
1 tbl. fresh lime juice
1/3 c. olive oil
3 tbl. butter
1 onion (medium), halved and thinly sliced
1 tbl. gingerroot, grated or finely minced
1/2 c. white wine or vermouth
2 tbl. sherry
pinch saffron
2 tsp. fresh thyme or 1 tsp. dried
6 tbl. chicken stock
1/2 c. heavy cream
salt and freshly ground pepper

In a bowl, combine mustard, garlic, lime juice, and oil. Pour into a resealable plastic food-storage bag, add tuna, and marinate in refrigerator for 1 hour. In a sauté pan, cook onion and gingerroot in melted butter until soft. Add vermouth, sherry, saffron, and thyme. Reduce liquid by half over high heat.

Mustard

Mustard is an herb cultivated for its pungent seeds or leaves (mustard greens). The greens are easily prepared by washing several times and cooking in a small amount of boiling water with a slice of salt pork or bacon. Cook for 15-30 minutes, drain, and serve.

The seeds are used in pickling mixtures, fish dishes, sauces, and vegetable gratins and as a crunchy garnish.

In powdered form mustard can be transformed into flavorful sauces. Mix the powder with water or champagne and add your choice of dried herbs. To make it crunchy, add a few seeds—whole or crushed.

147

Remove tuna from marinade and broil until done. Add marinade to sauce, along with stock and cream. Cook and reduce slightly. Taste and adjust seasoning with salt and freshly ground pepper. Serve over warm tuna.

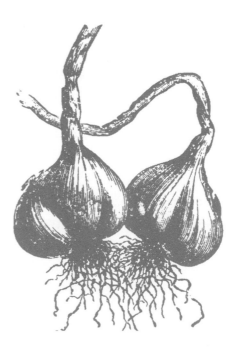

We prefer to grill the mahimahi over an open flame, but if weather or time doesn't allow this procedure, the broiler will do just fine.

Mahimahi with Spicy Asian Pesto
serves 4

2 lb. mahimahi (or firm, thick-fleshed fish)
1/3 c. oil
3 tbl. *Asian Vinegar* (See Index) or rice vinegar
2 cloves garlic, minced
1 tsp. dried red pepper flakes
1 tbl. gingerroot, minced
1/4 tsp. salt
freshly ground pepper
1 recipe *Spicy Asian Pesto* (See Index)

In a bowl combine all the above ingredients except the fish. Pour into a resealable plastic food-storage bag, add fish, and marinate in refrigerator at least 1 hour. Broil fish until done. Serve with pesto.

Grilling Tips— Wood Chips

Instead of using chemically treated briquette-type charcoal in your grill, try the different types of wood chips available, commercially or from your own yard.

Fruit Woods: Impart a pleasant sweetness, rather mild as opposed to a smoky flavor. Any fruit trees will do: apple, cherry, peach.

Oak: Burns slow and long, food doesn't need to be added until the last minute.

149

A quick entrée to make in spring and summer when you find you can't grill outside. Round it out with some South-of-the-Border side dishes and icy-cold beer.

Walleyed Pike Veracruz
serves 4

2/3 c. onions, chopped
4 garlic cloves, minced
1 tbl. olive oil
2 jalapenos, cut in slivers
5-6 Italian tomatoes, chopped, or 1 16-oz. can,
    undrained and chopped
1/4 tsp. salt
1/2 tsp. sugar
1/4 tsp. cinnamon
1/4 tsp. ground cloves
dash dried oregano
1 tbl. fresh lime juice
1/2 c. pimento-stuffed olives, cut in rings
2 tsp. capers
2 tbl. cilantro, chopped
2 lb. walleye fillets, cleaned
lime wedges

In a skillet large enough to hold the fish fillets, sauté onion and garlic in olive oil until soft. Add jalapenos, tomatoes and their liquid, salt, sugar, cinnamon, cloves, oregano, and lime juice. Cover and simmer 10 minutes. Stir in olives, capers, and cilantro. Add fish. If the fillets are

Grilling Tips— Wood Chips, continued

Mesquite: *A Southwestern and Mexican hardwood that is cured to produce charcoal. It burns hot and long, imparting a distinctive smoky flavor. If using chips, soak in water and add at the moment of grilling, since they burn up fast.*

Herbs: *When trimming plants in the garden, save the cuttings and place on the grill at the last moment. Any combinations will add that extra aroma.*

150

different thicknesses, place the largest in first—cook 1-2 minutes, then add the rest. Cover and poach for 10 minutes per inch of thickness.

Remove the cover, place fish on a platter, and keep warm. Turn up heat and reduce sauce until slightly thick, 2-4 minutes. Spoon over fillets and serve at once with lime wedges.

Marinated Olives

You can make your own oil-cured marinated olives without owning an olive grove! Add your favorite herbs or spices to store-bought olives and cover with olive oil. Packaged in small decorative canning jars, these marinated olives make a wonderful holiday or hostess gift.

151

152

Suzanne's 22-year-old son, Ethan, doesn't think a meal is complete unless it contains some heat, and this dish certainly fits that category. Not being fond of seafood, he prefers that Suzanne substitute chicken, which is as tasty as this shrimp version.

Shrimp in Black Bean Pasta Sauce
serves 4

Black Bean Pasta Sauce
   3-4 tbl. Chinese black bean sauce with garlic*
   1/4 c. jalapenos, chopped, or to taste
   1 tbl. sherry
   1 1/2 c. chicken stock
   2 tbl. cornstarch + 3 tbl. water
   1 tsp. sesame oil

   1-1 1/2 lb. shrimp, peeled and deveined
   3 garlic cloves, minced
   1 tbl. fresh ginger, minced
   2 tbl. oil
   6-8 scallions, sliced
   1 red pepper, cut in julienne strips
   1/3 c. fresh cilantro, chopped
   hot cooked rice or pasta

   *available in Asian markets or the Asian sections of large grocery stores

Combine sauce ingredients in a bowl and set aside. In a skillet, sauté shrimp, garlic, and ginger in oil. Remove shrimp and set aside. Add scallions and sauce mixture. Heat until thick. Add shrimp and red peppers and heat through—don't cook. Add cilantro and adjust seasonings. Serve over warm pasta.

Hot Peppers

Size does not always indicate the intensity of heat. Generally smaller varieties are hotter than larger ones, because they have less flesh in proportion to the amount of veins.

Climate also affects the heat level. Peppers grown in cooler, wetter climates tend to be milder than ones grown in hot conditions.

153

Saffron

The most expensive spice in the world comes from the dried stigmas of a crocus grown in Southern Europe and Asia. It takes thousands of stigmas to make a pound. Harvesting is very labor intensive and can only be done by hand—hence, the high prices.

Fortunately saffron has a powerful flavor—very little is needed for most dishes. The flavor is earthy and pleasantly bitter, the color a rich golden yellow and highly prized.

Saffron is sold powdered or in what are called "threads." Keep it in tightly covered glass jars away from the sun. The flavor and color are released when the threads are added to a liquid and heated. Use in soups, rice dishes, breads, rolls, and sauces.

§

154

A very rich and exotic dish that would make an elegant first course. Use any shape of wonton skin—make them into squares, rounds, or triangles or use cookie cutters for festive shapes.

Shrimp Ravioli with Wonton Skins & Saffron Sauce
serves 4

Paste Mixture
> 2 tbl. flour
> 1/4 c. water

> Mix very well in a small bowl until smooth. Set aside.

> 1 pkg. 3" wonton skins, thawed

Filling
> 2 tbl. Canadian bacon, minced (could substitute smoked ham)
> 3/4 lb. fresh shrimp, shelled, deveined, and chopped into
>   large chunks
> 2 tbl. scallions, minced
> 1 tbl. fresh chives, finely minced
> 1 tsp. fresh ginger, very finely minced
> 3 tbl. Parmesan cheese
> 1 egg white
> 1/2 tsp. EACH salt and freshly ground pepper
> 1/2 fresh jalapeno, seeded and cut into tiny slivers

Combine all filling ingredients in a bowl and set aside. Place about 1 tbl. of filling on each wonton skin. Brush two sides with the paste mixture. Fold over and seal. Place on wax-paper-lined baking sheets. Cover with plastic wrap and use immediately or refrigerate for a few hours.

Saffron Sauce

1 tbl. butter
3 tbl. shallots, minced
1 c. dry white wine
1 1/4 c. chicken stock
a few saffron threads
1/2 tsp. sugar
3 sun-dried tomatoes, cut in slivers (reconstitute if dry)
2 tbl. heavy cream
salt and freshly ground pepper

Melt butter in a small pan and sauté shallots until soft. Add wine and chicken stock and reduce by one-third. Add saffron threads, sugar, sun-dried tomatoes, and cream and cook until slightly thick. Taste and adjust seasonings. Serve hot.

To cook, bring a large pot of water to a boil. Add 1 tsp. oil and place 8-10 ravioli in at a time. Cook 2-3 minutes or until they rise to the top. Don't overcook. Remove with a slotted spoon. Drain briefly on paper towels (they will stick to the paper towels if left too long). Place on one large platter or individual plates and top with Saffron Sauce. Serve immediately.

Pots & Pans

Having the right pan for the right job makes cooking much more fun. Our favorites are ones with aluminum clad outsides and stainless steel insides.

Aluminum is a good conductor of heat, and, with a stainless steel liner, you won't have discoloring from acidic foods like tomatoes.

Copper, of course, is the best. It conducts and distributes heat evenly and maintains temperatures longer. It's beautiful to look at and use, but it does have two obvious drawbacks—namely, the prohibitive cost and time-consuming upkeep.

Besides our everyday pans, we also have several nonstick skillets in large sizes. We also own a few heirloom cast-iron pans—indispensable for frying and making Sunday pancakes—and we have several stainless steel stockpots and pasta pans.

§

Jerk seasoning is quite popular today—it's actually a combination of spices and herbs with an added kick of chilies. The flavor is hot but sweet and spicy. Make your own (see Index) or use the one below. Don't forget, as with almost any herb combination, you can use it as a rub with grilled fish, chicken, or pork or add it to a vinaigrette when making robust salads like those with beans and corn.

Jerk Marinated Fish
serves 6

2 lb. mahimahi, striped bass, halibut, tuna, or other
   very firm fish fillets, not steaks

Marinade
   2 2" cinnamon sticks
   3 tbl. whole allspice berries
   4 scallions
   2 jalapenos, seeded
   4 garlic cloves, chopped
   1 1/2 tsp. dried thyme
   1 bay leaf, broken
   1/4 c. EACH water and vegetable oil
   1/2 tsp. freshly grated nutmeg
   1 tbl. sugar
   1 lime, juiced
   salt

Over high heat, toast cinnamon sticks and allspice berries in a skillet (cast iron works best) for 3-5 minutes.

Toss to keep from burning; it will smoke slightly. Remove and place in a blender or food processor with the remaining ingredients and puree until smooth. Place in a resealable plastic food-storage bag with the fish and marinate 1 hour in the refrigerator. Grill or broil to desired doneness.

Flake the meat and serve fajita-style with fresh flour tortillas and assorted salsas (see Index) or serve whole fillets with Fresh Herbed Lemon Rice (see Index) and a fruit salad.

Seafood Lover's Alert

Today, fish is fast becoming a popular addition to most American's diets. From appetizers to salads, soups to entrées—it's not just fish sticks or tuna salad—and we enjoy it at least twice a week. This is all good news.

Unfortunately the bad news is that almost 70% of the world's catch is nearly depleted. Overfishing, increased demand, irresponsible and illegal fishing, and just plain greed have driven a once plentiful protein source to nearly extinct levels.

To help you make an informed and ecological choice when purchasing fish for cooking or deciding on a dish in a restaurant, the Seafood Watch Program from the Monterey Bay (CA) Aquarium offers the following list:

Good Choices: Farm raised catfish, clams, mussels, oysters, rainbow trout, striped bass,

Use fish fillets, not fish steaks, for most of your cooking—there is very little waste, there are usually no bones, and it's easier to cut in individual portions.

Cajun Fish & Andouille Kebabs
serves 4

1 lb. fish (mahimahi, striped bass, halibut, cod, or tuna)
2 andouille sausages (precooked)
1/2 red onion, cut in large chunks
1 red pepper, cut in large chunks
1 zucchini, cut in chunks

Marinade
1/2 c. vegetable oil
2 tbl. Worcestershire sauce
1/4 c. EACH red wine and soy sauce
2 tbl. red wine vinegar
juice of 1/2 lemon, plus zest
3 garlic cloves, minced
1 tbl. dry mustard
1/4 c. Italian parsley, chopped
1 tsp. cayenne
1/4 tsp. EACH freshly ground black pepper and dried thyme

Combine marinade ingredients and place in a resealable plastic food-storage bag with fish (cut in large cubes). Marinate 1 hour in the refrigerator. On bamboo skewers that have been soaked in water 30 minutes (this prevents burning on the grill) thread equal amounts of fish, sausage, red onion, red pepper, and zucchini. Grill till fish is done and serve with an aioli or salsa (see Index).

Seafood Lover's Alert, continued

sturgeon, and tilapia; Pacific albacore tuna, calamari/squid, Dungeness crab, Alaskan halibut, mahimahi, salmon, and New Zealand cod

Bad Choices: Bluefin tuna, Chilean sea bass, Atlantic cod, monkfish, orange roughy, Pacific red snapper, butterfish, salmon (farmed), Atlantic sea scallops, shark, and swordfish

To keep up-to-date on changes in these lists, contact the Audubon's Living Ocean Program at 1-888-397-6649.

159

A quick dinner dish for last-minute entertaining or a work-night family meal. Just add a simple green salad and crusty fresh bread.

Pasta with Smoked Salmon & Dill
serves 4

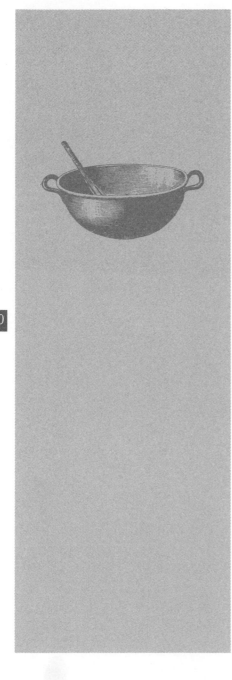

3/4 lb. fettucine or other pasta
3 tbl. butter
8 oz. smoked salmon
2 tbl. fresh lemon juice
1 tbl. red onion, chopped
1 c. sour cream (regular or low fat)
3 tbl. fresh chives, minced
1/4 c. fresh dill, chopped
8 oz. fresh asparagus, steamed and cut in 3" lengths
dill sprigs (for garnish)
freshly ground pepper

While pasta is cooking, combine butter, 6 oz. smoked salmon, lemon juice, and onion and whirl in a food processor until smooth. Add sour cream and blend. Remove and place in pasta serving bowl. Mix in chives, dill, and asparagus.

Drain pasta and reserve 1/2 c. water. Combine pasta and sauce, and if the mixture seems too thick, add small amounts of the pasta water. Garnish with remaining 2 oz. smoked salmon, cut in small pieces, and the dill sprigs. Sprinkle on a generous amount of black pepper and serve.

Even with all the ingredients in this dish, once the Cornish hens are stuffed, cooking time is under 45 minutes.

Cherry & Apricot Stuffed Cornish Hens
serves 4

Stuffing

2 thick slices of bacon, finely chopped
1 tsp. butter
1/2 c. shallots, minced
8-10 oz. fresh mushrooms (whirl in a food processor until very
    finely chopped; don't puree)
3/4 tsp. dried rosemary, crushed
3/4 tsp. dried thyme
1/2 c. Calvados (apple brandy) or brandy
1 1/2 c. fresh bread crumbs (2 slices fresh whirled in a food
    processor or blender)
1 egg yolk
2 tbl. EACH dried apricots and dried cherries, finely chopped
1 tbl. fresh chives, minced
salt and freshly ground pepper

2 Cornish hens, split in half, wing tips removed*
1 1/2 tbl. EACH butter and oil
apricot jam or other flavored jelly or jam
1/4 c. Calvados
1/2 c. beef stock
1 tsp. cornstarch mixed with 2 tbl. water
salt and freshly ground pepper

Kosher or Coarse Salt

Kosher salt sits in small bowls next to our stove. We use it daily and prefer it to regular salt because we tend to use less and it seems to have a lighter taste.

Coarse salt is the salt used in canning and pickling. The grains are rough and don't melt on contact with other food. It's the same kind that coats rolls, bagels, and pretzels.

Regular salt, available plain or iodized, contains sugar to make it free flowing—a fact most people aren't aware of.

To make stuffing, add bacon, butter, and shallots to a skillet and cook 1-2 minutes. Add mushrooms, rosemary, and thyme and cook until soft. Add Calvados and cook another minute. Remove to a bowl. Mix in bread crumbs, egg yolk, apricots, cherries, and chives. Combine well and season to taste.

Gently separate skin from Cornish hen breasts and legs and place 1/4 of the stuffing mixture inside. It will mound slightly. Repeat with other halves.

In an ovenproof skillet, melt the remaining butter and oil and place the hens skin side down. Brown well; turn over gently. Place in a 400-450° oven and roast 30-40 minutes. Baste occasionally with pan juices. For the last 15 minutes, brush with warmed apricot jam. Remove hens to a serving platter and keep warm.

Over high heat, place the skillet on top of the stove and add the remaining Calvados and beef stock. Scrape up all of the brown bits. Cook and reduce slightly. Add cornstarch mixture and whisk until smooth. Season to taste and pass in a separate bowl along with the Cornish hens.

*Use kitchen shears and cut down on either side of the backbone; remove. Use a large butcher knife and cut down the breastbone. It sounds difficult, but using heavy-duty kitchen shears will make the entire process easy.

Fresh shiitake mushrooms, many grown in Michigan, are a boon to cooks. Their meaty texture gives body to dishes, as well as a distinctive earthy taste. Be sure to discard their tough woody stems before using.

Chicken Marsala with Pancetta & Shiitake Mushrooms
serves 4

1 tbl. oil
1/4 lb. pancetta, finely minced
2 whole chicken breasts, halved, skinned, and boned
1/4 c. flour + 1 tsp. dried rosemary, crumbled
8 oz. fresh shiitake mushrooms, stems removed, cut into
   thick slices
1/2 lemon, juiced
4 garlic cloves, minced
1 tbl. fresh rosemary, minced
3/4 c. EACH marsala (or sherry) and chicken stock
salt and freshly ground pepper
1-2 tsp. beurre manié (equal parts flour and butter) if needed

163

Heat oil in a large skillet and add pancetta. Sauté over low heat until pancetta is cooked. Dredge chicken in seasoned flour and brown in same skillet, 2-3 minutes. Remove chicken and cover.

Toss mushrooms with lemon juice. Add to pan with garlic and cook 2-3 minutes. Add rosemary, marsala, and chicken stock. Increase heat and scrape brown bits from bottom of pan. Let mixture reduce slightly. Add chicken

Simple Vegetable Sautés

For quick vegetable side dishes, sauté 1-2 cloves minced garlic in 1-2 tbl. extra virgin olive oil. Toss in your choice of vegetables and cook until just slightly limp. This should take only a few minutes.

Add a dash of coarse salt and freshly ground pepper and sprinkle with 1 tbl. Parmesan cheese or 1 tbl. finely minced fresh herbs such as rosemary, tarragon, basil, dill, thyme, or marjoram.

Vegetables that work well are finely julienned or coarsely grated zucchini or other summer squash, shredded carrots, chopped fresh Swiss chard or spinach, thinly sliced fennel, or any cabbage. With cabbage, we usually add 1 tbl. of heavy cream and a generous amount of freshly grated nutmeg.

164

and cook 4-5 minutes longer or until chicken is just done. Taste and adjust seasonings. If sauce is too thin, add 1-2 tsp. beurre manié and whisk well. Serve immediately with oven-fried potatoes and a colorful salad.

Michigan boasts both sweet and sour cherries, which are available fresh and dried. This recipe is a fine example of how you can use dried cherries in an entrée, adding a wonderful flavor and texture.

Pecan Chicken Breasts with Michigan Dried Cherry Sauce
serves 4

2 whole chicken breasts, halved, skinned, and boned
3 tbl. minced fresh parsley
3/4 c. ground toasted pecans
2 tbl. flour
salt and freshly ground pepper
1 egg beaten with 1 tbl. water
3 tbl. butter
3 tbl. chopped red onion
1 1/2 tbl. Dijon mustard
1 tsp. dried thyme
3/4 c. dry white wine
1/2 c. chicken stock
1/2 c. crème de cassis
1/2 c. dried cherries
2 tbl. red currant jelly
2 tbl. balsamic vinegar
2 tbl. cornstarch mixed with 4 tbl. chicken stock
salt and freshly ground pepper

In a bowl mix together parsley, pecans, flour, salt, pepper, and chicken breasts. Dip chicken breasts in egg

Valentine's Day Menu

Shrimp Phyllo Purses

❤

Boston Lettuce & Goat Cheese Salad with Honey Vinaigrette

❤

Pecan Chicken Breasts with Michigan Dried Cherry Sauce

❤

Soft Herbed Polenta with Gorgonzola

❤

White Chocolate Cheesecake with Dark Chocolate Basil Crust and Michigan Cherry Sauce

❤

Serve with a Brut Rosé Champagne, California Zinfandel, or French Red Rhone wine

165

Dried Cherries

Dried cherries are usually the tart sour variety commonly used in cooking and baking, not the large sweet Bing cherries that are better known as "eating cherries" grown in Michigan. To make these succulent morsels a little more palatable and not as tart, fructose is added, making them more appealing for snacking. Even though we have both tart and sweet cherry trees in our backyards, we enjoy using the dried variety because of their intense flavor, chewy texture, and pantry storage convenience.

166

mixture one at a time, coating both sides. Toss in pecan mixture. Set aside.

In a large sauté pan melt 2 tbl. butter; cook chicken carefully on both sides. Cover skillet, turn down heat, and continue cooking 3-4 minutes (keep chicken warm).

While chicken is cooking, place additional 1 tbl. butter in new saucepan and sauté red onion until transparent. Add mustard and whisk; add thyme, wine, and chicken stock. Reduce by half and add crème de cassis, cherries, and currant jelly. Whisk until jelly has melted. Add balsamic vinegar and whisk in cornstarch mixture. Continue until sauce is thick and transparent. Season to taste with salt and pepper.

Serve warm chicken breasts with sauce poured over the center in a strip, with remaining sauce in a sauceboat.

When Marge worked in a carryout restaurant, this was one of her most requested dishes. An easy-to-make piquant recipe that's good for family suppers and company dinners.

Chicken Piccata with Fresh Italian Herbs
serves 4

1 1/2 c. onion, halved and sliced
4 large garlic cloves, minced
4 tbl. olive oil
2 c. mushrooms, sliced
1 tbl. lemon juice
1/2 to 3/4 c. sherry
2 whole chicken breasts, skinned, boned, and halved
1/2 c. flour
1/2 tsp. salt
1 tsp. paprika
1/2 to 3/4 c. chicken stock
6 tbl. Mediterranean vinegar or red wine vinegar
1/4 c. fresh parsley, minced (extra for garnish)
2 tbl. minced mixed fresh herbs (basil, marjoram, chives, thyme, or oregano)
2 tsp. honey (or to taste)
1-2 slices fresh bread whirled in a food processor
1 tbl. capers
salt and freshly ground pepper

Sauté onions and garlic in 2 tbl. olive oil until soft.

167

Capers

A frequently used Italian and French condiment that should be in everyone's pantry. Capers are the unopened flower buds of a small bush that grows wild in the Mediterranean region.

168

Capers have a sharp, tart flavor that adds crunch to sauces, mayonnaises, and salads. The tiny buds are dried and pickled in vinegar. The larger buds often sold as capers are sometimes pickled nasturtium buds.

Toss mushrooms with lemon juice and add to pan. Pour in sherry and cook, covered, over low heat 5 minutes. Remove all to a dish and set aside.

Dredge chicken in flour, salt, and paprika. In same pan, add more oil and sauté—browning chicken breasts. Add stock and vinegar and lower heat. Cook until chicken is springy and just tender. Remove to a platter and keep warm.

Add reserved mushroom-onion mixture, parsley, and mixed fresh herbs and cook to reduce liquid by half. Scrape bottom of pan to remove brown bits. Taste and add honey, if needed. To thicken mixture, add a little of the fresh bread crumbs. Taste and adjust seasonings. Add capers and pour mixture over chicken. Garnish with additional minced parsley.

For a delightful picnic, serve this entrée cold and accompany it with both Dried Blueberry Couscous and Tropical Melon Salsa salads (see Index).

Lime-Marinated Chicken with Fresh Herb Béarnaise Sauce
serves 4

4 whole chicken breasts, halved (boned and skinned optional)
or 1 whole chicken, cut up

Marinade
1/2 c. salad oil
1/2 c. fresh lime juice (include squeezed limes in marinade)
1 small onion, chopped
3 scallions, chopped
2 tbl. fresh chives, chopped
2 tbl. fresh tarragon, chopped, or 4 tsp. dried
1 tsp. coarse ground pepper
1 tsp. hot pepper sauce

Combine all marinade ingredients; place in a resealable plastic food-storage bag with the chicken. Toss. Marinate in the refrigerator several hours or overnight.

Grill 30-45 minutes, basting frequently. Serve with Fresh Herb Béarnaise Sauce.

Marinating

For the past 12 years, we have been marinating meats, fish, and vegetables in commercially available plastic food-storage bags. It sure has taken the mess and effort out of marinating. Simply take your marinade and the item to be marinated and place in a resealable plastic bag. Secure tightly. No longer will you have to turn the meat or clean up messy bowls.

169

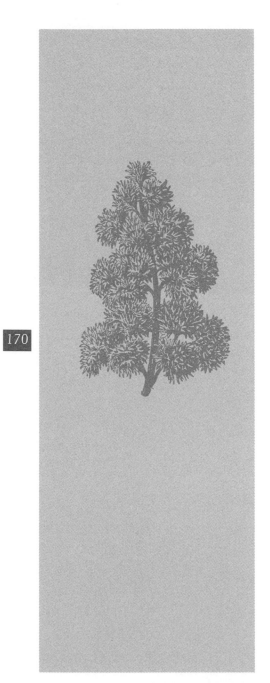

170

Fresh Herb Béarnaise Sauce

1 clove garlic
3 scallions, chopped coarsely
1/4 c. rice vinegar
1 egg yolk
1 1/2 c. assorted fresh herbs (parsley, basil, chives, savory,
    and tarragon or sage)
6 tbl. butter, melted
1/2 tsp. salt
freshly ground pepper

While blender or food processor is running, add garlic and mince. Add scallions, vinegar, egg yolk, and fresh herbs. Slowly add butter and blend well. Season to taste and refrigerate until ready to serve with chicken.

This is a great South-of-the-Border recipe. Serve over pasta for a quick and satisfying dinner.

Southwest Chicken with Chipotle Chili Sauce
serves 6

3 chicken breast halves, skinned, boned, and cut in strips
1 tbl. butter
1 tbl. oil
2 garlic cloves, chopped
1/2 medium onion, chopped
1 tsp. dried oregano
1/2 tsp. cumin powder
2-3 tsp. chili powder, commercial or homemade
2-3 chipotle chilies with sauce
1 large sweet red pepper, julienned
1 can chicken stock
1 c. white wine
3 tbl. cornstarch mixed with 1/3 c. stock
1 1/3 c. grated queso quesadilla or Monterey Jack cheese
    mixed with 1/4 c. flour
1/3 c. fresh cilantro, chopped
cooked pasta
grated Asiago cheese

In a sauté pan put butter, oil, garlic, onion, and chicken. Sauté 2-3 minutes or until chicken is almost done. Add oregano, cumin, chili powder, and chipotle. Set aside.

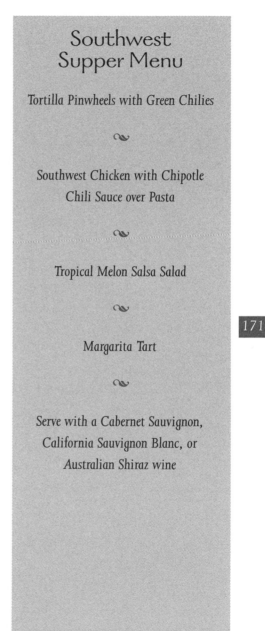

Southwest Supper Menu

Tortilla Pinwheels with Green Chilies

∾

Southwest Chicken with Chipotle Chili Sauce over Pasta

∾

Tropical Melon Salsa Salad

∾

Margarita Tart

∾

Serve with a Cabernet Sauvignon, California Sauvignon Blanc, or Australian Shiraz wine

171

Chicken Safety

In recent years we have become more aware of the dangers of Salmonella and how to prevent the contamination. Raw chicken is one of the biggest culprits in carrying Salmonella, but any poultry or fish is suspect. Items that come in contact with raw poultry, including its juices, must be washed with a mixture of hot soapy water and bleach. Cutting boards, especially in the crevices and seams, are a depository for Salmonella.

Some research recommends wood cutting boards rather than plastic, suggesting that wood counteracts Salmonella. We suggest having separate boards for poultry and the rest of the foods you chop.

In a saucepan put chicken stock and wine; reduce to three-quarters volume (1 1/2 c.).

Return chicken to heat; add stock; combine well. Stir in cheese; continue stirring until dissolved. Add cornstarch mixture and red pepper; continue to stir until it thickens and smooths. Season to taste; sprinkle in cilantro. Pour over pasta and garnish with Asiago cheese.

Depending on the occasion, use all chicken breasts, all wings, a cut up whole chicken, or half Cornish hens for this dish. Save some of the sauce and pass along with the cooked chicken.

Michigan Peach-Glazed Chicken
serves 6

3 whole chicken breasts, split
1/4 c. dried marjoram

Peach Sauce
1/4 tsp. chili oil
3 large ripe peaches, peeled, pitted, and chopped
   (about 3 c.)
1/4 c. EACH brown sugar and orange juice
1 tbl. grated orange rind
2 tbl. crystallized ginger, chopped
3 scallions, chopped
3 tbl. dry white wine (dry vermouth)
1 tsp. curry powder, commercial or homemade (or to taste)
2 garlic cloves, minced
1/4 c. vegetable oil
salt and freshly ground pepper

173

Rub chicken with marjoram and set aside 30 minutes to 1 hour in the refrigerator.

Combine all sauce ingredients in a stainless steel saucepan and simmer until thick, about 15-20 minutes. Remove and whirl in a blender or food processor. Taste and adjust seasonings.

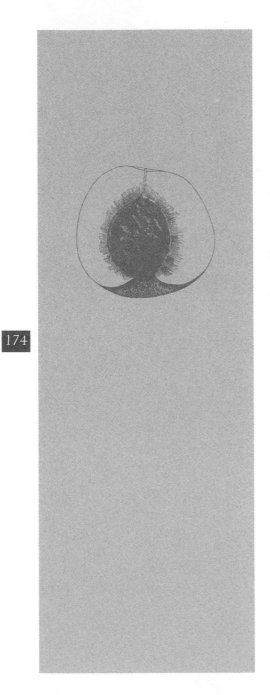

174

Prepare grill and cook chicken, using the indirect method.* Begin brushing with sauce halfway through grilling and continue until nicely glazed.

*The indirect method of grilling refers to the placement of coals to meat. The charcoal is at one end of the grill and the food at the other end. Cover your grill and leave the vents open. This method prevents the food from burning, yet it still gives it that smoky color and taste.

Flavorful fresh sausages are "in" and now they come in great selections like Tuscan chicken or chicken verdi. Try different meats such as turkey or pork or even tofu. Many flavors are available from health food grocery stores.

Chicken Sausage & Sun-Dried Tomatoes on Pasta
serves 6

2 tbl. olive oil
3/4-1 lb. fresh chicken sausages, sliced in 3/4" pieces
1 onion, cut in wedges
3 garlic cloves, minced
1 jalapeno, seeded and minced
1 red pepper, seeded and cut in slices
1/2 c. sun-dried tomatoes, reconstituted in hot water
  and sliced thinly
1 can (15 oz.) artichoke hearts, drained and quartered
2/3 c. EACH dry white wine (dry vermouth) and
  chicken stock
1/2 tsp. dried oregano
1/3 c. chicken stock mixed with 1 tbl. flour
2/3 c. fresh basil, destemmed and julienned
1/2 c. cured olives, halved
salt and freshly ground pepper
cooked pasta

In a large skillet place oil, sausage, onion, and garlic and sauté 3-4 minutes on high heat. Add jalapeno and red pepper and sauté an additional 2 minutes. Add tomatoes,

Italian Herbed Olives

1 1/2 lb. green olives
4 cloves garlic, peeled and placed
  on a skewer
4 sprigs EACH fresh thyme and
  oregano
1 small sprig rosemary
2 slices lemon
1/2 tsp. whole allspice berries
peppercorns
olive oil to cover

Place all in a glass jar and refrigerate 2 days. Remove the garlic and discard. Taste and add more herbs if needed. Keeps for months in the refrigerator.

175

Pasta Party

A fun dinner party to host during the winter months is a pasta party. Either make your own or buy several flavored varieties. Today most grocery stores and specialty shops stock interesting flavors—squid ink. saffron, chili peppers, herbs, wine-flavored, and so on.

Preboil each kind of pasta until almost al dente—this is how restaurants do it. Remove, drain, and place in resealable plastic food-storage bags with a little olive oil to prevent sticking. Just before serving, bring some water to a boil, add the partially cooked pasta, and heat through. Drain.

Make several kinds of sauces—tomato marinara sauce, a rich seafood sauce, a simple herb sauce, and maybe an unusual vegetable sauce. Grate lots of Parmesan and Asiago cheeses and set out in bowls.

artichoke hearts, wine, stock, and oregano. Cook 4-6 minutes until flavors combine and wine reduces slightly. Stir in stock and flour mixture to thicken sauce. Add basil and olives; season to taste. Pour over cooked pasta and sprinkle with Parmesan cheese.

For easy entertaining, assemble the chicken a day ahead and refrigerate or make extra and freeze uncooked.

Chicken Breasts with Prosciutto & Fresh Sage
serves 4

4 boneless, skinless chicken breasts, halved, pounded
   to 1/2" thickness
12 fresh sage leaves
4 paper-thin slices of prosciutto
1 tbl. EACH butter and olive oil
1 small onion (1/2 c.), chopped
4 garlic cloves, minced
12 oz. mushrooms, sliced
2 tbl. fresh lemon juice
1 1/2 c. chicken stock
1/2 c. Marsala (or dry sherry)
1/2 tsp. dried thyme
1/2 c. dry white wine
salt and freshly ground pepper
1 tbl. cornstarch mixed with 1/3 c. chicken stock

Lay 3 sage leaves across each chicken breast, then top with 1 slice prosciutto. Place plastic wrap on top of prosciutto and pound to an even 1/4". Sprinkle with salt and pepper.

In a sauté pan melt butter. Add oil and cook chicken on both sides about 2 minutes or until done. Set aside and

177

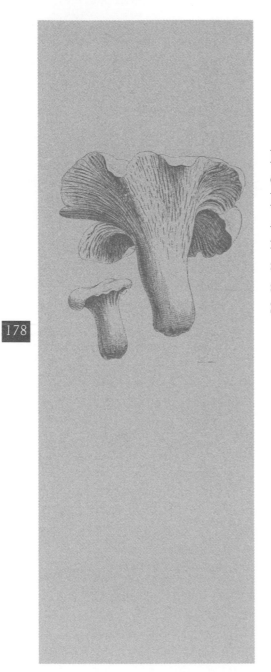

178

keep warm. In the same pan sauté onion and garlic and cook until transparent, 2-3 minutes. Toss mushrooms in lemon juice and add to onions, cooking 3 more minutes. Add stock, Marsala, thyme, and white wine. Cook and reduce about 10 minutes and season to taste. Add cornstarch mixture and bring to a boil. Rewarm chicken, prosciutto side up, and place on a warm platter with sauce. Serve with oven-roasted potatoes or pasta.

We use pork tenderloin more than any other cut of pork. It's lower in fat and more tender than most cuts and takes just minutes to cook. When grocery stores have them on special, we stock up and freeze them in plastic freezer bags.

Tequila Marinated Pork Tacos
serves 8

Marinade

1/2 c. tequila (or gin)
1/4 c. olive oil
1 tbl. chipotle chili (optional)
1 1/2 tsp. rubbed sage
2 tsp. cumin seed, crushed
1 1/2 tbl. Dijon mustard or herbed mustard
1/4 c. orange juice
1/2 tsp. cayenne pepper
3/4 c. chopped onion
1/2 tsp. hot pepper sauce
2 lb. pork tenderloin, trimmed of fat

Garnishes

lettuce, shredded
Asiago cheese, shredded
red onions, halved and sliced
flour tortilla, warmed
salsas (See Index)

Combine marinade ingredients in a resealable plastic food-storage bag and add pork. Marinate overnight in the refrigerator. Grill or broil until done (165°). Cut into long julienne strips and serve with taco garnishes.

Quick Tacos

One of our busy-day dinners, no matter what the season, inevitably features tortillas. We make quick fillings for tortillas from almost any leftover. Sauté onions and sweet peppers and add leftover cooked chicken, pork, or beef. Add some hot sauce, tomatoes, tomato sauce, salsa, chili powder, mole sauce, cumin seed, and oregano and you've invented a great fajita.

Serve with shredded garden lettuces, carrots, scallions, grated cheeses, salsa, hot sauces, and olives and your meal is complete.

Vegetarian versions are easily adapted when you have leftover Spicy Eggplant, roasted vegetables, or Spicy Black Beans.

Experiment and enjoy!

For large gatherings—like graduations or anniversary parties—this dish is perfect. It can be made a day ahead and refrigerated, but wait until just before serving to slice into rounds.

Saltimbocca (Pork Scallops with Prosciutto & Sage)
serves 4

1 1/2-2 lb. tied boneless pork loin

Filling

2 tbl. oil
1 tbl. butter
8 oz. mushrooms, chopped (squeeze 2 tbl. lemon juice over mushrooms)
1/2 c. onions, chopped
2 garlic cloves, chopped
1/4 c. Madeira or sherry
6 fresh sage leaves, chopped or 1 tbl. dried
1/4 c. toasted pine nuts (toast on a baking sheet in a 400° oven 4-7 minutes)
1/2 c. fresh Italian parsley
1/3 lb. Fontinella cheese, crumbled (or use *Asiago*)
5 slices prosciutto
salt and freshly ground pepper

Separate pork roast and cut into 1/3" slices. Place between wax paper and pound very thin (1/4"). Set aside.

(Don't worry about subsequent holes in flattened pork—
the prosciutto will cover.)

In a large skillet on low heat, place 1 tbl. oil and butter; sauté mushrooms, onions, and garlic until soft. Add
wine and cook 2 minutes more. Remove mixture to a bowl
and add sage, pine nuts, parsley, and cheese. Mix well. Taste
and adjust seasonings.

To Assemble:

Place 1/2 slice of prosciutto on each pork slice and
divide filling equally among slices. Fold in sides and roll
up. Secure with toothpicks, if desired. Place seam side
down on a large plate, cover with plastic wrap, and chill 1
hour to overnight.

In same skillet heat remaining oil and sauté the rolls,
a few at a time, until lightly browned all over. Remove to a
baking sheet, cover lightly with foil, and bake 10-15 minutes at 350°. Serve whole or cool slightly and slice. Serve
hot or cold with Sage Sauce.

181

Italian Cheeses

In Michigan, we have access to all kinds of cheeses. Besides the usual Swiss and cheddar, Italian cheeses are nice to serve as snacks or as toppings on food. Here are a few of our favorites:

Fontina—a mild, sliceable cheese with a buttery rich taste

Gorgonzola—a creamy blue cheese with a distinctive piquant taste

Fontinella—a firm cheese, like a cheddar, but with a little bite. Great with an antipasto platter.

Asiago—a hard, sharp cheese we often use in place of Parmesan or as a snacking cheese with red wine

Provolone—a smoky, creamy cheese with a mild, yet nutty flavor

Prepare this sauce a few days ahead for ease and convenience. Make extra for grilled chicken or spread on bread with leftover meat sandwiches.

Sage Sauce

3 cloves garlic, chopped
15 large fresh sage leaves (or 3 1/2 tbl. dried)
1 10-12-oz. jar roasted red peppers or 2 large fresh
    red peppers, roasted, seeds removed
1 1/2 c. Italian parsley, chopped
1/2 c. olive oil (more if needed)
3 1/2 tbl. red wine vinegar
1 c. fresh bread crumbs (made from 1 or 2 slices fresh bread
    whirled in a blender or food processor)
salt and freshly ground pepper

Combine all ingredients in a blender or food processor and whirl. Taste and adjust seasonings. Add more oil if too thick. Refrigerate several hours or overnight to blend flavors. Serve at room temperature.

This hearty autumn/winter entrée is excellent served with a Pinot Noir wine. It may also be made with a pork loin roast, sliced 1/2" thick and pounded to a thin 1/4" thickness.

Pork Tenderloin with Calvados-Lingonberry Sauce
serves 4-5

1 1/2 lb. pork tenderloin or pork loin, cut and pounded very thin
1 tbl. butter
4 shallots or 1/2 c. onion, minced
1 c. beef stock
1/2 c. Madeira
1/2 c. Calvados or pear brandy
2/3 c. port
1/2 tsp. dried thyme or 1 1/2 tsp. fresh
1 bay leaf
5 tbl. lingonberry preserves
1 tbl. balsamic vinegar
2 tbl. cornstarch + 1/2 c. beef stock
1/2 tsp. salt
freshly ground pepper
2 tbl. butter
1 tbl. olive oil
3 Granny Smith apples, peeled, cored, and sliced into wedges

In a large saucepan, melt 1 tbl. butter. Add shallots; sauté until soft and transparent. Add stock; then reduce on high heat 4-5 minutes. Add Madeira,

183

Deglazing

Deglazing is a sauce-making technique which uses the existing pan juices and particles from roasting meat, poultry, or vegetables.

To utilize the flavors, add your choice of liquid—wine, water, stock, or vinegar—to the roasting pan in which the food was browned. Stir over medium-high heat, scraping up browned particles with a whisk, fork, or spatula. Whisk in additional liquid, herbs, or cream and simmer to reduce. Dissolve cornstarch in cold liquid at a 1 to 4 ratio. Add cornstarch mixture to sauce, whisking constantly. Cook until transparent and thick; season with salt and pepper.

184

Calvados, port, thyme, and bay leaf; continue to reduce to half. Mix lingonberry preserves and vinegar into sauce and whisk in cornstarch mixture. Season to taste with salt and pepper.

In a large sauté pan melt butter and olive oil; cook apple slices on both sides until golden. Remove to a warm plate and set aside. Salt and pepper pork slices and, over medium-high heat, sauté on each side until golden. Serve pork and apple slices decoratively with Lingonberry Sauce on a warm platter.

This recipe uses a liqueur called crème de cassis (black currant liqueur). It's used to make delicious cocktails like Kir (white wine and cassis) or Kir Royale (champagne and cassis), but we find its fruity flavor good for sauces and desserts, too.

Pork Chops with Rosemary-Cherry Sauce
serves 4

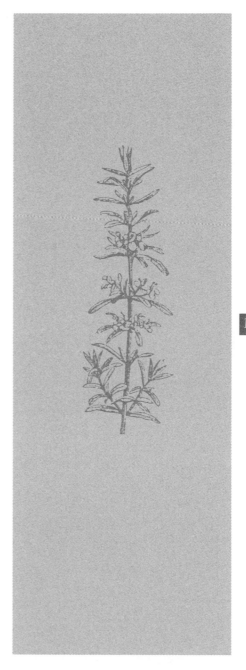

1/2 c. flour
1 tsp. dried rosemary, crushed
salt and freshly ground pepper
2 lb. boneless pork chops, 1 1/2" thick
1 tbl. oil + 1 tbl. butter

Rosemary-Cherry Sauce
3/4 c. red onion, chopped
1 garlic clove, minced
1 1/2 tsp. fresh ginger, minced
1/2 c. port
1/2 jalapeno, minced
1/4 c. crème de cassis (or substitute port)
1 c. beef stock
1/3 c. brown sugar
1 1/2 tsp. dried rosemary, crushed
1/2 c. dried sour cherries

Combine flour, rosemary, salt, and pepper and dredge pork chops in the mixture. Melt oil and butter and

185

Dried Cherries

Dried cherries were first introduced to the culinary world from here in Michigan. Credit is given to the famed American Spoon Food Company in Petoskey.

They're actually tart Montmorency cherries dried with the addition of sugar. These chewy, ruby-red jewels can be added to cookies, breads, muffins, cakes, pies, rice, couscous, and other grains, salads, stuffings or just for plain snacking—Yum!

You can find them in bulk at most health food or gourmet grocery stores or in packages from the American Spoon Food Company, 1-888-735-6700.

186

brown chops on both sides. Place in an ovenproof pan; cover with foil and bake at a low temperature (325°) for approximately 30 minutes. Don't overcook—check periodically.

Make sauce. To same pan in which the chops were browned, add the red onion, garlic, and ginger. Sauté until soft over low heat. Cover to release some of the liquid from the onions. Add jalapeno, crème de cassis (or port), beef stock, brown sugar, rosemary, and cherries. Cook over low heat about 20-25 minutes. Taste and adjust seasonings. Return pork to pan and heat. Serve immediately.

This entrée is spicy but flavorful, and if you prefer a little more heat, add some chopped jalapenos to the marinade. For summer months, cut the pork tenderloin into chunks and place on bamboo skewers with fresh whole okra, onion slices, and bell peppers for a unique shish kebab.

Curried Pork with Fresh Banana Chutney
serves 4

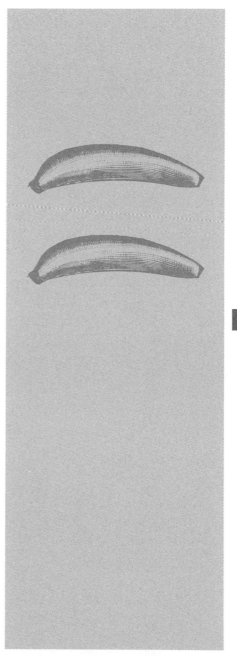

1 1/4-1 1/2 lb. pork tenderloin

Marinade
1 tbl. EACH cider vinegar and vegetable oil
1 tbl. curry powder, homemade or commercial (See Index)
2 garlic cloves, minced
1 tbl. fresh ginger, minced
2 tbl. plain yogurt
1/4 c. fresh cilantro, chopped

Combine marinade ingredients and place with pork in a resealable plastic food-storage bag. Marinate 1-2 hours in the refrigerator or overnight. Remove and grill or broil. Serve with Fresh Banana Chutney or Fresh Herb Salsa and warm pita bread.

Fresh Banana Chutney
3/4 c. onions, finely chopped
3 garlic cloves, minced
1 jalapeno, seeded and minced

187

Dad's Night

Marinated Roasted Peppers with
Herbed Goat Cheese

❧

Beef with Herbes de Provence

❧

Garlic Mashed Potatoes

❧

Fresh Green Beans with Dill Pesto

❧

Bourbon Brownies with Coriander

❧

Serve with a Cabernet Sauvignon
or Italian Barolo wine

1 tbl. curry powder, homemade or commercial (or to taste)
   (See Index)
1 tbl. vegetable oil
1 tbl. fresh ginger, minced
1 tbl. sugar
1/2 c. golden raisins
2 firm, ripe bananas, chopped
3/4 c. water
1 tbl. honey
1 tbl. fresh lemon juice
1/4 tsp. salt

In a large saucepan, cook onion, garlic, jalapeno, ginger, and curry in oil for 2-3 minutes or until onions are soft. Add rest of ingredients and simmer on low 20 minutes. Mixture should be soft and moist but with a crunch. Taste and adjust seasonings. Chill 2-4 hours.

❧

Every once in awhile we get a craving for beef—and this dish satisfies that craving.

Beef with Herbes de Provence
serves 6

3 tbl. Herbes de Provence (See Index)
1 tsp. coarsely ground black pepper
1 1/2-2 lb. beef tenderloin, trimmed and cut into
   1"-thick steaks
1 tbl. butter
1 tbl. oil
2/3 c. brandy
1/3 c. beef stock
salt
1 tbl. beurre manié (equal parts flour and butter)

Combine Herbes de Provence and black pepper. Press into both sides of each steak. Cover with plastic wrap and chill for 30 minutes or overnight.

Heat butter and oil in a heavy-bottomed skillet and sear steaks on both sides. They should be slightly pink inside. Remove to a platter and keep warm.

Add brandy and stock to the skillet and bring to a boil. Continue cooking to reduce liquid by half. Scrape bottom to loosen brown bits. Taste and adjust seasonings. Whisk in 1 tbl. beurre manié to thicken sauce. Pour over steaks and serve immediately.

❦

Baked Tenderloin

On many catering jobs, one of our most requested entrées was baked sliced tenderloin.

To make: trim a 2-4 lb. whole tenderloin (or cut in half) of excess fat. Press a handful of Herbes de Provence all over the tenderloins. Cover with plastic wrap and refrigerate 30 minutes or overnight. Preheat your oven to 450°. Put tenderloin (one or more) on a baking sheet and roast for 20-25 minutes.

Remove. Let cool completely. Wrap very well in aluminum foil and refrigerate overnight. Slice before serving with assorted aiolis and mustards.

❦

One of our favorite meals to make on cold, wintry days. Use a good quality thick-cut hickory-smoked bacon for a rich flavor.

Belgian Beef with Beer
serves 4-6

3 lb. lean chuck roast or rump roast in 1" cubes
1/4 c. flour mixed with 1/2 tsp. freshly grated nutmeg
4 slices thick hickory-smoked bacon, chopped
   in 1/2" pieces
oil (if needed)
3 c. halved and sliced onions
1 1/2 c. dark beer
1 1/2 c. water or beef stock
1/4 tsp. EACH ground cloves and freshly grated nutmeg
1/4 c. EACH fresh dill and parsley, finely chopped
1 tsp. dried thyme
6 tbl. red wine vinegar (plain or herbal)
3 tbl. brown sugar
6 parsnips, cleaned, peeled, and cut into 1 1/2" lengths
salt and freshly ground pepper

Dredge meat in flour and nutmeg mixture. Place bacon in a Dutch oven and fry a few minutes. Add meat and brown on both sides. Add onions and cook 2-3 minutes.

Blend in beer, water, spices, herbs, vinegar, brown sugar, and seasonings. Bring to a boil, place in a 350°

oven, and cook, covered, for 1 hour. Check level of liquid and add parsnips. Return to oven for another hour or until meat is fork-tender and some of the liquid has evaporated. Remove cover the last 30 minutes of cooking. Taste and adjust seasonings. Serve with boiled potatoes or noodles.

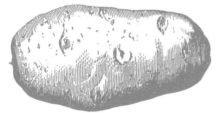

Bouquet Garni

Traditionally a bouquet garni was just a few sprigs of fresh parsley, thyme, and a bay leaf tied with string or placed in a cheesecloth bag. Today we use small reusable muslin bags or tea balls and fill with any combination of dried herbs and spices that fits our needs. We never use dried parsley, although many recipes call for it.

191

Indoor Grilling

It's possible to have your grill and eat inside too! Cookware shops all over sell several new kitchen tools that enable you to grill indoors—well, almost.

There are several styles of grills. Some are heavy cast-iron flat squares or rectangles; another is a round domed apparatus with grill grooves. All have the distinctive grill patterns so your food will really look authentic.

Most are made of heavy cast iron and usually coated with a nonstick surface. They fit directly over one burner and sometimes over two.

Be sure your kitchen has adequate ventilation because these grills really heat up.

Chipotles are smoked jalapenos and are available dried or canned in a tomato-type sauce called Adobo. Be careful, these chilies are quite "lethal." Use them sparingly or just use a teaspoon of the sauce to spice up almost any dish.

Grilled Flank Steak
serves 4

Chili Rub
    2 tbl. chili powder, homemade or commercial
    2 tbl. vegetable oil
    1 tbl. chili oil (available in Asian grocery stores)
    1 tbl. red wine vinegar
    1 1/2 lb. flank steak

Mix herbs, oils, and vinegar to a fine paste. Rub on both sides of the steak and cover with plastic wrap. Refrigerate several hours. Grill or broil—just till it's medium rare; this will only take minutes. Overcooking flank steak makes it tough. Remove meat and keep warm. Slice on a diagonal, across the grain.

Shallot, Shiitake & Chipotle Sauce
    4 very large shallots, sliced
    1 tbl. EACH olive oil and butter
    1 tsp. sugar
    3/4 c. red wine
    10-12 oz. fresh shiitake mushrooms, stems removed,
       cut in large slices
    2 tsp. chili powder, homemade or commercial

honey (if needed)
1 c. chicken stock
1/4 c. cilantro, minced
1 chipotle with a little sauce, minced
salt

Sauté shallots in oil and butter over low heat about 10-15 minutes or until very soft and beginning to caramelize. Sprinkle with sugar and cook, covered, 2-3 minutes longer. Add mushrooms, red wine, spices, and stock. Cook slowly till mushrooms are very soft and some of the liquid has evaporated, about 15 minutes. Add chipotle and heat through. Taste and adjust seasonings. Add honey if too acidic. Stir in cilantro and serve with sliced Grilled Flank Steak.

Harvesting Herbs

Choose a sunny morning to harvest herbs and wait until the dew is off of the leaves. Cut flowers or leaves with a sharp knife but be sure to leave enough foliage so the plant can continue to grow.

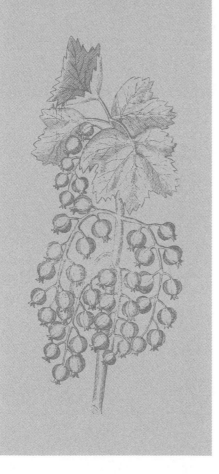

This dish contains anchovies—an acquired taste for some. We use them in lots of dishes. They're available packed in salt or olive oil or in paste form. Added to dishes, they give a piquant flavor without the fishiness.

Fresh Tomato Pasta Sauce
serves 4

4 oz. pancetta, cut in large cubes, or 3 thick slices bacon, diced
1 1/2 lb. Italian tomatoes, peeled or unpeeled, seeded and coarsely chopped in large chunks—about 5 (canned may be substituted but drain well)
1/2 c. fresh basil, chopped
1 1/2 tbl. sherry vinegar
2 tbl. capers
1/3 c. olive oil
6 oz. marinated artichoke hearts, sliced and drained
salt and freshly ground pepper
12-16 oz. cooked small-shaped pasta
Parmesan cheese
6-8 anchovies (if packed in salt, rinse well and pat dry)

Cook pancetta or bacon until crisp. Remove and set aside. In a large nonreactive bowl, place all ingredients except pancetta and anchovies. Mix gently. Taste and adjust seasonings. Pour sauce over hot, drained pasta and mix well. Add pancetta or bacon. Sprinkle with cheese and garnish with anchovies.

We've discovered that taco parties are a fun, easy, and colorful way to entertain. Provide a variety of fillings—Tequila Marinated Pork Tacos, Jerk Marinated Fish, and this vegetarian black bean mixture. Have plenty of hot flour tortillas and several fresh salsas (see Index). Of course, a pitcher of margaritas wouldn't hurt either!

Black Bean & Oregano Burritos
serves 4

1 large onion, chopped
1/2 c. EACH dry white wine and sherry
4 bay leaves
4-6 large garlic cloves, minced
1 tbl. whole cumin seeds, crushed
2 tbl. dried oregano
1-2 tsp. chili powder, homemade or commercial
1/4 c. orange juice
3 15-oz. cans black beans (or homemade equivalent)
2 tbl. sherry or balsamic vinegar
1 tbl. chipotle sauce (from can of chipotle chilies)
salt
flour tortillas
salsas
sour cream
assorted grated cheeses
scallions, chopped

Place onion, wine, sherry, bay leaves, garlic, cumin, oregano, and chili powder in a deep skillet or Dutch oven. Cook over low heat, covered, till soft, about 10 minutes.

Balsamic Vinegar

Balsamic vinegar, or aceto balsamico, is produced in Modeno, Italy. It's a sweet-sour vinegar prized by cooks. The process of fermentation takes approximately 25 years, during which the red wine vinegar is steeped in oak, chestnut, mulberry, and juniper kegs to give the characteristic deep-brown color.

The process is as much a family secret as are wine-making techniques, and the product is as costly. Its marvelous flavor is used sparingly in sauces, stews, and vegetables.

196

Add beans (drain half) and orange juice. Simmer, covered, on low heat for 30 minutes. Remove cover, raise heat, and cook till most of the liquid has evaporated. Mash beans with a potato masher or whirl in food processor. Stir in sherry or vinegar and chipotle sauce. Taste and adjust seasonings.

To Assemble:

Place some of the black bean mixture in a flour tortilla; sprinkle with scallions, salsas, and cheese. Fold like a burrito, taco, or fajita.

Vegetables & Side Dishes

Both Marge and I have joined a farm group that sells membership shares in weekly fruits, vegetables, and herbs. The produce is outstanding, and the variety of vegetables is staggering. Often we receive produce that normally wouldn't have been on our shopping list, but it has given us an opportunity to expand our usual green bean and broccoli recipes to include new dishes like Acorn Squash Spoonbread and Braised Fennel.

We have also discovered that many of our vegetable recipes serve double duty. Not only are they delicious side dishes and accompaniments to our meals but when served at room temperature with crusty bread, they become notable appetizers, like our Spicy Eggplant, Braised Leeks Italian Style, and Caramelized Onions with Sun-Dried Tomatoes & Walnuts. See if you don't agree!

197

A wonderful side dish to serve in the heat of the summer. We find it also tastes great in omelets or as a sandwich filling in pita bread.

Green & Red Tomato Ratatouille
serves 6

1 large eggplant, peeled and cut into 1/2" cubes
1 tbl. salt
1/4 c. olive oil
water
1/2 lb. (about 2-3) firm green tomatoes, very coarsely chopped
1 red or green pepper, chopped
1/2 lb. (about 2 large) onions, chopped
2 large garlic cloves, minced
1 lb. (about 3-4) ripe red tomatoes, peeled and coarsely chopped
1/2 tsp. freshly ground pepper
dash cayenne pepper
1 tsp. dried basil
1 tsp. dried oregano
1 6-oz. can tomato paste
1 tbl. honey
1 medium zucchini, unpeeled, cut in thin rounds (optional)
2 tbl. balsamic vinegar
1/3 c. fresh Italian parsley, chopped

Sprinkle eggplant with 1/2 tbl. salt and let stand 30 minutes. Rinse, drain, and pat dry. Place 2 tbl. oil in a very large skillet or Dutch oven and sauté eggplant. Add a small amount of water to the pan, reduce heat, and cover. Cook until eggplant is still firm yet tender. Remove from pan with a slotted spoon.

Add green tomatoes, pepper, onion, and garlic and sauté until wilted, about 5 minutes. Add the remaining oil if needed. Add red tomatoes and cook another 4-5 minutes. Add black pepper, remaining salt, cayenne, basil, oregano, tomato paste, and honey and increase heat. Scrape bottom of pan often to prevent sticking or scorching. Add zucchini, cover, and cook until firm yet tender. Return eggplant to pan and heat through. Add balsamic vinegar and parsley. Taste and adjust seasonings. Serve cold or at room temperature. Flavor improves if prepared one day ahead. Use as a side dish, as an omelet filling, or in pita bread sandwiches.

Honey

During the summer, there are farmers' markets all over the state and many that sell honey. Honey varies in color from dark amber to almost white with flavors to match.

For one pot of honey, bees have to visit more than 2 million flowers, and the honey taste depends on the flowers they choose. Clover is the mildest, but some prefer exotic choices like basswood, lavender, fruit blossoms, herb flowers, alfalfa, and mixtures from different fields.

Honey keeps for months in a cool cupboard. When refrigerated, it crystallizes and thickens, but placing the container in a pan of hot water will bring the honey back to spreading consistency.

199

Shallots

Shallots are a member of the onion family and like leeks are also classified as herbs. They range in color from orange-copper to the French gray cylinder-shaped ones. Mild in taste but more flavorful than scallions, they're an expensive item and don't keep as well as onions. We use them in vinaigrettes, in fish dishes, and in sauces (particularly butter, vinegar, or wine sauces).

In Cajun and New Orleans Creole cookbooks, the shallots referred to in recipes are actually scallions.

200

These are best made from firm, not overly ripe, tomatoes. But, we have to admit, we have even used those hockey pucks they call winter hothouse tomatoes and have had great results!

Baked Tomatoes
serves 8

4 tomatoes
salt
4 tbl. olive oil
1/2 c. minced shallots
2 tsp. minced garlic
1 1/2 c. fresh bread crumbs (place 1-2 slices of bread in a
    blender or food processor and whirl)
1/4 c. chopped fresh herbs or 1 tbl. dried herbs or herb mix*
1 tbl. minced fresh parsley
1/3 c. Parmesan cheese, grated
salt and freshly ground pepper

Preheat oven to 400°. Halve the tomatoes and remove the seeds. Lightly salt and drain upside down on paper towels 5 or 10 minutes. Meanwhile, heat 3 tbl. oil in a skillet and sauté shallots and garlic until soft. Add crumbs and sauté until golden. Remove from heat and add herbs, cheese, and salt. Mixture should not be dry—add more oil to bind, if needed. Spoon mixture into tomatoes, pressing gently. Drizzle with a little more oil.

Place in buttered or foil-lined pan and bake for 10 minutes or until heated through and skins start to shrivel. Don't overcook or the tomatoes will collapse.

*herbs to choose from: basil, dill, thyme, tarragon, Italian mix

This is the best way we've found to get kids to eat green beans and carrots! Roasting vegetables isn't a new technique, but it's effective in bringing out their natural sweetness.

Roasted Green Beans & Carrots
serves 4

1 1/2 tbl. garlic-flavored olive oil or regular olive oil
1 lb. green beans, trimmed
1 lb. carrots, peeled, cut into 1" chunks
1 tbl. butter
2 large garlic cloves, finely minced
1 tsp. EACH fresh savory and thyme, minced
salt and freshly ground pepper

Preheat oven to 475°. Add oil to large 10" x 15" baking sheet. Add green beans and carrots and turn to coat completely with oil. Roast in oven for 30-35 minutes, turning frequently. Continue baking until almost tender.

Meanwhile, melt butter in a saucepan and sauté garlic until soft. Toss with the vegetables and the herbs. Season to taste. Serve hot or at room temperature.

Green Beans

Living in the city, we have very small backyard vegetable gardens, but we use intensive gardening techniques to get the maximum use from small spaces. One of those vegetables that fits into this type of gardening is French green beans, or haricot vert (pronounced ary ko VERT). We grow both bush varieties such as Finaud, Astrelle, and Fin des Bagnols and pole types such as Emerite.

With just a few plants, the bush beans produce more than we can use for our families. Unfortunately, haricot vert do not freeze well, so our season is brief but, oh, so good.

Vinegar

In French, "vinaigre" means sour wine—which is where it originally came from—either intentionally or accidentally. Vinegar is made from fermented liquids such as apple cider, rice wine, malted barley, sherry, and red wine (balsamic) with the addition of a bacteria called a "mother."

A dash of herbed or balsamic vinegar after gently steaming or sautéeing broccoli, carrots, asparagus, or green beans brings out their sweet flavors.

When a pasta sauce or entrée dish seems to lack sparkle, add a dash of red wine vinegar while it's simmering.

The secret to this pesto is the cider vinegar—we've tried others as substitutes, but the flavor is never quite the same.

Fresh Green Beans with Dill Pesto
serves 4

Pesto

3/4 c. scallions, including green tops, chopped
3 tbl. fresh parsley, chopped
3-4 tbl. fresh dill weed, chopped
3 tbl. cider vinegar
3 oz. walnuts, coarsely chopped
1/2-3/4 c. olive oil
salt and freshly ground pepper
1 1/2 lb. fresh green beans, trimmed and cleaned
dill sprigs

In a blender combine scallions, parsley, dill, vinegar, walnuts, and 1/2 c. oil. Whirl until the mixture is smooth, adding more oil as needed. Pesto should be smooth but with a slight coarse texture. Season with salt and pepper and set aside. (Can be frozen.)

Cook green beans in a large skillet in 1"-2" water. When tender crisp, drain and remove to platter. Pour enough Dill Pesto on green beans just to coat them. Toss gently. Chill mixture for several hours or overnight.

To serve, bring back to room temperature. Taste and adjust seasonings—you may have to add a little more pesto. Garnish with dill sprigs.

This dish is so subtle, sweet, and earthy tasting, it reminds us of what dining in Tuscany must be like. See if you don't agree. Include it in your menu when grilling marinated chicken or whole pork roasts.

Braised Leeks, Italian Style
serves 4

5 large leeks
2 tbl. pine nuts
1/4 c. olive oil
1/3 c. currants
1 14-oz. can Italian tomatoes, chopped (reserve liquid)
    or about 6 fresh tomatoes
salt and freshly ground pepper
1/4 c. red wine vinegar
2 tbl. brown sugar

Trim leeks. Remove tough outer leaves, leaving only 1"-2" of pale green tops. Cut lengthwise and clean well. Slice in 1/2" pieces. Sauté pine nuts in 2 tbl. oil. As they begin to color, add the currants and tomatoes. Sauté a few minutes and add the leeks. Add remaining oil and water, enough to come halfway up the sides of the leeks.

Bring to a boil and simmer, partially covered, and braise for about 15 minutes or until the leeks are tender. Remove leeks gently and place on serving dish. Increase heat and reduce the pan juices. Add vinegar and brown sugar, tasting to adjust seasonings to your liking. Add salt and pepper. Continue to reduce until slightly thick. Pour over leeks. Chill. Remove and bring to room temperature and adjust seasonings.

Pine Nuts

Pine nuts actually come from a type of pine tree—the Stone Pines that grow in the Mediterranean area. Pine nuts are small and delicate and shaped like a corn kernel. They are delicious in pesto, pasta sauces, and tarts, but their price tag usually prohibits frequent use. They're found in Italian delicatessens or Asian markets. Store them in the freezer because their resinous oils spoil easily.

In New Mexico and Arizona a variety of the pine nut is also cultivated, called piñon. They grow on low bushy piñon trees and are less sweet and drier tasting than the Mediterranean kind. However, they can be used interchangeably.

Sweet Corn

In the Midwest sweet corn celebrations are annual events, reminding us that we grow probably the best corn around.

There are so many varieties it's hard to choose a favorite. Sweet, extra sweet, white, yellow, or bi-colored—you pick.

If you want to grow it yourself, you'll need plenty of room—this isn't a plant for intensive or container gardens, even if all you want is the newest food fad—baby corn. Actually baby corn isn't a special variety. It's really only sweet corn that is picked when it's very immature.

204

Marge's 16-year-old daughter, Dana, requests this colorful dish at Halloween because it looks just like candy corn!

Gingered Corn & Carrots
serves 6

1 tbl. butter
1 tbl. fresh ginger, very finely minced
6-8 garlic cloves, finely minced
2 1/2 c. carrots, peeled and cut into 1/4" cubes
1/3 c. chicken stock
1 tsp. sugar
2 1/2 c. corn
salt and freshly ground pepper

Melt butter in a deep saucepan. Add ginger and garlic and cook 1-2 minutes or until beginning to soften. Add carrots, stock, and sugar and bring to a boil. Reduce heat, cover, and cook 6-8 minutes. Add corn and heat through. Taste and season. Serve hot.

A quick side dish that rounds out a Mexican, Southwestern, or Caribbean meal. Serve with sangria or cold beer. To make this dish vegetarian, omit the bacon and cook onions and garlic in 2 tbl. vegetable oil.

Spicy Black Beans
serves 8

3 slices thick bacon, cubed
1 1/2 c. onion, minced
2 large garlic cloves, minced
1 1/2 tsp. EACH crushed cumin seeds and oregano*
1/2 tsp. EACH ground allspice and ground cloves
1 chipotle chili, minced with seeds, or 2 jalapenos**
2 15-oz. cans black beans (reserve some liquid)
salt
1/4 c. scallions, minced

Cook bacon in a deep skillet 2-3 minutes. Add onion and garlic and cook over low heat until soft. Add herbs, spices, and chilies and mix well. Add beans and cook until most of the liquid is absorbed. Try not to smash beans. Taste and adjust seasonings. Serve hot with scallions sprinkled on top.

*Or omit cumin, oregano, allspice, and cloves and substitute 1 1/2 tbl. jerk seasoning.

**Chipotles are smoked jalapenos. They're available either dried or canned in a tomato sauce called adobo.

Allspice

An interesting spice native to the Caribbean, sometimes called a Jamaican pepper. Although it's grown on the evergreen pimento tree, it's not to be confused with the pimento pepper. The whole berry, round and hard, is like a peppercorn and tastes faintly like a mixture of cinnamon, cloves, and nutmeg—hence the name "allspice."

Available whole or ground, allspice is used in patés, pickling spices, cakes, cookies, steamed puddings, sweet rolls, and as a mulling spice ingredient.

205

Anise

Anise is of Mediterranean origin and is one of the first aromatic plants to be written about. The Greeks, Hebrews, and Romans valued anise for its reputed medicinal properties. Anise belongs to the parsley family and is very similar to fennel—so much so that they are often interchanged and mislabeled in grocery stores.

Known for its distinctive licorice flavor, anise grows to reach 2 feet and has long, feathery leaves. The fruit of the plant, when dried, is called aniseed. It's used in liquors in Italy and breads in Germany and Scandinavia. We also use the seeds in baking and candy making, especially licorice confections. Remember to crush the seeds to release their flavor.

Fennel is a not-so-common vegetable often mistakenly labeled anise in grocery stores. Sliced in salads or pureed in velvety cream soups, the licorice flavor is refreshing and delicious.

Braised Fennel
serves 4

3 fennel bulbs
2 tbl. olive oil
1 tbl. pancetta,* diced, or 1 slice thick hickory bacon, diced
4 large shallots, cut in large chunks
1/2 c. white wine or vermouth
2 tbl. fennel leaves
3 tbl. balsamic vinegar
1 tsp. sugar
water (if needed)
freshly ground pepper
fennel sprigs for garnish

Trim fennel. Cut off ends and any brown areas. Chop into large chunks, reserving sprigs for garnish. Place oil in a large skillet and add pancetta, shallots, and fennel. Heat over low flame and cook until shallots begin to soften, about 4-5 minutes. Add rest of the ingredients and raise heat slightly.

Cover and braise until fennel is tender but still has a crunch. If liquid begins to evaporate, add a little water.

*Pancetta is an Italian bacon.

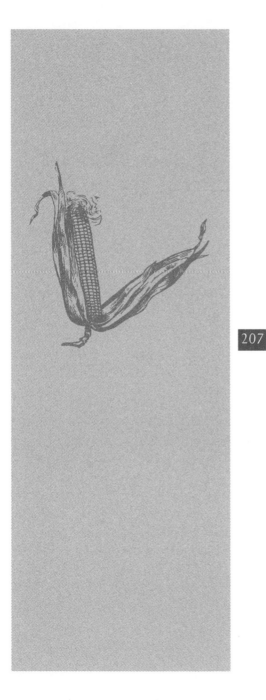

Turn and mix often. When fennel is done, remove with shallots and set aside. Reduce liquid to 1/4 c. and pour over vegetables. Sprinkle with freshly ground pepper and serve hot or at room temperature. Garnish with fennel sprigs.

Winter Solstice Dinner

Wild Rice Blinis with Caviar

❧

Cherry & Apricot Stuffed Cornish Hens

❧

Parmesan-Rosemary Potatoes

❧

Braised Fennel

❧

Artichoke Salad with Sun-Dried Tomatoes

❧

Apple-Orange Coriander Tart

❧

Serve with a Pinot Noir, California Chardonnay, or French White Burgundy wine

Suzanne's sister, Mary, lives in Texas and frequently likes to serve Midwestern dinners. She often serves Pecan Chicken Breasts with Michigan Dried Cherry Sauce and Parmesan-Rosemary Potatoes to wow her Texan friends.

Parmesan-Rosemary Potatoes
serves 6-8

3 tbl. olive oil
6 garlic cloves
2 tbl. fresh rosemary, minced
2 1/2-3 lb. potatoes, cleaned and cut in wedges or
    large chunks, unpeeled
1/2 c. Parmesan or *Asiago* cheese, grated
salt and freshly ground pepper

Combine oil, garlic, and rosemary. Place potatoes on a baking sheet and pour oil mixture over. Toss to coat. Place in a 450-500° oven for 15 minutes. Remove and toss. Sprinkle on half of the cheese and return to oven to bake an additional 10-15 minutes. Remove and toss again. Potatoes should be crispy. Add remaining cheese and salt and pepper. Toss and serve.

An easy potato dish to make for Thanksgiving and Christmas—best of all it can be prepared hours ahead and reheated.

Garlic Mashed Potatoes
serves 6-8

3 lb. boiling potatoes, peeled and quartered

2 bulbs of roasted garlic*

4 oz. goat cheese (plain or herbed)

1/2 c. warm milk (or more to reach desired creaminess)

2 tbl. low fat cream cheese

2 tbl. butter

1/8 tsp. freshly grated nutmeg

salt and freshly ground pepper

fresh chives

Boil potatoes until soft. Drain and return to pan. Add roasted garlic, goat cheese, milk, cream cheese, and butter. Mash, using a hand masher, and add more milk as needed. Season well with nutmeg, salt, and pepper. Garnish with chives.

Can be prepared ahead of time. Place in a glass oven-proof dish, cover with foil, and chill several hours. To serve, place in a preheated 350° oven and bake 30-35 minutes or until heated through.

Once garlic is roasted, squeeze the cloves to release the puree. Cover and set aside until ready to use.

Roasted Garlic

An appetizer that's become popular in homes and restaurants across the country is roasted garlic. In its raw state, garlic is strong and very pungent, but when slow-roasted in an oven it becomes sweet and succulent.

Roasted garlic is served with French bread, salt, and freshly ground pepper. Guests pull apart the cloves and press the soft interior onto a slice of bread, season well, and then eat. Yum!

Here's how to prepare:
On a 12" square of heavy duty aluminum foil place an entire bulb of garlic (be sure there are no soft spots or bruised cloves). Don't peel, but either separate the cloves or leave the bulb intact with 1/2" of the top cut off. Pour about 2 tsp. of extra virgin olive oil all over and toss to coat evenly. Gather the foil into a ball and place on a small pie plate. Bake in a 400-450° oven for 30-35 minutes. Toss occasionally. Remove from foil and serve immediately or cool and store in the refrigerator for later use.

209

Hazelnuts

Also known as filberts, hazelnuts are prized as one of the supreme dessert nuts by pastry makers. Grown in the Northwest and Midwest, they are widely available. Since hazelnuts are perishable, store in the freezer as you would other nuts.

Remove the skins before using by toasting. This is done by baking them in a 350° oven for 10-12 minutes or until flesh is golden brown and skin is a dark brown color. Cool slightly, then put in a cloth towel and rub to remove skins.

210

The interesting addition of hazelnuts and dried cherries to wild rice makes this dish flavorful—truly a Michigan treat.

Wild Rice Pilaf with Hazelnuts & Michigan Dried Cherries
serves 4

3 scallions, chopped
3/4 c. wild rice, washed
2 tbl. butter
2-3 c. chicken stock
2/3 c. white rice
1/2 c. dried cherries
1/2 tsp. dried rosemary or 1 tbl. fresh, minced
1/2 c. toasted (and skinned) hazelnuts, chopped coarsely
1/4 c. parsley, minced
1/2 tsp. salt
freshly ground pepper

Sauté scallions and wild rice in butter 3-4 minutes. Add 2 1/2 c. stock and bring to a boil; reduce heat and cover; simmer 20 minutes or until rice begins to soften. Add white rice and cook for 10 minutes. Add cherries and rosemary and cook until rice is tender. You may not use all the liquid—don't overcook wild rice. Add nuts and parsley and heat through. Season to taste and serve hot.

Lemon rice is easy to make and goes with practically any meal. We particularly like its tart-sweet flavor with curries, Caribbean, Thai, and spicy Southwestern foods.

Lemon Rice with Fresh Herbs
serves 4

2 tbl. oil
1 garlic clove, minced
2 large shallots, minced
1 1/2 c. long grain rice
3 c. chicken stock
1 tbl. grated lemon rind
2 tbl. fresh parsley, chopped
1/3 c. assorted fresh herbs, chopped (basil, chives, dill,
    tarragon, marjoram, mint, oregano)
salt and freshly ground pepper
1/3 c. toasted coconut (place on a baking sheet in a 400°
    oven for 5 minutes or until just starting to turn golden)

Melt oil in a deep skillet and sauté garlic, shallots, and rice for 2 minutes. Add stock and bring to a boil. Add lemon rind and parsley and lower heat. Cover and simmer 25 minutes.

Remove cover and mix in other herbs. Taste and adjust seasonings. Just before serving, sprinkle with coconut.

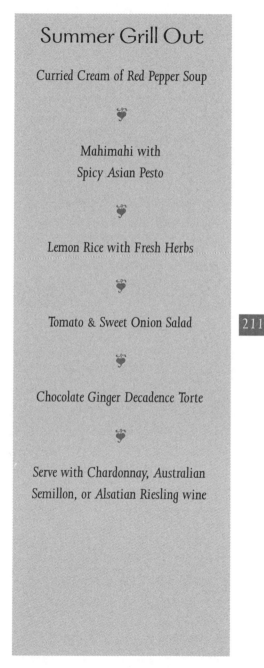

Summer Grill Out

Curried Cream of Red Pepper Soup

♥

Mahimahi with
Spicy Asian Pesto

♥

Lemon Rice with Fresh Herbs

♥

Tomato & Sweet Onion Salad

♥

Chocolate Ginger Decadence Torte

♥

Serve with Chardonnay, Australian
Semillon, or Alsatian Riesling wine

211

Lemons

Lemons are a must in everyone's pantry—store at room temperature to obtain the most juice, but refrigerate if you're planning to keep them for some time.

Lemons provide a tart accent to sauces, vegetables, salad dressings, marinades, and seafood. A little squeeze will intensify and perk up flavors. It also keeps freshly sliced mushrooms, cut-up apples, pears, avocados, and bananas from turning brown.

Freeze leftover juice in ice cube trays or small plastic containers—they'll add sparkle to ice tea, lemonade, club soda, and wine spritzers.

Try lemon juice as a substitute for vinegar in dressings—the taste is clean and refreshing.

212

Risotto has become a popular dish in recent years. An Italian comfort food, it's great with pork roasts, lamb, or baked chicken. We usually make this recipe as an entrée on cold winter nights, often substituting sautéed spinach, greens, or mashed winter squash for the mushroom mixture.

Wild Mushroom Risotto
serves 6-8

1/2 oz. dried wild mushrooms, assorted
1/2 c. boiling water
5 c. beef stock*
2-3 tbl. olive oil
2 oz. pancetta, cut in cubes (or use 1 slice of very thick bacon)
1 tbl. butter
10-12 oz. assorted fresh mushrooms, sliced
1/2 lemon, juiced
1/3 c. onions, minced
1 1/2 c. Arborio rice
1/2 c. dry white wine
1/3 c. freshly grated Parmesan cheese
salt and freshly ground pepper
1/4 c. fresh Italian parsley

Pour boiling water over the dried mushrooms and soak for 20-30 minutes or until soft. Cut in strips, set aside, and strain soaking liquid. Reserve. Heat beef stock in a large saucepan and keep warm over a low flame.

*Keep the stock constantly hot. Cold liquids chill the mixture and make the risotto mushy.

In a deep skillet cook the pancetta until crisp, 3-5 minutes. Remove to a bowl and set aside. Sprinkle fresh mushrooms with lemon juice. Add 1 tbl. oil and the fresh mushrooms and cook until soft. Add dried mushrooms and cook until mixture is slightly reduced. Place in bowl with pancetta.

In same skillet, add butter and the remaining oil. Sauté onions 1-2 minutes. Add rice and stir with a wooden spoon about 1 minute. Add wine, 1/2 c. hot stock, and the reserved soaking liquid. Cook over medium heat. Add stock, 1/2 c. at a time, stirring frequently and waiting until most of the liquid is absorbed before adding more. This should take 18-20 minutes. When rice is tender but firm, add reserved mushroom mixture, Parmesan cheese, salt, pepper, and parsley. Mix and taste to adjust seasonings. Serve at once.

Arborio Rice

To make a perfect risotto, it's essential to use the correct kind of rice. Not just any rice but a short grain rice that can absorb a great deal without becoming mushy. That's Arborio.

Italian-grown Arborio has a distinctive flavor and texture that are ideal for the long gentle-cooking risottos. It's more expensive than the regular short grain rice, but worth it. At one time it was only available in Italian markets, but today we can find it in any large grocery store.

It's also a good rice to use in paellas and jambalaya. Follow the package directions and add your own flavorings—saffron, shellfish, and sautéed vegetables.

Spoonbread

Spoonbread is a Southern specialty, a baked dish made with white or yellow cornmeal, milk, eggs, and shortening, which is served with a spoon. Historically, spoonbread is an adaptation of an Indian method of preparing native white cornmeal, called "Suppawn." This porridge-like dish was cooked in pots and was later refined by the English colonists, who added milk and eggs. Then, some unknown cook left the mixture too long in the oven by mistake—spoonbread was the result.

214

Even though this is called a bread, you should think of it more as a side of mashed potatoes—moist and served with a spoon.

Acorn Squash Spoonbread
serves 6

1 c. cornmeal
2 tsp. salt
1/2 tsp. paprika
2 c. pureed cooked acorn squash
1 1/2 c. water
2 tbl. butter
1 jalapeno, halved, seeded, and chopped
4 eggs
1 c. milk
2/3 c. grated Swiss or Parmesan cheese
1/3 c. fresh chives or green onions, sliced

Preheat oven to 425°; grease rectangular oven pan (9" x 12"). In a small saucepan, combine cornmeal, salt, and paprika. Add squash and water; stir well. Cook over medium heat, stirring constantly, 3-5 minutes or until thick. Remove from heat; add butter and jalapeno.

In a mixer beat eggs until frothy and lemon colored. Add milk, cheese, and chives or green onions. Stir to blend. Add cornmeal mixture and mix until smooth. Pour into pan, smooth even, and bake 25 minutes or until tip of knife inserted in center comes out clean.

We usually double this recipe since the earthy mixture tastes great the next day on toasted Italian bread—like a Crostini.

Caramelized Onions with Sun-Dried Tomatoes & Walnuts

serves 4

2 lb. small pearl or baking onions, peeled*
3 tbl. good olive oil
1 1/2 tbl. fresh rosemary, coarsely chopped
salt and freshly ground pepper
1/3 c. walnut halves
2 tbl. sun-dried tomatoes, cut into strips

Place onions in a 9" x 13" pan. Drizzle with olive oil and sprinkle with rosemary. Bake uncovered in a 375° oven for 25-30 minutes. Remove and add walnuts and sun-dried tomatoes. Return to oven and continue to bake, tossing occasionally, until onions are soft and caramelized—about 30 minutes more. Don't let them burn. Serve warm or at room temperature.

*Place onions in boiling water 2-3 minutes. Remove and cool and the peels will slip off easily.

Drying Tomatoes

During the late summer when the markets are flooded with tomatoes, we oven-dry a few of our own for snacking.

Here's how:
4 lbs. Italian or plum tomatoes, core end cut off and halved lengthwise
1 to 1 1/2 tbl. good olive oil
coarse salt and freshly ground pepper

Lightly brush the skin side of the tomatoes with oil and place skin side down on large baking sheets. Sprinkle with salt and pepper. Place in a 200° oven to bake to about 1/4 of their original size. This takes 5-6 hours. Be sure they remain a little soft. Remove pan from the oven and let cool completely. Store in covered containers in the refrigerator.

215

Julienning Vegetables

Juliennes are matchstick-size strips of food, such as carrots, leeks, turnips, or other foods. We use julienne strips in salads, soups, and vegetable dishes and as little bits of color in garnishes.

❧

216

Polenta is a centuries old Northern Italian food made from coarse cornmeal. There are two ways to prepare it, and we offer both. The traditional soft version can be made up to 1 hour before serving and can be varied with the herbs and kinds of cheese incorporated.

Herb Polenta with Gorgonzola
serves 4

1 c. onions, chopped
6 garlic cloves, minced
1 1/2 tbl. olive oil
5 1/2 c. chicken stock
1 tbl. butter
1 1/2 c. polenta (coarse yellow cornmeal)
1/2 c. Gorgonzola cheese
1 tbl. EACH fresh thyme, Italian parsley, and oregano, minced
1/2 tsp. chili powder, homemade or commercial (optional)
1 tsp. salt

Sauté onions and garlic in oil till soft, about 4 minutes. Remove to a bowl and set aside. In same saucepan, bring chicken stock to a boil. Add butter and cornmeal slowly, whisking well to prevent lumps. Cook and whisk 20 minutes over medium heat till thick. Add onion-garlic mixture, cheese, and herbs and stir. Taste and adjust seasonings. Serve immediately or cover and let sit 1 hour. Reheat with a little chicken stock if too thick.

Firm Polenta

The other way to prepare and serve polenta is slightly firm. It's made ahead and prepared as Herb Polenta with Gorgonzola but placed in a 11" x 7" or 9" x 13" greased pan, covered with plastic wrap, and chilled overnight. Just before serving, cut the firm polenta into triangles or squares or rounds. Fry in a little butter over low to medium heat and turn once. Serve with a mushroom sauce, tomato sauce, or poached eggs, as a side dish with beef, pork, or lamb roasts.

In the summer, try grilling the triangles or squares. Brush each piece with a little olive oil and grill till heated through. This is best done on nonsticking grids usually used for vegetables or seafood.

Gratins

Gratins are both a baking method and a type of cookware, French in origin. They're prepared and served in the same dish. Choose a shallow pan so that everyone gets a healthy share of the crusty top. Heat-conducting materials are best, such as earthenware, porcelain, or cast-iron enamel pans. When baked, the top should be crusty golden brown, with almost burnt edges for a rustic look, and the inside soft and creamy.

Potatoes

Buy or grow a specific potato for your specific purpose. Low starch or waxy potatoes are best for boiling or frying—Norland, Early Ohio, or Red Pontiac. They'll hold up in salads or just boiled and tossed with herbed butter. Tiny new potatoes, by the way, aren't a variety of potato but simply the earliest crop. For baking, try Kennebec or russet—the potato sometimes referred to as Idaho.

218

All potatoes, no matter what kind, should be stored somewhere cool, layered between newspapers so that if one turns bad the rest won't spoil. Refrigeration should be avoided—cold temperatures cause the starch in the potatoes to turn to sugar. With proper storage, potatoes will keep for months.

For vegetarians, these potatoes are great without the ham. They make an easy meal for 2 to 20.

Baked Potatoes with Sage & Ham
serves 4

8 small baking potatoes
1 lb. smoked ham, 1/4" thick slices
32 fresh sage leaves
1 onion, thinly sliced
1/3 c. chicken or vegetable stock
4 tbl. butter
salt and freshly ground pepper

Cut each potato into 4 diagonal slices—don't cut through base. Cut ham into pieces a little larger than potato slices. Place a piece of ham and a fresh sage leaf in each cut. Put potatoes in a shallow ovenproof dish and cover with onion slices. Pour stock over potatoes; sprinkle with salt and pepper and dot each potato with butter. Cover dish with foil and bake in a preheated 350° oven for 30 minutes. Remove foil and allow topping to brown an additional 15 minutes. Serve hot.

This versatile dish can be used as a vegetarian entrée by substituting vegetable stock for the chicken broth. If meat isn't an issue, you can add crumbled sautéed Italian sausage for a flavorful and filling entrée.

Quinoa & Wild Rice Stuffed Squash
serves 6

6 sweet dumpling, carnival, delicata, or acorn squash
   (about 3/4 lb. each), halved
1 tbl. olive oil
2 c. onions, chopped
1 c. celery, chopped
3 c. chicken stock
3/4 c. wild rice, rinsed and drained
1 1/2 tbl. chopped fresh sage or 2 tsp. dried
1/2 tsp. thyme
3/4 c. quinoa, rinsed and drained
1/2 c. dried apricots, chopped
1/4 c. EACH dried cherries and dried cranberries, chopped
1/2 c. chopped pecans, toasted
1/4 c. fresh Italian parsley, chopped
salt

Rinse squash; pierce each with a fork several times and set in a 10" x 15" pan. Add 3/4 c. water to pan and cover tightly with foil. Bake in a 350° oven until the squash is tender when pierced, 45 minutes to 1 hour.

Add olive oil, onions, and celery to a skillet and stir

219

220

over medium heat until the onions are limp, about 6 minutes. Add stock, wild rice, sage, and thyme. Bring to a boil over high heat. Cover, reduce heat, and simmer for 40 minutes. Stir in quinoa; cover and simmer until both of the grains are tender, about 15-20 minutes longer. Stir in apricots, cherries, cranberries, pecans, and parsley. Add salt to taste. Set aside and keep warm.

Cut 1/2" to 3/4" off tops of cooked squash (or sides of delicata) to form lids. Scoop out and discard seeds. If needed, trim a little off squash bases so they sit steady and level. Mound grain stuffing into squash cavities. Set squash lids on filling and serve.

If Fingerling potatoes are not available, use Yukon Gold or baby new potatoes.

Green Beans, Fingerling Potatoes & Sun-Dried Tomatoes
serves 4

1 lb. thin green beans, uncut
2 cloves garlic, minced
2 tbl. olive oil
1/4 c. sun-dried tomatoes (reconstituted if dried)
4 tsp. fresh thyme, chopped
4 Fingerling potatoes, unpeeled, cooked, and thinly sliced
1/4 c. walnuts, roasted
salt and freshly ground pepper
1/4 c. Parmesan or *Asiago* cheese, grated

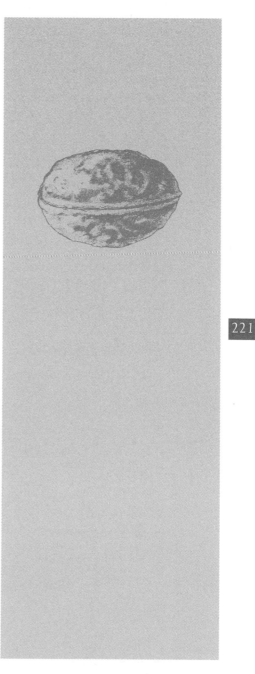

In a saucepan blanch green beans until barely crisp. Set aside. Sauté garlic in olive oil. Add sun-dried tomatoes, thyme, reserved beans, potatoes, walnuts, salt, and pepper. Warm and toss carefully. Serve sprinkled with grated cheese.

221

Thanksgiving Menu

Fines Herbes Cheese
Sage & Calvados Pâté
(Serve with a Sauvignon Blanc
or Beaujolais Nouveau wine)

❦

Roast Turkey
Garlic Mashed Potatoes
Broccoli with Garlic &
Sun-Dried Tomatoes
Acorn Squash Spoonbread
Fennel & Lychee Nut Salad
Pear Chutney
(Serve with a Beaujolais Nouveau,
Alsatian Gewürztramner, or
California Pinot Noir wine)

❦

Apple-Cranberry Tart with
Rosemary Streusel
Drunken Pumpkin Pie
(Serve with a Sauterne or
Tawny Port wine)

Every Christmas, Marge's family shares dinner with their good friends Sally and Mike Miley. Each family has two daughters who love broccoli—but this is the only recipe all four girls agree on.

Broccoli with Garlic & Sun-Dried Tomatoes
serves 4

1 lb. broccoli, broken into florets
3 tbl. sun-dried tomatoes, chopped with the oil they were packed in
1 tbl. olive oil
6 garlic cloves, minced
freshly ground pepper

Cook broccoli in your favorite way. We just fill a large skillet with about 1" water and let it come to a boil. Add the broccoli, turn so each floret turns bright green, reduce the heat, cover, and cook 2-3 minutes. Drain and keep warm.

Heat sun-dried tomato oil plus olive oil in same skillet and sauté garlic until soft, 1-2 minutes. Add sun-dried tomatoes, cut into slivers, and heat through. Pour over broccoli and toss gently. Sprinkle with fresh pepper and serve.

We like to use this recipe for a quick appetizer. Serve the spicy eggplant, roasted garlic, and goat cheese in small bowls with thin slices of baguette. Let your guests make interesting and creative appetizers with different combinations.

Spicy Eggplant
serves 8-10

3 tbl. olive or vegetable oil

1 tbl. sesame oil

1-1 1/2 lb. eggplant, peeled (or 4 Japanese eggplants, unpeeled), cut in 3/4" chunks

2 garlic cloves, minced

2 tbl. fresh ginger, minced

2 tsp. Chile Paste with Garlic (See Index)

2 tbl. sherry

2 tbl. soy sauce

1/2 tsp. sugar

1-2 tbl. seasoned rice vinegar

1/2 c. chicken stock

2-6 scallions, sliced thin

In a large skillet heat oils and add eggplant. Stir-fry 3-4 minutes or until slightly browned. Add garlic, ginger, Chile Paste, sherry, soy sauce, sugar, vinegar, and stock. Reduce heat, cover, and cook 10 minutes or until eggplant is tender. Remove cover. Taste and adjust seasonings with salt and pepper. Add scallions. Serve cold or at room temperature.

Sesame

Sesame is an annual tropical/subtropical herbaceous plant. It reaches up to 4 feet high and has been grown for its tiny grayish white or black seeds.

The seeds were brought to the American South by African slaves who called it "benne" or "bene" seeds. Sesame is still known by those names and is still popular in Southern cooking. Toast them to bring out flavor. The crunchy texture is good as a garnish for appetizers, salads, and almost any dish that requires nuts. If not toasted, use in baked dishes such as chicken, over bread before baking, in cakes and cookies, over noodles and vegetables, or crushed to make sesame oil.

223

Potatoes

Buy or grow a specific potato for your specific purpose. Low starch or waxy potatoes are best for boiling or frying—Norland, Early Ohio, or Red Pontiac. They'll hold up in salads or just boiled and tossed with herbed butter. Tiny new potatoes, by the way, aren't a variety of potato, but simply the earliest crop. For baking, try Kennebec or russets—the potato sometimes referred to as Idahos.

All potatoes, no matter what kind, should be stored somewhere cool, layered between newspapers so that if one turns bad the rest won't spoil. Refrigeration should be avoided—cold temperatures cause the starch in the potatoes to turn to sugar. With proper storage, potatoes will keep for months.

224

A versatile and aromatic dish. Instead of combining herbs, try using just one each time and see which flavors you like best.

Herbed New Potatoes
serves 6

1 1/2-2 lbs. small red potatoes, unpeeled
4-6 tbl. butter
3 tbl. fresh assorted minced herbs—tarragon, chives, mint, dill, chervil, or parsley, or 1 tbl. dried
salt and freshly ground pepper
lemon juice

Partially cook new potatoes. Remove from heat and drain. Cool slightly and slice with peels on. Melt butter in skillet and add potatoes. Cook until almost done and add herbs. Turn gently to coat—do not cook herbs. Season and sprinkle with lemon juice, if desired.

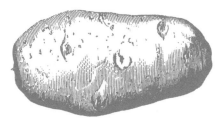

Desserts

It's hard to imagine any special evening meal, especially a dinner party, that doesn't include dessert. Yes, it's the last course to be served, but it is often the one by which the meal is remembered. We love desserts; who doesn't? But making them does take some time. With almost any other course in a menu you can adjust a little of this and a little of that in your recipe and still produce a great-tasting dish. But with desserts, there are more accuracy and precision involved. It's basic kitchen chemistry. To compound that fact, cooking desserts with herbs is even more of a challenge.

Suzanne and I are quite at home inventing dessert recipes with spices or other flavorings, but to use our kitchen herbs in desserts was new. How would we transfer the basil that's used in aromatic pestos to a pie, or pungent rosemary in potatoes and lamb dishes into a cake? Our families did raise their collective eyebrows; well, we experimented and experimented and found that indeed herbs did marry well with desserts. The recipes that follow are proof.

225

Use a mortar and pestle to crush the lavender buds. We have several kinds—ceramic and wooden. They both do a good job of pulverizing spices and herbs.

Lavender & Candied Ginger Shortbreads
makes 36

1/2 c. butter
1/2 c. sugar
1 1/2 tsp. dried lavender buds, crushed
1 1/4 c. flour
dash of salt
1-2 tbl. water
3 tbl. very finely minced candied ginger (also called crystallized ginger)
additional sugar for sprinkling

In a mixer bowl beat butter and sugar until well creamed. Add lavender, flour, and salt. Beat until combined. Mixture will be dry. Slowly add water until slightly moistened. (The mixture should stick together slightly.) By hand, mix in the candied ginger.

Press evenly into a 9" square pan. Bake in a 325° oven for 30 minutes. It will still be light but beginning to turn brown on the edges. Remove from oven and sprinkle with sugar. While still warm cut into 36 squares. Let cool completely before removing. Store in cookie tins or freeze for up to several months.

A Perfect Cup of Tea

Bring fresh cold water to a full rolling boil and pour over loose tea (1 tsp. per cup plus 1 tsp. for the pot). Cover and let steep 3-5 minutes; longer for herb tea. Don't judge the tea by color—taste it. You can always add water if it's too strong. Strain and serve with honey or sugar.

Marcel Proust is credited for making madeleines such a popular dessert—we're not disputing that, rather, applauding it. They're in between a cookie and a small cake and make a great dessert to serve with punch or tea. We make several flavors besides rose—including chocolate, lavender, and ginger.

Rose Madeleines
makes about 18

butter and flour for molds*
2 eggs
1/3 c. sugar
1/2 tsp. vanilla
2 tsp. rose water
3/4 c. cake flour
1/3 c. butter, melted and cooled
powdered sugar for garnish

Brush molds with soft butter and dust with flour.

In a bowl beat together eggs, sugar, vanilla, and rose water with an electric mixer until light colored and triple in volume—about 10-15 minutes. By hand, fold in cake flour. Fold in cooled melted butter.

Spoon into prepared pans, filling to top. In a 375° oven, bake 10-12 minutes or until cookie springs back when touched with fingertips.

Remove from molds and cool on a rack. While warm, sprinkle with powdered sugar. Store in cookie tins. Before adding batter, butter and dust molds with flour each time.

*Madeleine molds are small tin sheets with an indented scallop design. They can be found in most cookware shops.

Rose Water

Rose water is a liquid flavoring distilled from fragrant rose petals. In Middle Eastern and Indian cooking it's used for pastries and drinks. In its purest form, rose water is used as a basis for perfume—oil of rose. When diluted with water, it gives off a faint hint of roses—that's the type used in cooking.

It can be found in Asian and Indian grocery stores and through mail-order gourmet catalogs.

Add a dash to ice water for your next dinner party or use it in a simple syrup to be poured over pound cake for dessert.

227

Kathy's* Mint Julep Southern Style

In a silver mug or Collins glass, dissolve 1 tsp. powdered sugar with 2 tsp. of water. Then fill with finely shaved ice and add 2 1/2 oz. of bourbon.

Stir until glass is heavily frosted, adding more ice if necessary. (Do not hold glass with hand while stirring.) Decorate with 5 or 6 sprigs of fresh mint so that the tops are about 2" above rim of mug or glass.

Use short straws so that it will be necessary to bury your nose in the mint. The mint is intended for aroma rather than flavor.

*Kathy is Suzanne's sister-in-law.

228

These are definitely adult brownies and not for the Cub Scout meeting. Enjoy them either plain or with the chocolate glaze.

Bourbon Brownies with Coriander
2 dozen

8 oz. unsweetened chocolate
1 c. butter
5 large eggs
1 1/2 tbl. vanilla
2 tsp. almond extract
3 tbl. instant coffee
3 3/4 c. sugar
pinch of salt
3/4 tsp. ground coriander
5 tbl. bourbon (optional)
2/3 c. semi-sweet chocolate chunks
1/3 c. bourbon (for brushing)
2 c. flour
2 c. coarsely chopped pecans

Using a greased 9" x 12" pan lined with foil, butter and flour lightly.

Melt 8 oz. chocolate and butter in a small saucepan over low heat. Set aside. With an electric mixer beat eggs, vanilla, almond extract, coffee, and sugar on high for 2-3 minutes until light and fluffy. Mix in chocolate/butter mixture, salt, coriander, and bourbon. Blend in flour, pecans, and chocolate chunks. Pour into prepared pan. Bake in a preheated 350° oven 35-40 minutes. The brownies, when tested, should be moist and sticking somewhat to the toothpick or tester. Cool to room temperature. Invert brownies on a board, remove foil, and brush with additional bourbon. Coat with glaze.

Glaze

    2/3 c. sugar
    1 tbl. instant coffee
    1/2 c. heavy cream
    2 1/2 oz. unsweetened chocolate, finely chopped
    2 oz. butter
    1 tsp. vanilla

Combine sugar, coffee, and cream in a small heavy saucepan. Bring to a boil while stirring. Reduce heat and simmer 6 minutes without stirring. Remove from heat, add chopped chocolate, and stir until melted and smooth. Add butter and vanilla; whisk. Cool to room temperature; spread on brownies.

The apricot, brandy, and rum transform this cake from the traditional pound cake into holiday splendor.

Apricot Pound Cake with Fresh Thyme Glaze
serves 14-15

2/3 c. dried apricots, chopped
1/2 c. apricot brandy
2 sticks (1 c.) unsalted butter, softened
3 c. sugar
6 large eggs
1 c. sour cream (can use low fat)
1 tsp. vanilla
1 tsp. orange extract
1 tsp. rum extract or 1 tbl. dark rum
grated zest (peel) of 1 orange + grated zest of 1 lemon
1/2 c. diced crystallized ginger
3 c. sifted all-purpose flour
1/2 tsp. salt
1/4 tsp. baking soda
1 recipe Fresh Thyme Glaze

In small bowl, soak chopped apricots in 4 tbl. of apricot brandy. Set aside for 15 minutes.

In large bowl, cream butter. Add sugar a little at a time, beating well, until light and fluffy. Add eggs, one at a time, beating well after each addition. Beat in sour cream, soaked apricots, remaining apricot brandy, vanilla, orange

Fresh Thyme Glaze

1/3 c. fresh lemon juice
2 tsp. fresh thyme, chopped
1 tbl. apricot brandy
2 c. powdered sugar

In a small saucepan heat lemon juice, add thyme, and bring to a boil. Remove from heat. Cool. Add brandy and sugar; mix well until smooth. Spoon over cake 4 or 5 times.

extract, rum extract, orange and lemon zests, and ginger. In bowl, sift together flour, salt, and baking soda. Stir dry mixture into butter mixture. Transfer batter into well-buttered and floured 2 1/2-qt. bundt pan and bake cake in preheated 325° oven for 1 hour and 25 minutes or until cake tests done. Let cake cool in pan on rack for 45 minutes; invert on plate and drizzle on Fresh Thyme Glaze.

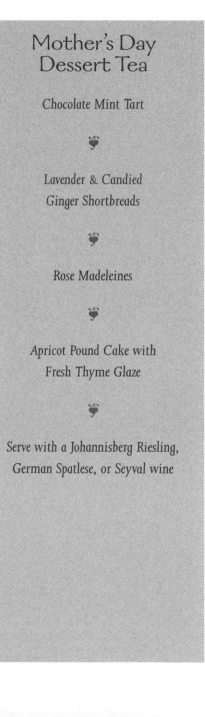

Mother's Day Dessert Tea

Chocolate Mint Tart

❧

Lavender & Candied
Ginger Shortbreads

❧

Rose Madeleines

❧

Apricot Pound Cake with
Fresh Thyme Glaze

❧

Serve with a Johannisberg Riesling,
German Spatlese, or Seyval wine

231

Raspberry Sauce

1 pint (2 c.) fresh raspberries or
    1 10-oz. bag frozen berries
4 tbl. sugar or to taste
3 tbl. kirsch, Grand Marnier, or
    other fruit-flavored liqueur
2 tbl. cornstarch, dissolved in
4 tbl. water
2 tsp. lemon juice

Combine raspberries with sugar in a food processor or blender; puree. Press through a sieve to remove seeds. Add liqueur and cornstarch mixture. Heat until raspberry mixture turns transparent and thickens. Add lemon juice.

232

When you're invited for dinner or luncheon, and there is a request for a dessert, take this cake. It's a winner! Not only does it travel well, but you can make it the day ahead.

Almond Ginger Torte with Fresh Raspberry Sauce
serves 12

3/4 c. sugar
1 stick unsalted butter, at room temperature
8 oz. almond paste
3 eggs
2 tbl. kirsch
1/4 tsp. almond extract
3 tbl. crystallized ginger, chopped into small pieces
2 tbl. minced fresh ginger
1/3 c. flour
1/3 tsp. baking powder
powdered sugar

Preheat oven to 350°. Butter an 8-1/2" round cake pan, line with wax paper, butter again, and dust with flour. With a mixer combine sugar, butter, and almond paste and blend well. Beat in eggs, kirsch, almond extract, and gingers. Add flour mixed with baking powder; combine well. Pour into prepared pan and bake 30-40 minutes until lightly golden brown and knife inserted in the center of the cake comes out clean. Cool in pan. Invert on serving platter, remove wax paper, and dust lightly with powdered sugar. Serve with Raspberry Sauce.

A very chocolatey dessert that freezes beautifully. Cut into quarters and wrap each section in plastic. Freeze for up to 1 year. Next time unexpected guests arrive, thaw one section for an hour and serve. Even one-quarter of this cake will serve 6 guests easily.

Chocolate Cranberry Torte
serves 12-14

1 1/2 c. fresh cranberries
1/3 c. sugar
2 tsp. grated orange rind
1/2 tsp. coriander seeds, crushed
3 tbl. crème de cassis or sweet vermouth
8 oz. semi-sweet chocolate
8 oz. butter
3 large eggs, separated
1/2 c. sugar
1/4 tsp. almond extract
1/2 c. ground toasted almonds
1/3 c. flour
1/8 tsp. salt

In a small saucepan place cranberries, 1/3 c. sugar, orange rind, and coriander seeds and cook until semi-soft, about 5 minutes. Don't be alarmed when you hear a popping noise—that's just the cranberries. Add the liqueur and set aside to cool slightly.

Melt chocolate and butter in a small saucepan and cool to room temperature.

Fresh Cranberries

The American Indians named the fruit "craneberries" because its blossoms resembled the crane. They used it in pemmican—a forerunner of beef jerky except it's made from venison.

The berries are grown in lowlands and boggy areas on evergreen-looking bushes. As they grow, the berries change from white to the distinctive wine-color, but only after the weather cools down.

Cranberries are high in vitamin C, making them a great breakfast juice, and because they have so much natural pectin they thicken when cooked in a matter of minutes.

233

Cranberry Dessert Sauce

Here's a rich dessert sauce that's great with chocolate cakes, pound cakes, ice cream, and bread puddings.

2 c. cranberry juice
3/4 c. sugar
1 1/2 tsp. orange rind, grated
1 1/2 c. fresh cranberries (coarsely chopped in a food processor)
dash of salt
1/4 tsp. coriander seeds, crushed
1 tsp. cornstarch + 1 tbl. cranberry juice or water
1/4 c. orange liqueur or crème de cassis

In a large saucepan reduce the cranberry juice to 1 1/2 c. Add sugar, orange rind, cranberries, salt, and coriander seeds and cook 5-7 minutes. Mixture will thicken. Combine cornstarch with juice and add to mixture. Cook until glossy, 1-2 minutes. Remove from heat and add liqueur. Can be frozen and reheated.

In a large mixer bowl, beat egg whites with a pinch of salt until stiff. Set aside.

In another mixer bowl, beat egg yolks and 1/2 c. sugar until thick and light. Add chocolate mixture and combine well. Add almond extract and almonds. Combine and add cranberry mixture. Fold in flour and salt, then continue to gently fold in egg whites. Pour into a greased and floured 9" springform pan and bake 40-50 minutes at 350°. Cool on a rack.

Glaze

1/2 c. heavy cream
6 oz. semi-sweet chocolate, chopped

In a small saucepan bring cream to a boil. Remove from heat, add chocolate, and stir until melted. Cool to room temperature. Spread thin layer of glaze over torte, cool to set. Pour more glaze over torte, spreading over sides until all is used (if glaze sets, rewarm to spread). Refrigerate until ready to serve.

Suzanne is the chocoholic and loves ginger equally well. This torte was invented to satisfy both those passions.

Chocolate Ginger Decadence Torte

serves 12-16

12 oz. semi-sweet chocolate
1 1/2 sticks butter
1 c. sugar
2 tbl. grated orange rind
5 eggs
3/4 c. cake flour
1 tsp. ground ginger
1 c. chopped toasted almonds (toast in 400° oven for
   5-7 minutes)
3/4 c. candied or crystallized ginger, minced
3 tbl. finely minced fresh ginger
ginger marmalade (about 1/2 c.)

Butter a 10" cake pan. Line the bottom with wax paper or parchment paper. Butter again and dust with flour.

In the top of a double boiler, melt chocolate. Remove from heat. Add butter, 1 tbl. at a time, and whisk in. Add sugar and orange rind. Beat in eggs, one at a time. Add flour, ginger, toasted almonds, candied ginger, and fresh ginger. Stir well.

Pour into prepared pan and bake at 350° for 1 hour and 5 minutes or until just springy to the touch. Cool on

Ginger

Ginger is a plant cultivated in the tropics, although many people grow it indoors in this country. Dried or ground ginger is used in curry powders and pastry making. Ginger contains a volatile oil called gingerly that gives fresh ginger that sharp, piquant flavor. In other forms—dried, powdered, candied, or crystallized—the fire diminishes.

We keep fresh, unpeeled ginger in glass jars refrigerated and covered with sherry. It will keep for months with only a very faint hint of sherry transmitted to other foods. The sherry acts as a preservative. Candied or crystallized ginger is best kept in plastic containers to prevent drying out.

235

236

rack. Cut cake in half horizontally. Heat ginger marmalade and spread on layer. Cover with top. Pour on glaze and chill or freeze.

Glaze

    1/2 c. whipping cream
    2 1/2 tbl. orange liqueur
    11 oz. semi-sweet chocolate, chopped
    1 tsp. corn syrup
    4 tbl. butter

Scald cream and liqueur. Remove from heat and add chocolate, corn syrup, and butter. Whisk until smooth, thick, and spreadable.

Bruce, Suzanne's husband, lived in New York for many years and loves cheesecake. He never found any that he liked outside "The City" until Suzanne invented this one.

White Chocolate Cheesecake with Dark Chocolate Basil Crust
serves 12-16

Crust

1 1/4 c. chocolate wafer cookie crumbs, ground
3 tbl. ground pecans or walnuts
3 tbl. melted butter
4 tbl. sugar
1/4 tsp. cinnamon
1 tsp. dried basil
dash nutmeg

Preheat oven to 350°. Combine all the above ingredients in a food processor or bowl until well mixed. Pat crumb mixture on the bottom of an 8" springform pan. Bake 5-7 minutes until set and hard. Cool. Lower heat to 315°.

Filling

8-10 oz. fine white chocolate
1/4 c. heavy cream
2 8-oz. pkg. cream cheese, at room temperature
7 tbl. sugar
2 eggs
1/2 tbl. vanilla

237

238

1 1/2 tbl. *Amaretto or Frangelico (or any other flavored liqueur)*
2 tbl. *flour*

In a small saucepan melt chocolate with cream. Stir to keep smooth. Cool. With an electric mixer beat cream cheese and sugar together until smooth—4-5 minutes. Add eggs, one at a time, beating well after each addition.

Beat white chocolate mixture, vanilla, liqueur, and flour into cream cheese mixture until just blended. Carefully spread into baked crust. Place on baking sheet and bake 40 minutes until lightly golden. Turn off heat, cool in oven, and refrigerate overnight. Garnish with fresh fruit and white chocolate curls. Serve with Michigan Cherry Sauce.

Michigan Cherry Sauce

4 c. *fresh or frozen tart cherries, pitted*
1 c. *sugar*
2 tbl. *cornstarch mixed with 5 tbl. cherry syrup*
2 tbl. *lemon juice*
4 tbl. *orange-flavored liqueur*

In a saucepan place cherries and sugar; bring to a boil. Add cornstarch mixture. Mix and cook until transparent and thick. Cool slightly; add lemon juice and liqueur. Can be served warm or cold.

One of our favorite pies. The clean lemon taste seems even better the second day. If pie crusts or pastry worry you, roll them out between pieces of plastic wrap. It's easier and you use less flour.

Lemon Basil Buttermilk Pie
serves 6

Pastry
1 1/2 c. flour
1/2 tsp. salt
2 tbl. sugar
1/2 tsp. grated lemon rind
1/4 c. solid shortening
1/4 c. cold butter, cut in bits
4 tbl. ice water

Place flour, salt, sugar, and lemon rind in a food processor. Add shortening and butter and whirl. Add ice water 1 tbl. at a time, till soft dough forms. Don't overmix. Form into a flat circle, seal in plastic wrap, and chill 1 hour before rolling out. Fit into a 10" metal or glass pie pan and flute edges decoratively.

Filling
1 c. sugar
3 tbl. flour
1/2 tsp. salt
1 tbl. fresh lemon basil, minced
2 tsp. grated lemon rind

239

Buttermilk

Today's buttermilk is a type of skim milk readily available in almost every grocery store. Originally it was made from the sour liquid left over when butter was churned. It contained small bits of butterfat and children loved to drink it.

Today's version of this tart milk is cultured. A lactic-acid bacterial culture is added to skim or partly skim milk.

240

Buttermilk has a refreshing, slightly acidic taste, almost lemony. We use it in desserts, salad dressings, pancakes, muffins, and bread. It's available in powdered form—a real help for cooks—or fresh in the dairy case.

1/4 c. butter, melted and cooled slightly
2 1/2 tbl. fresh lemon juice
2 c. buttermilk
4 eggs
freshly grated nutmeg

In a mixer, combine sugar, flour, and salt. Add lemon basil, lemon rind, butter, lemon juice, buttermilk, and eggs. Beat until smooth. Pour into prepared pie shell and sprinkle generously with freshly grated nutmeg. Bake 10 minutes at 400°. Reduce heat to 325° and bake until custard is puffy and just starting to set—about 50 minutes. Insert knife 2" or 3" from edge, and it should come out clean if pie is done.

Cool on rack. Can be made 8 hours ahead. Refrigerate when cool but remove 1 hour before serving.

A savory, full-flavored pie with nuts and rum. Serve with whipped cream for a spectacular finale.

Drunken Pumpkin Pie
serves 8-10

pastry for a 10" bottom crust (*see Margarita Tart*)
1/4 c. butter, melted
1/4 c. brown sugar
1/2 c. chopped pecans
2 c. cooked pureed pumpkin
1 c. brown sugar
4 eggs, lightly beaten
1/3 c. + 1 tbl. dark rum
1 1/4 c. heavy cream
2 tbl. crystallized ginger, chopped
2 tsp. ground cinnamon
1/2 tsp. ground ginger
1/2 tsp. ground cloves
1/2 tsp. ground allspice
1/4 tsp. salt
1/8 tsp. freshly grated nutmeg

241

In a small bowl, combine melted butter, 1/4 c. brown sugar, and pecans. Pour mixture into prepared crust, prick crust edges with fork, and bake in preheated 425° oven for 5 minutes or until brown sugar mixture bubbles. Remove from oven.

In large bowl, combine pumpkin, 1 c. brown sugar,

Clove

Clove is the dried, unopened flower bud of the evergreen clove tree, belonging to the myrtle family; grown mainly on the islands of Zanzibar and Madagascar.

First references to cloves are found in oriental literature of the Han period in China, under the name "Chicken-tongue Spice."

It takes between 5,000 and 7,000 dried cloves to make 1 lb. of the spice after preparation and drying.

Clove oil is an essential ingredient in many perfumes, soaps, toothpastes, mouthwashes, and medicines, and it is used as a synthetic or artificial vanilla, as well as being a widely used culinary ingredient in recipes from entrées to desserts.

eggs, rum, cream, crystallized ginger, cinnamon, ginger, cloves, allspice, salt, and nutmeg. Mix well, pour into crust, and bake in a preheated 350° oven for 40 minutes or until filling is firm in center.

This pie also tastes good with fresh nectarines or a combination of fruit.

Fresh Peach Lattice Pie
serves 8-10

Pastry
>2 c. flour
>3/4 tsp. salt
>1/2 c. unsalted butter, chilled
>1/4 c. vegetable shortening
>1 tbl. grated lemon peel
>1-2 tbl. fresh lemon juice
>4-5 tbl. ice water

In a large bowl combine flour and salt. Cut in butter and shortening with a pastry blender or food processor. Mix until it resembles coarse meal. Sprinkle with lemon peel and toss lightly. Gradually add lemon juice and enough ice water to make a soft dough. Form into 2 balls, cover with plastic wrap, and chill.

Glaze
>2/3 c. peach preserves
>2 tbl. rum

Combine peach preserves and rum in small saucepan. Cook over medium heat until boiling; keep warm.

244

Filling

1/2-3/4 c. sugar (*depending on sweetness of peaches*)
1/4 c. brown sugar
3 tbl. cornstarch
8 medium peaches (about 2 1/2 lb.), peeled
    and cut in 1/2" slices
2 tbl. fresh lemon juice
1/2 tsp. cinnamon
1/8 tsp. freshly grated nutmeg
1/8 tsp. salt
1 egg beaten with 2 tsp. water

In a large bowl, combine sugars and cornstarch; set aside. Add sliced peaches. Toss with lemon juice, cinnamon, nutmeg, and salt.

Line a 9"-10" pie pan with dough. Brush bottom and sides of pastry with glaze. Pour filling into pastry. Roll out remaining dough and cut into strips. Arrange in a lattice design. Brush pastry with beaten egg mixture. Bake 40-45 minutes in a 375° oven or until golden and bubbly in center. Cool.

This tart is rich and almost brownie-like in texture. Besides using the mint flavor, we've made this tart with Grand Marnier and grated orange peel, coffee-flavored liqueur and espresso, dried cranberries and cranberry liqueur, dried cherries and kirsch, and framboise and raspberries.

Chocolate Mint Tart
serves 12

1 Pâté Brisée pastry recipe (See Index)

Prebake in a 400° oven for 10 minutes. Cool.

Filling

2 oz. unsweetened chocolate, melted
4 oz. semi-sweet chocolate, melted
1/2 c. butter, soft
1 1/2 c. sugar
3 eggs
1/4 c. fresh mint, finely minced, or 1 1/2 tbl. dried
1/2 tsp. peppermint extract
1/2 c. chopped walnuts, pecans, or almonds (optional)
3/4 c. flour

In a food processor or mixer, add melted chocolates and butter and blend well. Add sugar; mix well. Add eggs, one at a time, blending well after each addition. Mix in mint, peppermint extract, and nuts. Gradually add flour and mix. Pour into prebaked pastry shell and bake until center is set (20-25 minutes). Don't overcook. Cool on rack. Sprinkle with powdered sugar and garnish with fresh mint sprigs.

Herb Honey

1 pint clover honey

2-5 tbl. fresh herbs or 1 tbl. dried (choose from mint, lemon balm, rose geranium, or lavender)

Heat honey in a pan over low heat. Pour into a large jar with the herbs on the bottom. Let sit on the counter overnight. Strain out herbs (if desired) and label. Store on pantry shelves and use for biscuits, muffins, pancakes, and toast.

Fruit & Herbs

Herbs have a remarkable natural affinity for desserts—especially fruit-based desserts. Basil with its clove-cinnamon flavor is wonderful with lemon or wherever cinnamon is used. Lavender is good in sugar cookies and custards and with berries, peaches, and apricots. Coriander seed is sparkling with citrus fruits with its orange-like flavor, and it also blends well in spice combinations for poaching fruit. Ginger tastes just great with chocolate and pears. Scented geraniums add an exotic perfumey taste to simple cakes, custards, muffins, cookies, sweet rolls, and jellies. Rosemary tames apples and cranberries, and mint is great with everything. Keep these flavor facts in mind and try some substituting in your favorite recipes.

246

When fitting the pastry dough into a tart pan, remember to compress the dough several times with your fingers against the side ring. This will help to keep the sides from shrinking while baking.

Apple-Orange Coriander Tart

Pastry
> 2 c. flour
> 1/3 c. sugar
> 1 1/2 sticks butter, cut into bits
> 1 egg yolk
> 1 tsp. grated orange rind
> 1 tbl. ice water (or as needed)

Combine flour, sugar, and butter in a food processor and whirl. Add butter in batches with egg yolk and orange rind, whirling until the mixture resembles coarse meal. Slowly add water until pastry particles adhere when pressed together with fingertips. Add water as needed to make dough smooth and pliable.

Form dough into a ball and knead lightly with heel of hand on a smooth surface for a few seconds to distribute butter evenly. Form into 2 flat circles, one slightly larger than the other. Chill 1 hour. Roll out and fit larger circle into a tart pan with removable bottom (10" or 11"). Reserve smaller circle.

Filling
> 5-6 Granny Smith or Golden Delicious apples, peeled, cored, and thinly sliced

1/3 c. sugar
1/2 tsp. ground cloves
1/2 tsp. ground coriander
2 tbl. grated orange rind
1 tbl. Grand Marnier or orange-flavored liqueur
1 tbl. flour
1 tbl. heavy cream

Toss apples with sugar, cloves, coriander, orange rind, liqueur, flour, and cream. Set aside. Arrange apples in pastry shell. Place reserved pastry circle on top of tart, pressing upper and lower pastry edges together. Bake in a 400° oven 45-50 minutes.

Glaze

3 tbl. powdered sugar
1 tsp. orange rind
1 tbl. orange juice
1 tbl. Grand Marnier

Combine all and blend until smooth. While tart is warm, drizzle glaze decoratively in strips across surface.

Coriander Seed

Coriander seed is the dried fruit of a foot-tall herb which belongs to the parsley family.

Coriander was one of the first spices to be used in cooking. Native to the Mediterranean area and the Orient, seeds have been found in Egyptian tombs of 960 to 800 B.C. and are mentioned in the Bible. The Romans introduced coriander into England, and it remained a favorite of the herb garden.

It has a pleasant flavor similar to that of aniseed, cumin seed, and orange. Like many spices, it can be used in a variety of foods. Ground, it flavors cookies, candies, soups, Danish pastries, gingerbreads, cheeses, and meats—even salads.

Herb Teas

Grow your own herbs for later use in teas. You don't need many, and they can be harvested anytime. Brew the dried herb teas singly or mix with black tea for unusual combinations. Create other blends with combinations of herbs such as sage-rosemary-mint. Plants to grow would be: mint, lemon balm, lemon verbena, chamomile, bergamot, anise, hyssop, sage, and rosemary.

When making tarts, we use "flan" pans, otherwise known as tart pans, with removable bottoms. They are metal pans (we prefer the heavy tin ones) and come in many sizes and shapes. These pans are easy to use and transport—the outer ring is removed before serving.

Cinnamon Caramel Nut Tart
serves 12-14

Pastry

        1 1/4 c. flour
        2 tbl. sugar
        1/8 tsp. salt
        1/2 c. butter, cut into bits
        1/2 tsp. almond extract
        2 tbl. milk

Preheat oven to 425°. In a food processor, combine flour, sugar, and salt. Add the butter in batches and whirl until the pastry resembles coarse cornmeal. Mix almond extract with the milk and slowly add to the pastry mixture until particles adhere when pressed together with fingertips, adding more liquid if needed. Knead with heel of hand several times, forming a flat disk. Seal in plastic wrap and refrigerate 30 minutes or until ready to use. Roll out dough to fit a 10" flan pan. Prick bottom several times with a fork and freeze until ready to use. Bake in a preheated 425° oven for 10-15 minutes, or until golden. Cool.

Filling

> 1 c. heavy cream
> 3/4 c. packed brown sugar
> 2 1/2 c. coarsely chopped pecans, hazelnuts, macadamia nuts,
>   almonds, pine nuts (a combination)
> 1 tsp. almond extract
> 1/4 tsp. EACH ground cinnamon and ground coriander*

While shell is baking, place cream and brown sugar in a heavy saucepan and cook over medium heat. Bring to a boil. Stir and continue boiling 1 minute. Add nuts, flavoring, and spices. Cook 2 minutes longer, stirring occasionally. Pour into shell and bake at 350° for 15-20 minutes or until top is set and nuts start to turn golden brown.

*You can replace the cinnamon and coriander with 1/2 tsp. crushed cardamom.

Nutmeg

Ground nutmeg straight from the jar is a rarely used spice—in demand most in the winter for hot drinks and cookies! But once you discover the aromatic flavor from grating your own fresh nutmeg, you'll be adding it to all sorts of dishes.

There are two types of nutmeg graters or grinders. One is like a pepper mill with a crank handle, and the other is a small tin gadget with teeth or grates that produce a fine dust when whole nutmegs are rubbed over it. Either device is good. The flavor is so fresh and intense you'll be using it in ways you never thought of.

Be sure the cranberries are below the apples and not poking through the streusel. They have a tendency to burn. This tart can be made ahead and keeps well, that is, if someone doesn't finish it off first!

Apple-Cranberry Tart with Rosemary Streusel
serves 12

Pastry

> 1 1/4 c. flour
> 1/4 tsp. salt
> 2 tbl. sugar
> 2 tsp. minced fresh rosemary
> 8 tbl. butter, cut in 1-tbl. slices
> 3 tbl. water

In a food processor combine flour, salt, sugar, and rosemary; whirl until well combined. Add butter; whirl until the pastry resembles cornmeal. Add water slowly until crumbs just start holding together when pressed between fingers.

Knead a few times with heel of hand; form into a flat ball. Seal in plastic wrap and refrigerate 30-60 minutes. Roll out to fit a 10" flan pan. Prick with a fork and freeze until ready to use.

Prebake at 425° for 10-15 minutes until lightly golden.

Streusel

> 1/2 c. + 1 tbl. flour
> 1/8 tsp. salt
> 4 tbl. oatmeal
> 2 tbl. white sugar
> 3 tbl. brown sugar
> 4 tbl. melted butter
> 1/3 c. coarsely chopped toasted hazelnuts

In a bowl combine all dry ingredients except nuts. Add butter, mix with a fork, add nuts, and continue mixing until crumbs form. Set aside.

Filling

> 5 Granny Smith or other baking apples, peeled, cored, and sliced
> 2/3 c. dried cranberries
> 3 tbl. brown sugar
> 4 tbl. white sugar
> 2 tbl. flour
> 1/8 tsp. salt
> 2 tsp. grated orange rind
> 4 tbl. orange-flavored liqueur
> 1/2 tsp. cinnamon

In a large bowl combine all ingredients. Pour into pastry shell. Sprinkle with streusel topping and bake at 350° for 30-40 minutes until apples soften and juice forms. Watch crumbs so they don't burn.

Baking Apples

When baking, choose the type of apples that are suited for baking and not just eating. Select apples that are firm and tart, such as Greening, Jonathan, Cortland, or Granny Smith. Eating apples such as Delicious or MacIntosh soften too much when baked.

To keep fresh apples on hand in all seasons, they may be sliced, seasoned, and frozen in individual pie-sized packages, ready for use in baking a pie at any time.

251

This is a great make-ahead tart. Its shelf life is 1-2 days. Cut into small slices. It's dense and rich—a little goes a long way.

Pine Nut Tart
serves 12-14

Pastry

> 1 1/4 c. flour
> 1/8 tsp. salt
> 1 tbl. sugar
> 8 tbl. butter (1 stick), cut into thin slices
> ice water

In a food processor, whirl flour, salt, and sugar. Add butter in 2 batches, whirling after each addition until mixture resembles coarse cornmeal. Add 1 tbl. water; whirl, adding more water if necessary to hold mixture together when pressed between fingers. Knead with heel of hand a few times; form into a flat disk. Seal in plastic wrap and refrigerate. Roll out and fit into a 10" flan pan. Freeze 10 minutes. With a fork, prick bottom and bake in a preheated 425° oven 10-15 minutes or until pastry starts turning golden. Cool.

Filling

> 1/2 c. apricot preserves, warm
> 8 oz. almond paste
> 4 oz. butter
> 1/3 c. sugar
> 1/2 tsp. almond extract

1/8 tsp. anise extract
4 eggs
1/4 c. flour
1/2 tsp. baking powder
3/4 c. pine nuts

Spread apricot preserves over bottom of pastry. Set aside.

With mixer, combine until smooth the almond paste, butter, sugar, and extracts. Add eggs, one at a time. Mix until well combined. Mix flour and baking powder together; add to almond paste mixture; beat until smooth. Pour into pastry and sprinkle with pine nuts. Bake in a 425° oven for 10 minutes. Reduce heat to 375° and continue to bake 10-15 minutes until dark golden brown.

Almond Paste

Almond paste is a blend of ground almonds and sugar. It's available in specialty food stores in an 8-oz. can or 7.5-oz. soft bars or tubes. It should be kept in a cool place and should be stored in the refrigerator if opened. Almond paste may be used to make marzipan, macaroons, Danish pastry, coffee cake, and many of our desserts. We enjoy the taste as well as the moist texture that almond paste provides to the desserts we created. It blends well with many flavors and is distinctive on its own.

253

This is a fun dessert to serve at a Southwestern dinner. We don't consider it a children's dessert but more like a Margarita in a crust.

Margarita Tart
serves 12-14

Pastry
    1 1/4 c. flour
    1/3 c. powdered sugar
    1/3 tsp. salt
    1/4 tsp. ground cinnamon
    1/3 c. ground pecans
    9 tbl. butter, cut into bits
    2 tbl. water (optional)

In a food processor, mix flour, sugar, salt, cinnamon, and pecans; whirl. Add butter in batches and blend until it resembles coarse meal. Sprinkle with 1 tbl. water; whirl. Add additional water if needed to hold pastry together. Knead with heel of hand a few times. Form into a flat ball; seal in plastic wrap. Refrigerate 1/2 to 1 hour. Roll out to fit a 10" removable bottom flan pan. Prick bottom with a fork several times and freeze until ready to use. Bake completely in a 425° oven until dark golden, 15-20 minutes. Cool.

Filling
    1 1/4 c. sugar
    4 1/2 tbl. cornstarch

5 tsp. grated lime rind
8 tbl. fresh lime juice
1 c. half-and-half
pinch salt
6 tbl. tequila
5 tbl. triple sec
1/4 tsp. dried mint
1/2 c. sour cream
1 pint fresh strawberries
whipped cream (optional)

In a saucepan place sugar, cornstarch, lime rind, lime juice, and half-and-half. Combine well and bring to a boil while stirring. Remove from heat; stir in salt, tequila, triple sec, and mint. Cool and combine with sour cream. Place in baked pastry shell; smooth with a spatula. Decorate with whipped cream and sliced strawberries.

Tequila

Tequila is a Mexican liquor distilled from the fermented juice in the stem of the century plant.

Traditionally, tequila is drunk straight. While holding the glass in the left hand, one places salt in the crevice between the thumb and fore-finger; a lime wedge held in the right hand is sucked immediately before licking the salt and downing the small glass of tequila. In the United States tequila is best known as the main ingredient in margaritas.

255

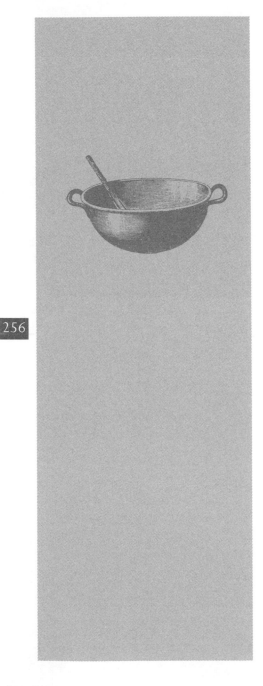

256

This is a great summer dessert decorated with fresh sliced fruit such as strawberries, kiwis, or raspberries. Glaze fruit with ginger or apricot preserves.

Triple Ginger Tart
serves 14

Pastry

    1 1/4 c. flour
    1/2 c. ground pecans
    3 tbl. powdered sugar
    1 tsp. powdered ginger
    1/8 tsp. salt
    9 oz. cold butter (1 stick + 1 tbl.), cut into thin slices
    1-2 tbl. water

In a food processor whirl flour, pecans, sugar, ginger, and salt. Add butter in 2 batches, whirling after each addition until the mixture resembles coarse cornmeal. Add 1 tbl. water; whirl, adding more water if necessary to hold mixture together when pressed between fingers. Knead with heel of hand a few times; form into a flattened disk. Seal in plastic wrap and refrigerate. Roll out and fit into a 10" flan pan. Freeze 10 minutes, prick bottom with a fork, and bake in a preheated 425° oven 10-15 minutes or until pastry turns golden. Cool.

Filling

    16 oz. cream cheese, at room temperature (regular or low fat)
    2/3 c. sugar
    2 eggs

6 tbl. chopped crystallized ginger*
1 1/2 tbl. fresh ginger, grated
1 tsp. vanilla extract
4 tbl. ginger preserves, warm
fresh fruit for garnish
ginger preserves, melted for glaze (optional)

In a large bowl, combine cream cheese and sugar with a mixer until smooth. Add eggs one at a time; beat in ginger and vanilla. Spread preserves on the bottom of the prebaked crust. Pour cream cheese filling on top. Spread and bake in a preheated 375° oven 30 minutes or until set and golden. Cool. Serve as is or arrange fresh fruit on top. Slice thin.

*Look for crystallized ginger in Asian food stores.

Dressing up a Tart

Instead of just placing the tart or torte on a plate, we place it on an attractive doily. We also decorate tarts with chocolate lace—which is melted chocolate placed in a pastry bag fitted with a small plain tip and randomly drizzled on top. We also decorate with fresh fruit on either the dessert or the plate. A slice of dessert can look very lonely on a plate. Try a light dusting of powdered sugar or fine cocoa on the plate or on the tart. Remember, do your dusting just before serving.

257

Cinnamon

Cinnamon, known as sweet wood, is the oldest spice known to humankind. Cinnamon is a reddish-brown spice that comes from the dried bark of shrub-like evergreen trees from the laurel family. This is one of the very few spices not obtained from the seeds, flowers, or fruits of a plant but rather from the bark.

The kinds of cinnamon most commonly used are cassia and Ceylon cinnamon. Cassia is native to China and is lower in quality and price. Now imported from Indonesia and Vietnam, it has an aromatic odor and a pungently sweet flavor and is mainly used in this country. Ceylon cinnamon is used more in other parts of the world.

258

❧

When pear season is upon us this is the dessert to prepare. It's elegant or casual in appearance, a wonderful traveler, and good to serve the second day.

Glazed Pear Tart with Ground Coriander
serves 10

Pastry

    1 1/4 c. flour
    1/4 c. sugar
    1 stick butter, cut into bits
    1 tsp. grated lemon rind
    1 egg yolk
    1-2 tbl. ice water

Combine flour, sugar, butter, and lemon rind in a food processor and whirl until just crumbly. Add the egg yolk and ice water and toss mixture with the on-off switch until just incorporated. (Can be done in a bowl with a pastry blender.)

Knead pastry lightly with heel of hand for a few seconds to distribute the butter evenly. Form into a flat disk, cover with plastic wrap, and chill for 1 hour.

Roll out on a floured surface and fit into a 10" flan pan with removable bottom. Prick bottom with a fork and freeze for 20-30 minutes. Prebake pastry in a 400° oven for 10 minutes or until golden. Remove and cool slightly.

Almond Crème

1/2 c. butter
1/2 c. sugar
1 egg
1 c. finely ground toasted almonds
3 tbl. Amaretto
1 tbl. flour
1 tsp. almond extract

In a food processor or mixer, cream butter and sugar until fluffy and light yellow. Add eggs, almonds, Amaretto, flour, and almond extract. Combine.

Filling

3-4 pears, peeled, cored, and sliced thinly
2 tbl. sugar
1/2 tsp. ground coriander
1/2-3/4 c. apricot preserves (heat and press through sieve)

To Assemble:
Pour crème into prebaked pastry shell; spread evenly. Place pear slices in a circular pattern, covering entire filling.

In a small bowl combine sugar and coriander, sprinkle over pear slices, and bake tart in a preheated 425° oven for 40-50 minutes or until golden brown and pears are tender.

Cool slightly and brush with apricot preserves.

Glazes

Glazes turn ordinary desserts into show-stoppers with very little effort. Use good jams, jelly preserves, or marmalades. Put 1/2-3/4 c. of desired preserves in a small saucepan and heat. Heating thins the mixture.

Add lemon juice or 1 tsp. of a liqueur if extra flavor is desired. If you don't like the small pieces of fruit in some of the preserves, press the mixture through a sieve.

259

With a pastry brush, lightly brush the top of your cake, tart, or fruit slices. Be sure to cover everything. Let it dry a few minutes and reglaze. The effect will make your dessert glossy and shiny.

This unique crust takes more time baking, and at a lower temperature than most pastries, but the end result is worth it. We make it in rectangular tart pans with removable bottoms—then we can just cut small slices of this rich tart.

Pumpkin Cheesecake Tart
serves 10-12

Pastry
    1 c. rolled oats
    1 c. chopped walnuts or almonds
    1 c. sweetened coconut
    1/3 c. sugar
    6 tbl. butter, cut into bits
    1/4 tsp. vanilla

In a food processor whirl oats, nuts, coconut, sugar, butter, and vanilla until dough holds together. Press evenly over bottom of 10" rectangular tart pan or 12" round tart pan.

Bake in a 300° oven until crust feels firm and is lightly browned, about 30-40 minutes.

Filling
    1 8-oz. and 1 3-oz. pkg. of cream cheese
      (regular or low fat), softened
    1 16-oz. can pumpkin
    3 eggs
    2/3 c. sugar

1 1/2 tsp. cinnamon
1 tsp. EACH ground ginger and vanilla
2 tbl. flour
3 tbl. finely minced crystallized ginger

In a food processor, place cream cheese, pumpkin, and eggs and whirl. Add sugar, cinnamon, ginger, vanilla, and flour and blend until very smooth.

Sprinkle crystallized ginger on bottom of prebaked pastry and pour filling over. Bake at 350° until center is set, about 25 minutes. Cool on rack to room temperature.

If you don't have a springform pan, a 10" tart pan with a removable bottom will work just as well.

Cherry-Blueberry Crumb Tart
serves 10

Pastry
> 1 3/4 c. flour
> 3/4 c. white sugar
> 1/2 c. packed brown sugar
> 1/2 tsp. cinnamon
> 3/4 c. almonds, toasted and chopped
> 2 tbl. crystallized ginger, minced
> 1/2 tsp. salt
> 3/4 c. butter

In an electric mixer or food processor combine flour, sugars, cinnamon, almonds, ginger, and salt. Mix or whirl until well combined. Add butter and whirl until crumbs begin to stick together. Press 3 c. of crumbs on the bottom and 1 1/2" up the side of a 9" springform pan. Set aside remaining crumbs for top. Bake pastry in a 375° oven until it begins to turn golden brown, about 18-20 minutes. Set aside to cool.

Filling
> 1 tbl. flour
> 6 tbl. white sugar

Flavored Ice Cubes

Freeze mint leaves, lemon balm, rosemary flowers, anise hyssop flowers, or unsprayed rosebuds in ice cube trays. Add them to iced tea, lemonade, water, and sparkling wine spritzers. Don't use tap water for these cubes or for decorative ice rings—the minerals in the water make them cloudy. Bottled distilled water works best.

262

1/4 tsp. *EACH cinnamon and salt*
1/3 *c. crystallized ginger, minced*
2 *c. pitted tart cherries*
1 *c. fresh blueberries*

In a medium bowl, place flour, sugar, cinnamon, and salt. Add ginger, cherries, and blueberries and combine well. Pour mixture onto pastry; spread evenly. Sprinkle with remaining crumb mixture. Bake 45-50 minutes in a 350° oven.

❧

263

Cardamom

Cardamom is a spice native to India and a member of the ginger family. The hard brown seeds are the prized feature and often sold in the pod. It is an expensive spice, with a flowery, aromatic, subtle taste.

Cardamom is used in Indian curry powders as well as in Scandinavian pastries, coffee cakes, and cookies. We use it with fruits such as plums, cherries, apples, and peaches and even to flavor coffee.

264

Free-form tarts are quick and easy to make because there's no pastry to fit into a pan, and the free-form shape gives a relaxed look to the end of a meal. The possibility of fillings is endless, but make sure you don't have any cracks in the dough or the filling may leak out.

Rustic Blueberry & Peach Tart
serves 10

Pastry

    1 1/2 c. flour
    1/4 tsp. salt
    2 tbl. sugar
    1 tsp. grated lemon zest
    10 tbl. butter, chilled and cut into bits
    2-3 tbl. ice water

In a food processor combine flour, salt, sugar, and lemon zest. Add butter in 2 batches. Whirl until it resembles coarse meal. Add 2 tbl. water and whirl. Add additional water if needed. The pastry should just hold together when pressed between fingers. Knead 2-3 times and form into a flat disk. Seal in plastic wrap and refrigerate for 30 minutes. On a floured surface roll dough into a 14" round. Transfer to a 14" x 17" cookie sheet (pastry will hang over edges). Set aside.

Filling

    4 peaches, peeled and sliced
    1 c. fresh blueberries
    1 tsp. almond extract

1 tbl. fresh lemon juice
1/3 c. sugar
1/4 c. flour
1/4 tsp. cardamom, crushed
1/3 c. sliced almonds
1 tbl. butter, cut into bits
2 tbl. sugar

In a bowl combine peaches, blueberries, almond extract, and lemon juice. In a small bowl combine sugar, flour, and cardamom. Add half of the sugar mixture to peaches and blueberries and sprinkle remaining half on pastry, leaving a 3" border. Place peaches and blueberries evenly on top of sugar mixture. Dot with butter. Fold 3" border over fruit. Sprinkle with almonds and sugar. Bake on center rack in a 400° oven until pastry is golden brown, about 45-60 minutes. Serve warm or at room temperature.

265

Make sure that you use a baking sheet without sides—it's easier to slide the tart onto a serving platter after baking.

Country Peach & Plum Tart
serves 10

Pastry
> 1 1/2 c. flour
> 2 tsp. grated orange peel
> 2 tbl. brown sugar
> 1 tsp. white sugar
> 1/2 tsp. salt
> 1/2 tsp. ground coriander
> 8 oz. + 3 tbl. butter, cut into bits
> 2-3 tbl. ice water

Combine flour, orange peel, sugars, salt, and coriander in a bowl or food processor. Add butter in 2 batches; process after each until mixture resembles coarse meal. Add water 1 tbl. at a time, until pastry just starts to hold together when pinched with fingers. Knead 2-3 times and form into a disk. Seal in plastic wrap and chill 30 minutes.

Frangipane
> 1 c. toasted almonds
> 2 egg whites
> 3/4 c. powdered sugar
> 1/2 tsp. almond extract
> 1/4 tsp. salt

266

Process almonds (pulverize), then add egg whites, powdered sugar, almond extract, and salt until blended. Set aside.

Filling

1 lb. dark plums, pitted, halved, and sliced
3/4 lb. peaches, peeled and sliced
2 tbl. sugar
1 tsp. cinnamon
1/2 tsp. ground coriander
2 tbl. flour
2 tbl. butter
1 tbl. orange-flavored liqueur
1/2 c. apricot preserves
1/2 tsp. grated orange rind

In a large bowl combine plums, peaches, sugar, cinnamon, coriander, and flour. Preheat oven to 400°. Roll pastry to a 16" x 12" rectangle or 12" round. Transfer to a large cookie sheet (pastry will hang over edges). Spread frangipane on pastry with a 2" border on all sides. Arrange fruit on top; fold 2" border over filling. Dot tart with butter, then bake 50-60 minutes. Stir liqueur, preserves, and orange rind and cook over low heat until melted. Drizzle over fruit when tart is removed from oven.

268

A deep-dish ginger crust adds a special twist to this delicious dessert.

Pumpkin & Pear Tart
serves 8-10

Pastry

1 1/4 c. flour
1/4 c. sugar
1/4 tsp. salt
8 tbl. butter, chilled, cut into bits
1 egg yolk, beaten
1/3 c. crystallized ginger, finely chopped
1 tsp. vanilla
2 tbl. ice water

In a food processor or with a pastry blender, combine flour, sugar, and salt. Add butter; combine until mixture resembles coarse meal. Add egg yolk, ginger, and vanilla. Using a quick on-and-off pulse with the food processor, add water, then gather pastry together and knead with heel of hand on a flat surface. Form into a flat disk. Seal in plastic wrap and chill.

Roll pastry to fit a 10" tart pan with removable bottom. Freeze or chill pastry 30 minutes. In a 425° oven, prebake pastry for 10-12 minutes or until golden brown. Cool.

Filling

    2 eggs
    1 c. sugar
    1 15-oz. can pumpkin
    1/4 c. heavy cream
    3/4 tsp. EACH ground ginger and ground coriander
    1/2 tsp. freshly grated nutmeg
    1/4 tsp. salt
    2 pears, peeled, halved, and cored
    1 tbl. lemon juice
    2 tsp. sugar
    1/2 tsp. cinnamon
    1/4 c. ginger preserves
    2 tbl. brandy

Beat eggs and sugar in a large bowl. Whisk in pumpkin, cream, ginger, coriander, nutmeg, and salt. Pour into prebaked crust. Slice pears 1/2" thick and toss with lemon juice. Arrange in a circular design over the filling. Sprinkle pears with sugar and cinnamon. Bake at 350° for 1 hour and 15 minutes or until knife inserted in center comes out clean. Cool on rack 10 minutes.

Combine ginger preserves and brandy in a saucepan over low heat until melted and smooth. Cut the large chunks of ginger into smaller pieces. Brush mixture over pears and let cool.

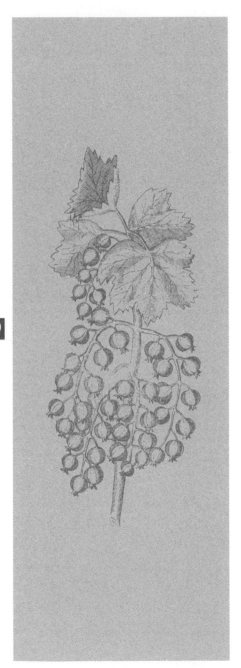

270

Because of the natural pectin in cranberries, this chutney thickens quickly. It's such a hit at Thanksgiving, we often give some in festive jars as gifts.

Pear Chutney
makes 2-3 cups

2 lb. fresh cranberries
3 apples, pared, cored, and diced in 1/2" cubes
3 pears, pared, cored, and diced in 1/2" cubes
1 c. golden raisins
1 c. currants
2 c. sugar
1 c. fresh orange juice
2 tbl. grated orange peel
2 tsp. ground cinnamon
1/4 tsp. coriander seeds, crushed
1/2 tsp. freshly ground nutmeg
1 1/2 c. walnuts, coarsely chopped
2/3 c. orange-flavored liqueur

In a large nonaluminum saucepan, combine all ingredients except walnuts and liqueur. Bring to a boil, reduce heat, and simmer uncovered, stirring frequently, until mixture thickens—about 45 minutes. Stir in walnuts and liqueur. Refrigerate covered 4 hours or overnight. Keeps 2 weeks refrigerated.

A very colorful chutney with just a little heat. Use it to accompany grilled chicken, lamb, or pork kebabs.

Michigan Dried Fruit Chutney
makes 2-3 cups

2 c. dried apricots, chopped
1 c. pitted dates, coarsely chopped
1 c. dried sweet or sour cherries
1/4 c. dried blueberries
1 c. EACH brown sugar and white sugar
1 c. cider vinegar
1/3 c. onions, minced
1 tbl. fresh ginger, minced
2 dried chilies, crushed
juice from 1 lime
1 garlic clove, minced
1 1/4 c. water
2-3 tbl. honey (if needed)

In a stainless steel saucepan, combine everything except dried fruit. Bring to a boil, reduce heat, and add fruit. Simmer 20 minutes until soft. Taste and adjust seasonings. Chill.

271

Mint Syrup

1 qt. cider or malt vinegar (or
    half-and-half)
1 c. sugar
2 c. fresh spearmint or peppermint
    leaves, packed

Place vinegar in a nonaluminum pan
and bring to a boil. Add sugar and
mint. Stir and crush leaves. Boil 3-5
minutes. Strain and cool. Place in
bottles and store in refrigerator.

Use as a base for iced tea, punch, or
with mineral water.

Finally, a dessert that can be prepared in under one hour and still be impressive. Try substituting pears for the cherries when your supply is low.

Quick Cherry Turnovers
serves 4

1 sheet frozen puff pastry—purchased or homemade
1 1/2 c. pitted sweet or tart cherries
1/2 lemon, juiced
1/4 c. golden raisins
1/2 c. sugar (or to taste)
3 tbl. rum or brandy
1 1/2 tbl. flour
1/4 tsp. aniseed, crushed
1/2 tsp. ground allspice
1/4 tsp. cardamom, crushed
powdered sugar
Flavored Whipped Cream

Remove one sheet of dough from package. Rewrap remaining dough and refreeze.

Place cherries, lemon juice, golden raisins, sugar, liquor, flour, aniseed, allspice, and cardamom in a bowl and mix well. Taste to adjust seasonings.

On a floured board, roll pastry out into a 16" square. Divide into fourths. Place about 3-4 tbl. of the filling in the middle, plus a little of the juice. With fingers, wet the pastry edge on two sides. Fold over to form a triangle. Press to seal edges. Prick top 1 or 2 times with a fork for air vents.

272

Place on parchment paper or aluminum-foil-lined baking sheet. Bake at 400° for 20 minutes or until golden. Remove and sprinkle with powdered sugar. Serve with a dollop of Flavored Whipped Cream.

Flavored Whipped Cream
    1/2 c. whipping cream
    2 tbl. powdered sugar
    1/4 tsp. cardamom, crushed

Whip cream with sugar and cardamom. Chill till serving time.

273

Curd is a tart, custardlike filling that is used as a spread on scones, muffins, toast, and cookies. It's great as a cake or pastry filling even with the addition of strawberries, raspberries, or blueberries. And when placed in small tart shells, it becomes an essential component of English teas.

Honey Lemon-Lime Curd with Thyme
makes 2 cups

1 1/2 c. light honey
4 whole large eggs
2 large egg yolks
1/2 c. fresh lemon juice
1/2 c. fresh lime juice
1 tbl. EACH lemon and lime zest
1/2 c. unsalted butter, cut into bits
1 tsp. fresh thyme leaves, chopped

In a saucepan whisk together the honey, whole eggs and egg yolks, lemon and lime juice, zest, and butter. Cook the mixture over moderately low heat, whisking constantly, until curd is thick and the first bubbles appear on the surface. Transfer the curd to a small bowl and let cool, covered with plastic wrap. Chill until ready to serve. Refrigerated curd lasts for weeks.

We've tried many citrus curds, and this is a foolproof recipe. Line small tartlette pans with a dough from one of our many pastry recipes. Bake until golden, cool, and fill with curd. Top with fresh fruit and berries and whipped cream. Yum!

Lemon Curd
makes 2 cups

1 c. sugar
2 tbl. cornstarch
2 tbl. finely shredded lemon peel (or orange, tangerine, lime)
1 c. fresh lemon juice (or 1 c. orange/tangerine +
   2 tbl. lemon juice)
1/4 c. butter
6 beaten egg yolks

In a saucepan, stir together sugar and cornstarch. Stir in citrus peel, juice, and butter. Cook and stir over medium heat until thickened and bubbly. Slowly stir about half of citrus mixture into beaten egg yolks. Bring to a gentle boil. Cook 2 minutes. Remove and cover surface with plastic wrap. Chill until ready to serve. Refrigerated curd lasts for weeks.

May Wine

May Wine is not an actual type of wine, but a drink made from German wines and sweet woodruff.

❦

May Wine Punch

1 c. dried sweet woodruff
1 c. superfine sugar
1 gal. Rhine or Moselle wine
1 bottle chilled champagne
1 qt. fresh strawberries,
   lightly sugared

275

In a large container, combine woodruff, sugar, and wine. Cover and let steep overnight in the refrigerator. Strain mixture into a punch bowl or a large pitcher. Add ice cubes or a decorative ice ring, champagne, and strawberries. Mix and serve.

❦

276

This is a quick and yummy low fat dessert to be made ahead of time.

Honey Coriander Brûlée
serves 4

1 12-oz. can evaporated low fat milk
1 c. milk
2 eggs
1/2 c. honey
2 tsp. grated orange peel
1/2 tsp. ground coriander
1 tsp. vanilla
3 tbl. sugar

Preheat oven to 325°. In a medium bowl, whisk together evaporated milk and eggs until well blended. Mix in honey, orange peel, coriander, and vanilla. Divide mixture evenly among 1-cup ramekins or custard cups. Place cups in baking pan and fill halfway up side with boiling water. Bake until knife inserted in center of cup comes out clean, about 1 hour. Remove cups from baking pan and allow to cool. Cover and refrigerate about 4 hours or overnight.

Just before serving, sprinkle sugar evenly over custards. Place under broiler and broil until sugar melts and caramelizes. Serve immediately with Michigan Cherry Sauce (see Index).

Condiments & Little Extras

In this chapter we've added what we call staples. They're in the form of dried herb blends, flavored vinegar blends, salsa recipes, aiolis (flavored-garlic mayonnaises), and pestos.

The herb blends are fresh and vibrant versions of the common grocery store types. Use them whenever you want to add a unique flavor to just about anything—or package them as gifts. The salsas are our favorites. We use them in place of relishes or chutneys. They're always fresh, and the ingredients are flexible, so that if you don't have one fruit or vegetable, you may substitute another.

The aiolis are the closest we get to a restaurant's "signature dish." We have fun inventing new flavors, and we serve them with all kinds of dishes—from appetizers, to soups, to entrées.

Last is pesto, our all-purpose recipe. Not only do pestos stand alone with just crusty bread, but adding any one of them to a simple salad vinaigrette will transform yesterday's leftovers into a delicious main dish salad or an accompaniment to grilled fish, meats, poultry or a sauce to serve over flavored hot pasta.

In a word, or words, we couldn't do without this chapter. Once you try some of the recipes, you'll be saying the same thing.

Herbes de Provence #1

2 bay leaves, crushed

1 tbl. EACH basil, rosemary, and thyme

1/8 tsp. EACH ground coriander, nutmeg, savory, cloves, and white pepper

Combine and store in glass or ceramic jars. Use in pâtés, omelets, meat loaf, and breads.

Herbes de Provence #2

Equal portions of the following: thyme, sage, fennel seeds, rosemary, basil, oregano, lavender, and mint

Combine and store in glass or ceramic jars.

278

Pâté Seasonings

1/4 c. salt

2 tsp. ground cinnamon

1 tsp. EACH crushed bay leaves, thyme, rosemary, and basil

3/4 tsp. paprika

1/2 tsp. ground cloves

1/2 tsp. freshly ground pepper

1/4 tsp. ground allspice

Combine and store in a glass or ceramic jar.

Homemade Chili Powder

4 large dried ancho or other mild chilies

2-4 small hot dried peppers

4 tsp. cumin seeds

1/2 tsp. whole cloves

1 tsp. coriander seeds

1/2 tsp. whole allspice berries

1/4 c. dried oregano

2 tbl. garlic powder

1 tbl. salt

1/2 tsp. sugar

Remove stems from peppers and break into small pieces. Place in cast-iron or other heavy skillet. Add cumin, cloves, coriander, and allspice. Stir over low heat until it begins to crackle and gives off an aroma. Cool to room temperature and put with the rest of the ingredients in a grinder or blender and whirl until it becomes a fine powder. Store in glass or ceramic jar in a cool, dry place.

Red Chili Seasonings

12 dried hot chilies

9 dried ancho or mild chilies

3 tbl. cumin seed

1 tbl. ground coriander

1 tbl. garlic powder

1 1/2 tsp. whole cloves

2 tsp. dried basil

1 1/2 tbl. salt

1/2 tsp. freshly ground pepper
1/4 tsp. ground allspice

With rubber gloves, remove seeds from dried chilies and place in a blender or spice mill. Whirl until mixture is a fine powder. Add rest of ingredients and whirl again. Store in glass or ceramic jars in a cool, dry place.

❦

Italian Blend

3 tbl. EACH oregano, marjoram, savory, and basil
1 tbl. EACH thyme and sage
2 tbl. rosemary
2 tbl. salt

Combine all and store in glass or ceramic jars. Use with meatballs, salad dressings, tomato sauces, eggplant dishes, rice, cheese, vinegars, and butters.

❦

Creole Seasonings

8 tsp. salt
2 tbl. freshly ground pepper
2 tbl. garlic powder
8 tsp. sweet paprika
8 tsp. cayenne pepper
4 1/2 tsp. onion powder
1 tbl. dried thyme

Combine all and store in glass, ceramic, or tin jars away from heat. Use in gumbos, rice, sauces, cheese dips, and marinades.

❦

Curry Powder #1

12 cardamom pods, seeds removed
2 tbl. coriander seeds
1 tbl. EACH turmeric and ground ginger
1 1/2 tsp. EACH cumin seeds, ground allspice, ground cinnamon, freshly ground pepper, and ground cloves

Crush with mortar and pestle or in a spice grinder or blender until powdery. Store in airtight glass or ceramic jars.

279

❦

Curry Powder #2

6 whole cloves
1 tsp. EACH cumin seeds, whole peppercorns, mustard seeds (black or yellow), ground ginger, and ground cardamom
1 tbl. coriander seeds
6 bay leaves
2 tsp. EACH chili powder and turmeric
1/2 tsp. EACH ground cinnamon and cayenne

Toast in a hot heavy skillet until some of the seeds pop. Cool and grind to a powder. Store in airtight glass or ceramic jars.

Poultry Spice Blend

1 1/2 tbl. dried basil
1 tbl. EACH dried marjoram, tarragon, and rosemary
1 tsp. EACH dried thyme, lovage, paprika, and sage
1/2 tsp. garlic powder
2 tsp. salt

Combine all the ingredients; store in a glass, ceramic, or tin jar.

Jerk Spice Blend

1 tbl. EACH dried thyme, chives, ground cinnamon,
    allspice, ginger, and sugar
2 tsp. EACH ground nutmeg, coriander, and cloves
1/2 tsp. EACH ground garlic powder, freshly ground
    pepper, and dried grated lemon peel
2 bay leaves, crushed
1 tbl. salt

Combine all of the ingredients; store in a glass, ceramic, or tin jar. Use on chicken, pork, or fish.

Garam Masala

1/4 c. coriander seeds
1/3" cinnamon stick
1 tbl. black peppercorns
2 tbl. cumin seeds

1/2 tsp. turmeric
1 small dried hot red chilie or red pepper flakes
1/4 tsp. ground ginger
1 whole allspice berry
2 tsp. cardamom seeds
6 bay leaves

Combine all in a spice grinder or blender and whirl until finely blended. Store in glass, ceramic, or tin jars. Use whenever curry powder is called for.

Tandoori Masala

1 tsp. chili powder, homemade or commercial
1 tsp. cumin seeds, ground
1 tsp. ground coriander

Combine all. Store in glass, ceramic, or tin jars. Used to season chicken, beef dishes, and other curry foods.

Southwest Spice Blend

3 tbl. ground coriander
2 tbl. ground cumin
1 tbl. EACH dried oregano and ground red chilies
2 tbl. chili powder
1 tsp. dried basil
1/2 tsp. garlic powder

280

1 bay leaf, crushed
1 1/2 tbl. salt

Combine all ingredients; store in a glass, ceramic, or tin jar. Use on chicken, pork, fish, or rice.

č

Dried Herb Vinegar

1 qt. white vinegar
1 1/2 tbl. dried herbs (assorted)

Bring vinegar to an "almost" boil. Pour over herbs, cover, and let stand 2 weeks. Shake daily, strain, and decant with a sprig of fresh herbs, if desired.

Combinations: tarragon, basil, chives, Italian mixes, dill, fines herbes, rosemary-thyme.

č

Fresh Herb Vinegar

1 gal. white vinegar
2 c. crushed fresh herbs*

Pour cold vinegar over crushed fresh herbs. Cover and let stand in a warm place for 2 weeks. Check periodically for strength and aroma. Decant in glass bottles with fresh herb sprigs.

*combinations: same as in previous recipe

č

Asian Vinegar

3 sprigs marjoram
3 sprigs sweet woodruff
1 tbl. sliced fresh ginger
1/2 tsp. peppercorn
4 c. rice vinegar

Combine all ingredients and place in glass jars. Let sit for 3-5 weeks. Shake or stir periodically. Check for strength and aroma. Decant into more decorative bottles with fresh sprigs of herbs.

č

Provençal Vinegar

2 sprigs EACH rosemary, lavender, thyme, and marjoram
2 bay leaves
2 garlic cloves
2 hot chilies, dried
3 1/2 c. white vinegar

Combine all ingredients and follow directions for Asian vinegar recipe. Place in glass jars.

č

Mediterranean Vinegar

5 hot chilies, dried
3 garlic cloves
2 sprigs EACH basil, thyme, and lemon thyme
1 sprig rosemary
3 1/2 c. red wine vinegar

Combine all and follow directions for Asian vinegar recipe. Place in glass jars.

❦

French Blend Vinegar

1 clove garlic, peeled and coarsely chopped
2 sprigs fresh tarragon
2 sprigs fresh thyme
1 sprig fresh rosemary
2 bay leaves, broken
1 shallot, peeled and chopped
2 1/2 c. white wine vinegar

Place garlic, herbs, and shallot in a stainless steel pan. Heat half the vinegar to a boil, pour over the herbs, and steep until cool. Mix with the remaining vinegar. Pour into a wide-necked bottle, seal tightly, and keep for 2 weeks. Shake every few days. Pour through a strainer; rebottle with fresh tarragon and rosemary sprigs.

❦

Italian Blend Vinegar

1 clove garlic, peeled and chopped
3 sprigs fresh basil
2 sprigs fresh oregano
1 sprig fresh rosemary
1 small sage sprig
1/2 tbl. black peppercorns
2 c. red wine vinegar

Place garlic and herbs in a stainless steel pan. Heat the vinegar to a boil, pour over the herbs, and steep until cool. Mix with remaining vinegar, pour into a wide-necked bottle, seal tightly, and keep for 2 weeks. Shake every few days. Pour through a strainer; rebottle with fresh basil and rosemary sprigs and a small garlic clove.

❦

Spicy Asian Oil

2 garlic cloves
2 small hot dried chilies
1 slice, 1/4" thick, fresh ginger
1/2 cinnamon stick
1/4 tsp. star anise
1/4 tsp. coriander seeds
1/4 tsp. whole allspice berries
grated rind of 1/4 orange
1 c. flavorless oil—canola, safflower, etc.

Combine all in a glass jar and let sit 2-3 weeks. Discard garlic after 4-5 days. Use oil to marinate pork or chicken or for stir-frys.

❦

Herb Butter

1/2 c. room temperature butter
1/2 tbl. fresh lemon juice
1 tbl. fresh parsley, minced

282

2-3 tbl. fresh herbs or 1-2 tsp. dried*
salt and freshly ground pepper

Cream the butter in a bowl. Add lemon juice slowly. (Can also be made in a food processor or blender.) Mix in herbs and season. Place on foil and roll into a cylinder. Label; chill or freeze until needed. Use in vegetables, fish, omelets, baked potatoes, pita triangles, etc.

   * suggested herbs: dill, tarragon, basil, savory, Italian mixes

ॡ

Quick Herbal Mustard
   1 1/2 c. Dijon, coarse Dijon, or Dusseldorf mustard
   1/4 c. chopped fresh herbs or 2 tbl. dried,
      crushed herbs*
   3-4 tbl. mild flavored honey

Mix all ingredients in a nonaluminum bowl. Taste and adjust seasonings. Store in refrigerator. Serve with hot pretzels, pâtés, or sausages; or on sandwiches; or package as gifts in small fancy bottles or jars.

   *suggested herbs: basil, mint, thyme, chives, rosemary, tarragon, or combinations

ॡ

Tangerine Salsa
   2 tangerines, peeled, seeded, and diced
   1 yellow pepper, finely diced

1 red pepper, finely diced
1-2 jalapenos, finely chopped and seeded
1 tbl. rice vinegar or mild herb vinegar
3 scallions, finely diced
1-2 tbl. oil
1 tbl. fresh ginger, finely chopped
2-3 tbl. cilantro, finely chopped
honey (if needed)
salt and freshly ground pepper

Combine all ingredients in a bowl and adjust seasonings. Keeps in refrigerator for several days.

ॡ

Cucumber Salsa

   1/2 c. rice vinegar
   1 stalk lemon grass, cut into small pieces
   1/4 c. sugar
   1/2 c. water
   1/2 tbl. red pepper flakes
   2 cucumbers, peeled, seeded, and diced
   1 red pepper, diced
   3 jalapenos, minced
   3 tbl. fresh basil, minced
   2 tbl. fresh mint, minced

In a small saucepan, bring vinegar, lemon grass, sugar, water, and pepper flakes to a boil. Boil down to 1/2 c. Strain and cool. In a bowl add cooled liquid and remaining ingredients. Taste and adjust flavors. Refrigerate.

Fresh Herb Salsa

1/2 c. red onion, minced
1/8 tsp. chili oil
1 large green pepper, minced
1/4 c. scallions, minced
6 tbl. oil
1 1/2 tsp. lime juice
2 tbl. fresh basil, minced
1/4 c. fresh parsley, minced
1 jalapeno, minced
2 tbl. tarragon vinegar
1 tsp. honey

Combine all in a bowl and taste to adjust seasonings. Cover and chill 1 hour.

Fresh Tomato Salsa

See page 119.

Mango Salsa

2 ripe mangoes, chopped
1/2 c. cilantro, chopped
1 red pepper, chopped
1 1/2 c. Daikon radish, chopped
1 cucumber, peeled, seeded, and chopped
3-4 jalapenos, chopped
1/4 c. fresh basil, chopped
4 tbl. salted peanuts, coarsely chopped*
3 tbl. red onion, chopped
2 1/2 tbl. rice vinegar
2 tbl. oil
1 1/2 tbl. honey
salt and freshly ground pepper

In a large bowl, combine mango, cilantro, pepper, radish, cucumber, jalapeno, basil, and red onion. In a jar, mix vinegar, oil, and honey. Pour over salsa mixture and toss gently. Taste and season with salt and pepper. Serve chilled or at room temperature.
* Place peanuts in salsa just before serving.

Cilantro Salsa

1/2 c. fresh cilantro
2 tbl. fresh basil
2 tsp. fresh ginger, minced
1-2 jalapenos, minced, or other fresh hot chili peppers
2 garlic cloves, minced
1/2 c. pine nuts, walnuts, or peanuts
1/2 lime, juiced
1/4 c. oil
salt
1 tsp. brown sugar

Put cilantro, basil, ginger, jalapeno, and garlic in food processor. With motor running, add nuts and lime juice and whirl. Add oil, salt, and brown sugar. Chill until serving time. Mixture should not be watery.

284

Cranberry-Jalapeno Salsa

1 1/2 c. fresh or frozen cranberries, picked over

1 orange, grated, peeled, and coarsely chopped

4 tbl. sugar

salt

2-3 jalapenos (or to taste), chopped

1/4 c. vegetable oil

1/4 c. scallions, minced

1/4 c. cilantro, chopped

1 tbl. fresh ginger, finely minced

In a food processor chop cranberries and orange. Do not liquefy; mixture should be coarse. Remove to a bowl and add sugar, jalapenos, oil, scallions, cilantro, and ginger. Taste and adjust seasonings. Keeps in refrigerator for up to 3 weeks.

SAFETY WARNING ON RAW EGGS

Because of the potential risk of Salmonella, pregnant women, young children, and anyone with a weakened immune system should avoid eating raw eggs. Make sure you use only the freshest (preferably organic) eggs.

Aioli

2-3 large cloves garlic, chopped

1 large egg or 3 egg yolks

1 tsp. Dijon mustard

3 tsp. lemon juice

1 c. oil (olive, vegetable, corn, or a combination)

salt and freshly ground pepper

honey (if needed)

In a food processor or blender with motor running, whirl garlic until very finely minced. Add egg, mustard, and lemon juice and whirl until smooth. Keep motor running and very, very slowly drizzle the oil into the mixture until thick. Taste and adjust seasonings. Store in glass jars in the refrigerator.

Quick Aioli

1 1/2 c. mayonnaise (regular or low fat)

2-3 garlic cloves, finely minced

1/2 lime, juiced

1 tbl. desired herb or herbs or other flavorings

honey (as needed)

salt and freshly ground pepper

Combine mayonnaise, garlic, lime juice, and flavorings in a bowl. Add honey if too harsh or acidic. Taste and adjust seasoning and chill.

Chipotle Aioli

3 garlic cloves

1 chipotle chili (drained)

1 tsp. EACH dried oregano and ground cumin

1 tbl. chili powder, homemade or commercial

285

1 tbl. lime juice

1 large egg

1 c. oil

honey

salt and freshly ground pepper

In a food processor or blender with motor running, whirl garlic and chipotle until finely minced. Add oregano, cumin, chili powder, lime juice, and egg and whirl until smooth. With motor running very, very slowly add oil as needed. Taste and add honey if too acidic. Add salt and pepper. Store in glass jars in the refrigerator.

❦

286

Jalapeno Aioli

3-4 garlic cloves

2 fresh jalapenos, chopped

1 egg

1 egg yolk

2 tbl. lime or lemon juice

salt

1 tsp. Dijon mustard

1 tsp. dried oregano

1 c. oil (approximate)

honey (if needed)

In a blender or food processor with motor running, whirl garlic and jalapenos. Add eggs and egg yolk, juice, dash of salt, Dijon, and oregano and whirl until smooth. While motor is running

add oil to desired thickness. Taste and add honey if too acidic. Adjust seasonings, store in glass jars, and chill.

❦

Sun-Dried Tomato Aioli

See page 65.

❦

Red Chili Aioli

4 garlic cloves, chopped

1 tbl. chili powder, homemade or commercial

1 large egg

1 1/2 tbl. lime juice

3/4 c. olive oil

honey (if needed)

salt and freshly ground pepper

In a food processor or blender with motor running, whirl garlic until finely minced. Add chili powder, egg, and lime juice and whirl until smooth. Keep motor running and very, very slowly drizzle in olive oil until desired thickness. Taste and add honey if too acidic. Add salt and pepper to taste. Store in glass jars in the refrigerator.

❦

Soy Aioli

2 garlic cloves, chopped

1 tbl. fresh ginger, chopped

1 egg

1 tbl. EACH rice vinegar and soy sauce
1 tsp. sesame oil
3/4-1 c. vegetable oil
honey (if needed)

With motor running, in a food processor or blender whirl garlic and ginger until finely minced. Add egg, vinegar, soy sauce, and sesame oil. With motor running, add oil very, very slowly until desired thickness. Add honey if too acidic. Store in glass jars in the refrigerator.

🌶

Roasted Red Pepper Aioli

2 garlic cloves, chopped
1 small roasted red pepper, patted dry
1 jalapeno, chopped
1 whole egg
1 egg yolk
3 tbl. rice vinegar
1/3-3/4 c. oil
honey (if needed)
salt and freshly ground pepper

In a food processor or blender with motor running, whirl garlic, red pepper, and jalapeno until finely minced. Add egg, egg yolk, and vinegar and whirl. With motor running, very, very, slowly drizzle in oil until desired thickness. Taste and add honey if too acidic. Season with salt and pepper. Store in glass jars in the refrigerator.

Basic Basil Pesto

2 garlic cloves
2 c. packed fresh basil
2 tbl. pine nuts or walnuts
1/2 c. Parmesan cheese, grated
1-1 1/2 c. olive oil (approx.)
salt and freshly ground pepper

In a food processor or blender with motor running, put garlic and pulse until minced very fine. Add basil, nuts, and Parmesan cheese and whirl until smooth. Slowly add olive oil until desired consistency has been reached. Taste and season. Store in refrigerator with a little film of oil on the top (this prevents the mixture from turning black). The blackening doesn't affect the flavor—just the visual appeal! The pesto can also be frozen for up to one year.

🌶

Winter Basil Pesto

2-3 cloves garlic
2 tbl. dried basil
2 c. parsley, stems removed
1/4 c. Parmesan cheese, grated
2 tbl. pine nuts or walnuts
1-1 1/2 c. olive oil (approx.)
salt and freshly ground pepper

In a food processor or blender with the motor running, pulse garlic until minced very

287

fine. Add basil, parsley, nuts, and Parmesan cheese; whirl until smooth. Slowly add olive oil until the desired consistency is achieved. Taste and season. Store in refrigerator with a little film of oil on top. May also be frozen.

❦

Sun-Dried Tomato Pesto

See page 70.

❦

Tarragon Pesto

2 garlic cloves
2 c. packed fresh tarragon
1/2 c. parsley
3 tbl. walnuts
1/4 c. Parmesan cheese, grated
1/2-3/4 c. olive oil
salt and freshly ground pepper

In a food processor or blender with motor running, whirl garlic. Add tarragon, parsley, walnuts, and Parmesan cheese. Add 1/2 c. oil and whirl until smooth. Add more oil if a looser consistency is desired. Adjust seasonings. Store in glass jars. Refrigerate or can be frozen. Use with chicken, fish, and potato salads.

❦

Dill Pesto

3/4 c. scallions, including tops
3 tbl. fresh parsley
1/4 c. minced fresh dill or 2 tsp. dried
3 tbl. cider vinegar
3-4 oz. walnuts, chopped
1/2-3/4 c. olive oil
salt and freshly ground pepper

Place scallions, parsley, dill, vinegar, walnuts, and 1/2 c. oil in a blender or food processor and whirl. Process until mixture is smooth. Add more oil if too thick. Season. Serve over cooked green beans, asparagus, carrots, or potatoes. Refrigerate or can be frozen.

❦

Red Chili Pesto

2 garlic cloves, chopped
2 tbl. chili powder, homemade or commercial
1/4 tsp. ground cumin
1/4 c. walnuts
1/4 c. Parmesan cheese, grated
1/2-3/4 c. olive oil
salt and freshly ground pepper
1/4 c. cilantro, chopped

With motor running, put garlic into a food processor or blender. Add chili powder, cumin, walnuts, and Parmesan cheese. Slowly add oil and process until desired thickness. Taste and season.

Mix in cilantro by hand. Good with grilled fish and chicken, fajitas, or fresh tortilla chips. Refrigerate or freeze.

ॐ

Cilantro Pesto

2-3 garlic cloves, chopped
2 c. fresh cilantro, chopped
dash chili oil (optional)
1 tbl. lime juice
3 tbl. walnuts
1/4 c. Parmesan cheese, grated
1/2-3/4 c. olive oil
salt and freshly ground pepper

With motor running, put garlic into a food processor or blender. Whirl until very fine. Add cilantro, chili oil, lime juice, walnuts, Parmesan cheese, and 1/2 c. oil. Whirl until smooth. If too thick, add more oil. Taste and adjust seasonings. Store in glass jars in the refrigerator. Can also be frozen. Use on pasta salads or potato salads; with fresh tortilla chips; on grilled chicken, fish, or pork; and on fajitas.

ॐ

Rosemary Pesto

2 large garlic cloves
1/4 c. fresh rosemary, chopped lightly
1/4 c. pine nuts or walnuts

1/4 c. Parmesan cheese, grated
1/2-3/4 c. olive oil
salt and freshly ground pepper

With motor running, put garlic in a food processor or blender. Whirl until finely minced. Add rosemary, nuts, Parmesan cheese, and 1/2 c. oil. Whirl until smooth. Add more oil if too thick. Taste and adjust seasonings. Store in glass jars in the refrigerator. Can also be frozen.

Use with beef, lamb, chicken, or potato salads.

ॐ

Thai Pesto

2 garlic cloves
2 tbl. fresh ginger, chopped
2 tbl. fresh basil
1/2 c. fresh coriander
1/4 c. fresh mint
2 hot chilies, chopped
1/2 c. walnuts
1/2 lime, juiced
1/2-3/4 c. olive oil
salt

With motor running put garlic and ginger in a food processor or blender. Add remaining ingredients and whirl until smooth. Add more oil as needed. Use with grilled fish, chicken, or Asian noodles.

ॐ

289

Spicy Asian Pesto

2 garlic cloves, minced
3 tbl. fresh ginger, chopped
2 tbl. jalapeno, chopped
2 large bunches fresh cilantro, chopped
1/2 c. walnuts or pine nuts
1/4 c. Parmesan cheese, grated
1 tsp. sesame oil
1/2-3/4 c. olive oil
dash of honey
salt and freshly ground pepper

In a food processor or blender with motor running, put garlic, ginger, and jalapeno. Whirl until very fine. Add cilantro, nuts, Parmesan cheese, sesame oil, and 1/2 c. olive oil. Whirl until smooth. Add more oil if too thick. Taste and add honey if too acidic. Add salt and pepper to taste. Store in glass jars in the refrigerator. Can be frozen.

Use on grilled seafood or as a dip with homemade tortilla chips or Indian pappadums (lentil crackers).

290

Mulling Spice

4 sticks cinnamon
1 tbl. dried orange peel
2 tsp. whole cloves
1 whole nutmeg, broken
1 tsp. whole allspice berries
1/4 tsp. cardamom pod, crushed

Break up cinnamon sticks and pound other ingredients with a meat cleaver. Place in a covered jar. When ready to use, put 1 heaping tbl. of the mixture into a muslin bag or tea ball and add to a quart of cider or red wine. Add 1 orange, cut in rounds. Simmer mixture until hot but do not boil. Taste before serving; add a small amount of sugar if too tart.

Rosemary Walnuts
makes 2 cups

2 tbl. butter
2 c. walnut halves
1 1/2 tsp. dried rosemary
1 1/2-2 tsp. salt
1/8 tsp. cayenne

Preheat oven to 350°. Heat butter in baking dish or cookie sheet. Add walnuts and toast 10 minutes. Add remaining ingredients and toss well. Return to oven for 10 minutes or until toasted. Stir frequently. Remove and cool on paper towels. Season according to taste. When cool, store in an airtight container.

Index

291

The Authors

Suzanne Breckenridge and Marjorie Snyder began their careers together in the 1970s. Their young daughters were at the beach taking swimming lessons and, as waiting mothers are inclined to do, they began talking. One thing led to another and they soon discovered their mutual interest in cooking, gardening, and herbs.

The two began cooking professionally with "Herb Cooking" classes conducted in Marge's kitchen. As their reputation as teachers grew, they moved to conducting herb classes in several Madison, Wisconsin, gourmet cookware shops. They soon began to cater parties and to produce herbal mustards and vinegars.

Marjorie and Suzanne wrote a food column for *Wisconsin Trails* magazine for more than 10 years and for *Isthmus*, a popular Madison weekly newspaper. They have sponsored public forums on herbs, helped to design Madison's public herb gardens, demonstrated herb cooking techniques on TV, and contributed to numerous cookbooks. In 1988, they saw their own cookbook, *The Wisconsin Country Gourmet*, published by *Wisconsin Trails*.

Marjorie and Suzanne are self-taught cooks whose educational backgrounds have influenced their approaches to cooking. Suzanne is a food stylist with a Master of Fine Arts degree from the University of Wisconsin-Madison and has worked as a graphic designer. Marge graduated from Bradley University with a degree in English and Business and is a former English teacher. She is currently president of the Madison Herb Society.

Both cooks feel that good food, prepared with imagination and sensitivity, should not be just for company. Their secrets include the use of the freshest seasonal foods, the subtle incorporation of herbs and spices into recipes, and imaginative visual presentation.

The authors live in Madison, Wisconsin. Suzanne lives with her husband, Bruce. They have a daughter, Sarah, and a son, Ethan. Marjorie lives with her husband, Chuck. They have two daughters—Ryan and Dana—and a great-chef son-in-law, Chris.